Storybook-Centered Themes

An Inclusive, Whole Language Approach

Interventionist's Guide

Janet A. Norris, Ph.D., CCC-SLP

Paul R. Hoffman, Ph.D., CCC-SLP

Communication Skill Builders ®

a division of
The Psychological Corporation

3830 E. Bellevue / P.O. Box 42050
Tucson, Arizona 85733
1-800-866-4446

Reproducing Pages from This Book

Many of the pages in this book can be reproduced for instructional or administrative use (not for resale). To protect your book, make a photocopy of each reproducible page. Then use that copy as a master for photocopying or other types of reproduction.

ISBN 0-88450-184-1   Catalog No. 3012

10 9 8 7 6 5 4 3 2 1
Printed in the United States of America

For information about our audio and/or video products, write us at: Communication Skill Builders, a division of The Psychological Corporation, P.O. Box 42050, Tucson, AZ 85733.

■ About the Authors

Janet A. Norris, Ph.D., is Associate Professor of Communication Sciences and Disorders at Louisiana State University. She has worked in the public schools as both a speech-language pathologist and a special education teacher and has consulted extensively with classroom teachers and special service providers. She has received ASHA's Clinical Achievement Award twice—once in the state of Nebraska and once in Louisiana. She was recently elected a Fellow of ASHA. Dr. Norris has developed specific assessment and intervention strategies to facilitate learning based on whole language principles and co-authored the book *Whole Language Intervention for School-Age Children* with Paul Hoffman.

Paul R. Hoffman, Ph.D., is Professor of Communication Sciences and Disorders at Louisiana State University. His research interest is in intervention strategies for children's speech and language disorders, and he received an ASHA Foundation grant for his work. *Language, Speech, and Hearing Services in Schools* honored him with the Editor's Award in 1991 and 1993. Dr. Hoffman has directed a series of studies demonstrating the effects of whole language intervention on phonological behaviors, including articulation and spelling and has authored the book *Children's Phonetic Disorders.*

■ Contents

■ List of Tables

■ List of Figures

■ Acknowledgments

The development of the Storybook-Centered Lesson Plans was supported in part by Louisiana Educational Quality Support Fund Award LEQSF RD-B-08 to Janet Norris and Paul Hoffman. Our special appreciation is expressed to the children who participated in this project, the classroom teachers who consulted with us to select topics and suggest activities, the graduate students who helped to assist the project at all stages of implementation and analysis, the elementary school that implemented the program and supported the research, and the board of regents that made the project possible.

CHAPTER 1

Purpose and Structure of the Storybook-Centered Curriculum

The Storybook-Centered Curriculum consists of this *Interventionist's Guide,* plus four books of lesson plans, each of which comes with four children's books. The primary books used within the curriculum are chosen from The Story Box® Series published by The Wright Group. These picture books are sold with the lesson plans. The same stories are also available in big book format from:

> The Wright Group
> 19201 120th Ave., NE
> Bothell, WA 98011-9512
> (800) 523-2371

The *Interventionist's Guide* outlines the S-D-S model of language intervention, explains the implementation and management of the approach, lists goals and objectives for treatment, and contains reproducible forms for assessing and monitoring the children in the program. The first book of lesson plans contains topic explorations for *Community and Society* and is ideally intended to be implemented during September and October. The second book contains topic explorations for *Holidays and Customs* and is best used between Halloween and Christmas. The third set of topic explorations, *Me and My World,* contains themes relating to the months of January, February, and March. The final set of explorations, *Spring and the Environment,* covers the final months of the school year.

■ Purpose

The Storybook-Centered Lesson Plans are designed to provide a well-balanced, comprehensive curriculum for young children. The curriculum and component lesson plans are based on principles of whole language learning (see Goodman 1986). They are designed for maximum flexibility in implementation to meet the needs of a broad range of children within a wide range of educational settings.

The books in The Story Box® Series are readable by emergent readers and present a variety of plots and levels of story complexity. The activities in the lesson plans support the content encountered in the story and can be implemented at many levels of language to meet the needs of children with special needs as well as children in regular education, making the lessons ideal for programs promoting the total inclusion of all children in the regular educational setting.

What Are the Characteristics of the Curriculum?

The Storybook-Centered Curriculum is designed to have the following characteristics:

- Integration of learning across all content areas

- Narrative-centered themes that allow for repeated readings

- Content based on predictable books that are readable by and interesting to emergent readers

- Reading and exploration óf good children's literature each day

- Balance between narrative and expository literature

- Presentation of information guided by developmental sequences

- Comprehensive exposure to social sciences, physical sciences, mathematics, arts, and language arts

- All activities centered around language development

- Maximum flexibility for use in the regular classroom, self-contained classroom, small-group intervention, and individual therapy

- Easy modification to meet individual teacher, classroom, or student needs

- Active participation and hands-on learning

- Large-group, small-group, and individual center-based learning activities

- Daily plans giving specific examples of dialogue used to facilitate a wide variety of language abilities

- Proven to work with at-risk learners

What Is a Whole Language Curriculum?

A whole language curriculum is consistent with whole language philosophy (Goodman 1986). This philosophy suggests that children learn best when these principles are followed:

- Language is used to talk about meaningful information.

- Language is used to accomplish purposes that make sense to the child.

- Language is "whole"; that is, it is presented in a context of meaning and use, not broken up and analyzed in small parts within an artificial setting.

- Language is used to help children understand concepts relative to their own experiences and insights.

- Children are active participants in their own learning, not passive, quiet listeners.

- Language is the primary vehicle for learning about the physical and social world, including all content areas (math, science, social studies, language arts, arts, and reading).

- Children use language to relate to one another and to become socialized as part of a culture and community.

- Learning involves active problem solving and critical thought about a topic, not memorizing information organized by others.

- Adults and peers provide as much assistance as necessary to learners who are attempting to talk about or understand new or complex information.

- Learning situations are designed to exploit the natural curiosity and intelligence of children.

- Learning accrues over time and involves repeated opportunities to interact and explore complex information.

- Learning emerges gradually across time, with the child forming, abandoning, refining, and modifying many hypotheses in the progressive development toward conventional form, content, and use.

- Learning occurs in a context that is sensitive to the needs of individual children and that supports risk taking.

Collaborative Reading –
Bring out skills
Get language
Is developmental

Not shared read'g

The Storybook-Centered Lesson Plans are carefully designed to be consistent with these whole language principles of learning. Language in this curriculum is an integral part of every activity, whether the activity is in a large group and teacher facilitated or is individual and self-directed. The lessons are organized to help children make sense of complex information while they acquire and use oral and written language (Goodman 1986; Norris and Hoffman 1993). They provide activities that integrate the content of the curriculum, so that children begin to see and understand how math, science, history, and geography all come together when whole, meaningful events or situations are examined (Pappas, Kiefer, and Levstik 1990). The curriculum exposes children to a wide variety of books throughout the day, some which are easily read by emergent readers because of their repeatable and predictable text and others which challenge listening and critical thinking abilities because of their more complex and abstract text. The Storybook-Centered Approach is designed to develop emergent literacy through repeated readings of the same readable book for the duration of a thematic unit and to support the events of the story through the exploration of a rich background of story-related knowledge across the domains of science, social studies, and the arts (Sulzby 1985; Sulzby and Zecker 1991; Yaden 1988).

The Storybook-Centered Curriculum supports the efforts of the teacher, speech-language pathologist, or special service provider implementing it. Daily lesson plans are provided for use in small-group or even individual intervention with children who have language and learning problems. The expanded plans can be used to structure an entire curriculum for an all-day regular classroom program. The Storybook-Centered Curriculum is ideal for school systems that implement total inclusion of children with special needs into the regular classroom. We have suggested specific ideas that children can talk about at a wide variety of language levels (Blank, Rose, and Berlin 1978; Monroe 1951). We also provide transition statements that help children see the interrelationships among activities explored on the same day, as well as across days.

But the curriculum itself is not whole language. Whole language is a *process* of children actively engaging and participating in learning (Goodman 1986; Smith 1990). This means that *how the curriculum is implemented is far more important than the activities within the curriculum.* The curriculum is only a product, and as such, it can be implemented using a directive style that places children in a passive listening and imitative role. The adult could model, elicit, and reinforce the "correct" art project, writing patterns, or answers to questions, thus robbing children of opportunities to learn how to solve problems, think critically, and learn through active involvement. Or the adult can present the curriculum in a more effective *transactional* style, in which problems and questions are raised and resources are collaboratively explored (Straw 1990; Vygotsky 1962; Wells 1985, 1986). This facilitated exploration enables children to engage in looking for information, recognizing the relevance of the information, using that information to solve problems, and reflecting on the problem and the solution, using language as the vehicle for learning and expressing that learning throughout the process.

This manual provides suggestions for *how* to implement the Storybook-Centered Lessons in a manner that is consistent with whole language. It describes how to build a learning environment based on active participation and problem solving. It explains why children should not be asked to copy or imitate well-formed art projects or written words, why children's incorrect answers are more important than their correct ones, and why the adult needs to continuously teach language as a natural part of every interaction. The manual also provides specific suggestions and strategies for implementing this transactional approach to learning.

Who Is the Storybook-Centered Approach Designed to Serve?

The Storybook-Centered Curriculum was originally designed for and researched in a regular kindergarten classroom environment where many of the children were considered at-risk for school failure because of low socioeconomic status. (See Hoffman and Norris 1994 for a review of these research findings.) Approximately 15 percent of the children were learning English as a second language. Speech-language pathologists developed the lesson plans in collaboration with classroom teachers who were interested in learning more about whole language. The speech-language pathologists worked with the teachers to meet the needs of children with speech, language, and other learning problems in the classroom.

The Storybook-Centered Curriculum also was used in a pull-out program for kindergarten, first-grade, and second-grade children with language and learning disabilities whose teachers were implementing other curricula. In this program, the speech-language pathologist completed the storybook reading, one topic exploration activity, and one writing activity in each session. Intervention was provided three times per week in groups of six to eight children.

Finally, the curriculum has been used in a preschool program for children with language and learning disorders. At the preschool level, greater emphasis was placed on discussing the storybooks at lower levels along the semantic and discourse continua, and more hands-on activities were selected. Thus, the Storybook-Centered Lessons are designed to be used flexibly depending on the needs of the children and the learning environment. They are appropriate for use:

- in a regular kindergarten classroom
- in a regular preschool program

- in a preschool program for children with special needs

- in a self-contained classroom for children with special needs

- in a pull-out program for children with special needs

- with children who are at-risk because of low socioeconomic status

- with children who are at-risk because of language and learning disabilities

- with early elementary low-ability readers who are at a stage of emergent reading and writing development

- in collaborative-consultative models of service delivery

- in classrooms where total inclusion of children with special needs is implemented

- with children who are learning English as a second language

The whole language principles on which the Storybook-Centered Approach is based allow for its flexible use within a wide variety of settings and for a broad range of children. The lesson plans enable the instructor to use the same materials and activities to implement discussions at many levels. Children who are younger or developmentally less advanced in their language acquisition and general knowledge can participate in lower levels of discussion, whereas children with more advanced language abilities can interact at higher levels. An accomplished teacher or speech-language pathologist can use the thematic storybook to simultaneously facilitate the development of oral and written language abilities for emergent readers, while promoting oral language development in children whose needs are related to language comprehension and expression and expediting written language acquisition in children with reading disabilities (Norris and Hoffman 1993).

Why Is the Curriculum Language Based?

Language is perhaps the most important ability children acquire. Language enables people to communicate with one another to accomplish goals, get needs met, express beliefs or feelings, plan for future events, reflect on past events, and negotiate actions and establish attitudes within ongoing events. Without language there is no means for learning about events from the past— we *talk about* history because we can't directly experience it (Bruner 1983; Hudson and Shapiro 1991). Similarly, we need language to learn about scientific principles that can't be seen or touched (such as "photosynthesis") and to think abstractly about concepts far removed from perception (such as "except" or "opinion"). Language allows us to communicate across distances of time and space; for example, reading enables the child to learn from an author who may have lived centuries earlier in a distant country (Bruce 1981). Language is necessary for understanding classroom rules, following a sequence of directions, listening to a lecture, participating in a discussion, assigning meaning to complex observations, reading a book, writing a paper, and spelling words (Cazden 1988). It is critical to forming friendships, solving problems, learning to share and take responsibility, and acquiring new knowledge. Language is part of everything that we do throughout the day. It is the aspect of the school curriculum that underlies all other learning.

Most children enter kindergarten with remarkably sophisticated language abilities. They have a vocabulary of as many as 26,000 words and speak in complete sentences (Brown 1973; White, Graves, and Slater 1990). They are able to use language to organize their ideas well enough to tell a complete story (Applebee 1978). They use language successfully to listen, discuss, plan, share, and learn. But much language development occurs throughout the school years as well. Research indicates that children with good literacy skills acquire up to 5,000 new words during each school year (Baumann and Kameenui 1991; White, Graves, and Slater 1990). In addition, they master metaphors, similes, and other figurative uses of language during the elementary grades. Grammatical development, especially the ability to coordinate many clauses within one sentence, continues to occur through grade twelve and beyond (Loban 1976). For this language acquisition to take place, children must have frequent, enriched opportunities to use language in many contexts, including oral discussion, peer interaction, problem solving, exposure to good literature, exploration of topics through reading expository text, and written language created for a wide variety of purposes (Applebee 1991).

But many children, either because of limited opportunities for language learning or because of presumed neurologically based language delays and disorders, enter kindergarten with underdeveloped language skills (Aram, Ekelman, and Nation 1984; Bryan 1986; Clay 1991; Loban 1976; Maxwell and Wallach 1984). Children with inflexible and unelaborated language systems experience difficulty with all aspects of school. They find themselves in trouble for violating classroom rules, not because they didn't listen, but rather because they cannot adequately process this difficult language. They exhibit short attention spans and disruptive behaviors in groups, not because they are undisciplined, but rather because they cannot make sense of the complex, rapid flow of speech produced by the teacher. Noise and surrounding movements or distractions common in a group setting further disrupt their ability to process the teacher's words.

Children with unsophisticated language abilities lack the linguistic abstraction needed to learn about historical events, scientific principles, or mathematical properties from definitions and verbal examples. Learning new language and concepts through definitions and verbal examples depends entirely on listening to language (Blank, Rose, and Berlin 1978). Learning to read is particularly challenging, as children who barely have competence in using language to communicate must use language to study language, breaking it apart into words, sounds, and rules for combining sounds (Goodman 1993). These children are confused and lost when the teacher asks the class to find an object that begins with the /b/ sound. When a classmate finds a boot and the teacher announces that it makes the /b/ sound, the confused child listens more carefully. Certainly, her own boots have never talked nor made any sounds, and the one held by the classmate doesn't appear to be producing a /b/ either. The child is in a quandary, believing that the teacher must be telling the truth, but puzzled because the teacher's statements don't make sense and violate actual experience.

Because of the importance of language to school success, facilitating language development is critical for children who enter school with excellent language abilities. It is even more critical for those who enter school with less flexible and elaborated language abilities. The Storybook-Centered Lesson Plans are designed to enable children to talk and learn using their present language abilities and to increase their language skill through actively reading storybooks, exploring story-related topics, acquiring information from a wide range of social studies, science, and mathematic content areas, and participating in numerous hands-on experiences that are developed through language. The lessons develop the following skills:

- **Knowledge** in the areas of history, geography, sociology, life sciences, earth science, mathematics, art, and more

- **Vocabulary** from a wide range of school-related content areas

- **Language concepts,** including size, shape, color, or position and the development of noun-phrase elaboration

- **Descriptive language,** including actions and states, and the development of verb-phrase elaboration and verb tense markers

- **Abstract language,** including the ability to understand and use modal verbs and complex sentences

- **Predictive language,** including making inferences, drawing conclusions, and using causal conjunctions

- **Critical thinking,** including evaluations, justifications, explanations, and the development of embedded clauses and "why?" "should?" "why not?" and "how do you know?" questions

- **Figurative language,** including understanding and using similes, metaphors, and grammatical comparatives and adverbial phrases

- **Metalinguistic awareness,** including phoneme discrimination, sound sequencing, sound blending, phoneme identification, rhyming, and letter-sound association

- **Articulation,** including auditory discrimination, phonological structure, and phonemic production in context

- **Narrative structure,** including organization by spatial location, temporal sequence, causality, intentionality, and purpose

- **Expository structure,** including procedural sequences, descriptive lists, comparisons and contrasts, and interactive events

- **Classroom discourse,** including turn taking, asking questions, contributing information, and following classroom rules

- **Contextualized language uses,** including talking about ongoing events and perceptually present information

- **Decontextualized language uses,** including talking about past events, predicting future events, and using literate language

- **Pragmatic language,** including expressing a range of communicative intentions, performing a range of communicative functions, and using appropriate conversational acts

- **Emergent reading abilities,** including awareness of print, concepts of "wordness," structure of written text, conventions of print, and word and letter recognition

- **Emergent writing abilities,** including letter formation, word structure, directionality of print, and meaningful communication through writing

- **Emergent spelling abilities,** including phonemic awareness, letter-sound correspondence, and representation of syllabic structure

How Can the Curriculum Be Used with Children Who Have Special Needs?

When children enter school with inflexible and unelaborated language systems, they have twice as much curriculum to master as other children. They must learn the language that their peers have mastered easily and naturally during the preschool years, and they must use their existing language to learn all of the content information and rules of conduct presented in school. Not only do they have twice the content to learn, but the process of learning is twice as difficult for them, because content learning is almost entirely dependent on language. There are not enough hours in the day to learn two separate curricula, and there is not enough time in the children's educational program that we can wait to teach content information until their language systems are better developed. Even if there were time, the language of classroom peers is developing rapidly throughout the school years, with high achievers adding vocabulary and grammatical structures at a rate more than 35 percent faster than low achievers (Baumann and Kameenui 1991; Loban 1976). Much of this language is learned through the exploration of content-area information and through mastery of reading, writing, and mathematical abilities.

Clearly, the only solution is to simultaneously teach language and content-area knowledge through the same curriculum. By carefully planning a curriculum to facilitate language development across a broad continuum of language skills using content-area topics and activities, both goals can be reached. The same information can be talked about at multiple levels, establishing basic vocabulary, grammatical competence, discourse structures, and communicative functions for children who need language development at this level, and establishing abstract vocabulary, complex grammatical and discourse structures, and nonliteral, critical language functions for children at more advanced levels. The children with less flexible and elaborated language systems are exposed to more complex uses of language, giving them a foundation for acquiring these abilities later on, while they are given opportunities to use language within their current level of competence, assuring them success in school and the development of greater language competence (Vygotsky 1962).

When the Storybook-Centered Curriculum is used in the regular classroom, the speech-language pathologist can consult with the classroom teacher, identifying individualized goals and objectives for the children with speech and language learning needs. This collaboration should result in specific strategies that the teacher can use to reduce the complexity of language used in the classroom so it is within the child's range of abilities (Norris and Hoffman 1993). The collaboration also should result in specific strategies the teacher can use to help the children meet their individual goals and objectives. In addition, the speech-language pathologist can provide small-group intervention within the classroom using the same curriculum. Children whose teachers are not using the Storybook-Centered Curriculum also can participate in these small groups. These small groups are an opportunity for the speech-language pathologist to provide intensive language facilitation.

Children with specific language learning needs will learn language rapidly when the lessons are adapted to meet their needs. These needs may include:

- Participation in small groups where children have multiple opportunities to talk and to receive feedback on their communications

- A minimally distracting setting

- Assistance in attending to the most important or relevant information

- A reduced level of language input

- Assistance in generating an appropriate response

- A higher frequency of responding

- A high level of direct feedback regarding language productions

- Frequent clarifications and reinterpretations

- Assistance in drawing necessary inferences or activating appropriate background information

- More numerous and more frequent exposures to information

- Assistance in establishing the appropriate temporal, spatial, causal, conditional, or other relationships among ideas and events

The information in focus under these modified learning conditions should be meaningful, purposeful, integrated, socially mediated, process oriented, and characterized by active problem solving and whole-to-part learning (that is, consistent with whole language philosophy).

These small-group intervention sessions *do not* involve targeting and repeatedly drilling specific vocabulary, grammatical forms, and articulatory productions. Rather, the interventionist makes learners aware of the significance and communicative value of language as they engage in real communicative situations. The language that they are made aware of depends entirely upon what is being communicated during each instance of language use. This awareness could occur in the form of a production model for a phoneme in a word that the child is attempting to use, or it could involve assistance in using word order to communicate the relationships of meaning between objects, agents, and events that are relevant to the context. The interventionist helps children see complex meanings and communicate these ideas (Norris and Damico 1990; Norris and Hoffman 1990).

An entire idea might be too complex and require too much sophistication in language for the child to communicate it independently. But by gradually helping the child to notice relevant ideas and to assemble the ideas into complex utterances, one helps the child simultaneously acquire knowledge, the language needed to talk about this knowledge, and the logical language patterns that can be used to express these and other ideas. The child then can use this content knowledge and the increased language abilities to more actively and successfully participate in classroom interactions.

■ Structure

The central theme of whole language philosophy is that language is a whole, the parts of which cannot treated separately if it is to remain language (Goodman 1986). Real language simultaneously expresses function, content, and form. Language is useful because it performs a number of *functions*, such as informing, persuading, commanding, and facilitating learning. Language is meaningful because it provides a vehicle for sharing *content*, or one's knowledge about the world (Bloom 1970). This knowledge includes an understanding of the physical nature of objects, the appropriate functions of objects, the actions of people, and the underlying plans and goals that motivate their actions. Much of this knowledge is reflected in the content areas of science, literature, and social studies (Smith 1990). Language is social because the members of a community share the same language *form*, including the words, syntactic structures (rules governing word order), and discourse structures (rules for forming stories, conversations, or expository text). These forms may be expressed in either the spoken or written modality, each of which has its own specific characteristics (Goodman 1982; Smith 1985).

What Is an Integrated Curriculum?

The whole language assumption that language and knowledge are essentially interrelated and indivisible leads to the practice of teaching in a whole-to-part manner. The Storybook-Centered Lesson Plans are integrated so that a single activity may simultaneously facilitate the learning of content and skills across many curricular areas. There are no separate teaching times that focus exclusively on, for example, printing, spelling, story structure, social studies, or art. Rather, a single meaningful writing activity may integrate all of these content areas as the children explore, write about, and illustrate a topic. The skills are focused on in context, when they are relevant to the process of researching, organizing, drafting, editing, or illustrating. This is the opposite of many traditional teaching strategies, in which each area of language arts and each content area of social studies, mathematics, and science is taught as a separate topic. The traditional division of knowledge into curriculum content areas often results in little or no relationship among the reading, language arts, math, and science goals for a particular day, week, or month. The burden of integrating knowledge across content areas rests with the children. They must figure out which concepts are common across class periods and what kinds of relationships might exist among the various classroom topics.

The Storybook-Centered Curriculum is designed to enhance the discovery of whole-to-part relationships by coordinating all language and content-area goals within integrated activities. The activities within and across the days of a narrative-centered thematic unit are interrelated, and a series of narrative-centered thematic units build on one another across an entire topical unit (Norris and Hoffman 1990, 1993). As described in the following section, these activities, narrative-centered thematic units, and topical units provide opportunities for meeting all of the social studies, science, math, reading, and language arts goals of the typical kindergarten curriculum, and for expressing this knowledge using increasingly more sophisticated language.

What Is a Narrative-Centered Theme?

Reading is more than the transmission of information from the text to the child. Rather, it is a *transaction,* a process whereby children combine their own rich background of knowledge with information present in the text as they read (Bruce 1981; Morrow 1988; Morrow and Smith 1990). Both the information provided by the author and that contributed by the child are needed to create the meaning of the text. The author cannot possibly provide every bit of information needed to interpret the text. The writer must make certain assumptions about readers' competence, including the information or knowledge they should already possess, the vocabulary they should be familiar with, and the complexity of the language they can understand (Bruce 1981). Readers need to read beyond the literal meaning of the words to interpret the information that is given and to make inferences and predictions based on their own background knowledge (Straw 1990; Sulzby 1985).

For example, one of the theme books, *Grumpy Elephant*, reads "Along came Monkey. 'Poor old Elephant. I'll play for you,' he said." The reader must extract information from the picture (which shows the elephant looking very grumpy and the monkey pounding on bongo drums) to interpret what "play" means and why the monkey refers to the pachyderm as "poor old Elephant." The reader must go beyond the information in the picture and use personal knowledge to infer that the monkey feels sorry for the elephant and is trying to cheer him up by playing the drum. The meaning of the word "grumpy" must be differentiated from the meanings of "sad" or "angry" to understand the elephant's mood, and knowledge about the destructive things a grumpy elephant could do is needed to provide a possible explanation for the monkey's interest in improving the elephant's mood. None of this is explicitly stated in the text, and without these interpretations and inferences the story does not make sense.

When readers do not have the extensive vocabulary; command of language; background of experiences; wealth of world, historical, and scientific knowledge; association of words to a continuum of feelings or emotions; and understanding of temporal, causal, intentional, conditional, and other links among characters, events, and outcomes, then their comprehension will be limited to literal facts. The more often that the assumptions made by the author do not match the actual knowledge possessed by the reader, the more difficulty the child will experience in learning to read, making sense of the print, and deriving meaning from the story (Bruce 1981). The transaction between the author and the reader will be minimal.

Narrative-centered themes are designed to help children engage in the transactional process (Norris 1992; Norris and Hoffman 1993). In a narrative-centered theme, one theme book is explored over a long time period (approximately two weeks). The adult facilitator guides the children in transactional exploration of the story (Roser and Martinez 1985). On the first day of the thematic unit, only the cover page of the book is explored. For example, the cover page for *Grumpy Elephant* shows a very unhappy elephant in the jungle being peered at by the other animals, who are hiding behind trees. One goal of the lesson plan is to talk about the picture at many levels of language, ranging from simply naming and describing the animals and the jungle depicted, through generating interpretations and inferences and reading the words. Once the ideas are established, the children then use this information to create simple stories about what might be occurring, such as:

> The animals heard a loud noise coming toward them in the jungle.
> They didn't know what it was, so they hid behind some trees to watch.
> Soon the elephant appeared. He looked very grumpy.

To understand the story at an expanded level, the children have to possess a good understanding of what it means to be grumpy. The lesson plans provide a variety of activities and experiences that are used to explore the concept of grumpiness throughout the day. Literature such as *The Three Billy Goats Gruff* is read and discussed to identify what a grumpy character is like and how he might behave toward others. Children are asked to talk and write about things that make them grumpy and relate the elephant's mood to personal experience. The children have opportunities to role-play grumpy behavior and talk about this feeling.

On the second day, the cover page is reread. The children now have a more elaborated background of knowledge and understanding of the concept "grumpy," which enables them to engage in a higher level of transaction. They can spontaneously contribute more of the ideas, and they begin to generate insights and questions that go beyond what they had previously noticed or understood.

The title page is then introduced in much the same way as the cover page was on the previous day. On this day, the class explores the pachyderm and his habitat to create an expanded understanding of elephants and the jungle. They discover and talk about facts about the elephant and use this information to measure and map out the elephant's dimensions and to collaborate in creating elephant heads from paper sacks. In musical games, the children move and behave like elephants, including elephants on a rampage.

Thus, in narrative-centered themes, important concepts from the story serve to coordinate the learning within the theme, and the explorations of these concepts function to develop the background of scientific, historical, psychological, and culture knowledge needed to understand the story at increasing levels of complexity. This reciprocity between the story and content-area knowledge results in an integrated curriculum. The narrative-centered themes in particular are designed to facilitate language and literacy development, following principles (such as repeated readings of the same book) that are found to enhance learning in nondisabled children. Repeated readings across periods of time enable the children to internalize more of the concepts and many dimensions of the language of the book with each examination. To each reexamination the children bring a more extensive network of concepts and language that they can use to independently interpret the pictures and text (Roser and Martinez 1985; Sulzby 1985; Teale and Sulzby 1986, Yaden, Smoklin, and Conlon 1989). This foundation allows for more abstract levels of understanding to be verbalized and for more attention to be directed at an analysis of the print, including letter-sound correspondences, syllable structure, and conventions of capitalization and punctuation.

The advantages of narrative-centered themes can be summarized as follows:

- Repeated readings of the same storybook are similar to the important practice of rereading favorite books every night at home.

- Repeated exposure to the same vocabulary in both familiar and changing contexts fosters learning and generalization.

- Repeated exposure to story events facilitates the learning of story grammar, temporal sequences, and causality between actions and the language used to mark these relationships.

- Repeated exposure to words in print enables learning of sound-symbol relationships, letter names and sounds, the function of punctuation, and other concepts about print.

- Repeated discussion of the same events allows for increasing abstraction and background knowledge to be introduced as more basic information becomes familiar.

- Repeated opportunities to use oral language to communicate information leads to more child-initiated, topic-relevant, and elaborated talk about a topic.

- The children are repeatedly exposed to literate forms of language modeling patterns of complex grammar, specific word use, and standard English morphology.

- The children are repeatedly exposed to sound patterns of English and have opportunities to refine articulation and phonemic awareness.

- Repeated exploration of a topic using multiple media and multiple perspectives results in an integrated and comprehensive curricular approach to learning.

What Is a Topical Unit?

Narrative-centered themes provide naturally occurring contexts for acquiring world and scientific knowledge and for using this knowledge to interpret and expand on literature. They enable beginning readers to experience fluent reading, to begin discovering how print functions to communicate meaning, and to internalize the patterns of letters that form words (Clay 1991). Narrative-centered themes serve as a means for addressing children's language and learning needs at multiple levels and provide a strategy for maintaining continuity across the curriculum and across time.

The narrative-centered themes are themselves embedded within larger themes called topical units (see Table 1-1). Topical units allow for an extended exploration of a general concept—such as holidays and customs or spring and the environment—and create an awareness of personal, cultural, seasonal, and environmental patterns that organize our experiences (Lehr 1991). The information explored within the topical units enables children to better understand themselves, their community, and their cultures, as well as the physical and biological nature of the world and the environment. Children must develop an understanding of both the cultural and physical aspects of the world to be able to fully communicate with others through language and literature, to understand how individuals and cultures use scientific and mathematical knowledge, and to understand the historical development of those communities and cultures (Bruner 1983; Wells 1986). Four topical units are developed in the Storybook-Centered Curriculum, each composed of four narrative-centered themes.

TABLE 1-1
Four Topical Units and Component Narrative-Centered Thematic Units

Community and Society

AUG.	SEPT.	SEPT.	OCT.
Stop!	Who Will Be My Mother?	Boo-hoo	Hairy Bear
School Community	Farm	Animals	Crime
Farm Community	Family Roles and Structure	Problem Solving	Police
City Community	Other Cultures and Societies	Cause-Effect	Safety
Community Helpers	Animal Care and Habitats	Buy-Trade	Fear
Transportation		Happy/Sad	Problem Solving
Calling 911			Fall
Accidents			

Holidays and Customs

OCT.	NOV.	NOV.	DEC.
The Monsters' Party	Meanies	The Jigaree	One Cold, Wet Night
Halloween	Friends	Thanksgiving	Holidays
Music	The Continents	Other People	Weather
Celebration	Other Countries	Oceans	Clothing
Talents	Other Customs	Solar System	Shelter
Customs	Other Climates	Planets	Animals
		Universal Friends	Adaptation

TABLE 1-1 (continued)

Me and My World

JAN. **The Grumpy Elephant**	JAN. **The Hungry Giant**	FEB. **To Town**	MAR. **Obadiah**
Moods and Feelings	Moods and Behavior	Hometown	Senses
Self-Concept	Communities	Travel	Vision
Self-Expression	Traditional Tales	Vehicles	Movement
Responsibility	Animals	Maps	Taste
Civil Rights	Cooperation	Geography	Touch
	Zoo Animals		Sound
	Learning a Lesson		Smell

Spring and the Environment

MAR. **Mrs. Wishy-washy**	APR. **Too Big for Me**	APR. **The Red Rose**	MAY **If You Meet a Dragon**
Seasons and Weather	Life Cycles of Insects	Life Cycles of Plants	Dinosaurs
Rain and Mud	Spiders	Prey and Predators	Life Cycles of Reptiles
Cleaning	Defenses	Colors	Jungle
Bathing and Hygiene	Size	Chain Reactions	Swamps
Health			Ecology

The first topical unit, **Community and Society**, explores the many layers of community and the society in which the children live. The school is one focus of this unit, intended to familiarize the children with the many different aspects of this community. The people who form the school community and their roles are explored, and children are helped to understand how these people fit into this world. A second focus in this unit is differences between urban and rural lifestyles and the roles that people and animals play within these communities. Other explorations include the many kinds of families and family structures, with an emphasis on understanding personal and family history. The children explore the roles played by animals both as pets and as producers of food and work. Problem solving is addressed within families and at the community level through police and other safety personnel.

Cultural aspects of the community are explored in the second topical unit, **Holidays and Customs**. The class discusses the historical origin of many holidays such as Thanksgiving and how these holidays are celebrated in the child's society and in other communities and countries. This unit is designed to be used from October through December during the holidays between Halloween and Christmas. Topical exploration of Halloween includes concepts of celebration and customs as well as emotions of fear and friendship. The topic is extended through Thanksgiving with explorations of customs from other countries. The transition from Thanksgiving into winter brings with it scientific discussion of the seasons, weather, the solar system, animals' adaptations to climate, and people's development of clothing. Thus, during this topical unit, the lessons continue to develop the theme of how children relate to their community by exploring aspects of their culture.

The third topical unit, **Me and My World,** explores many dimensions of the individual and the individual's relationships with others. One goal is to help children develop self-understanding, including self-concept, moods, feelings, and self-expression. These factors are related to the children's interpersonal relationships at home and in the community through exploring concepts such as fairness, defiance, independence, and cooperation. The child's relationship to the broader community is explored through the topic of people's civil rights. The broader community is further explored through travel, geography, and the many means of transportation. Understanding of oneself is further explored by an examination of the senses and how they are used to learn about the world and the community. Thus, this section continues the exploration of culture, but at more abstract and complex levels.

The fourth unit, **Spring and the Environment** increases children's awareness of the physical environment in which they live. Knowledge of the senses developed in the third topical unit is used to listen to, observe, and make discoveries about the world. These explorations include developing an understanding of the seasons and weather as the school year enters into spring. Life cycles of plants and animals are highlighted. The cultures and societies of animals and how these groups help them to survive are examined. The life cycle of the planet is introduced with an exploration of present-day animals and their relationship to the dinosaurs of the past. The need to protect the environment and to save forest and swamp areas is emphasized. The interrelationships of the many life forms on the planet are discussed, including predator-prey relationships and physical chain reactions. Cultural aspects of the spring season are interwoven throughout.

Each of the four topical units provides for repeated and overlapping coverage of important topic areas throughout the year. Rather than talking about farm animals only once (during a farm theme unit, for example) farm animals are revisited throughout the year. This intentional redundancy in the discussions enables children to meet topics repeatedly within different frameworks and to use the background knowledge they acquire in earlier units as a foundation for more advanced or complex explorations in later units. For example, the family is discussed in **Community and Society** in the contexts of the school environment, other cultures, and safety issues related to community helpers. In **Holidays and Customs,** the family is discussed in relationship to friends,

American customs, customs of other countries, and protection from the elements. In **Me and My World,** the family is explored in relationship to people's rights, obligations to others, cooperation, and personal feelings. In **Spring and the Environment,** the family is explored in animal life cycles and in protection from the elements and from predators.

One of the inherent characteristics of this approach is the broadening of concepts through their exploration in a variety of meaningful contexts. The concepts become deeper and more flexible as the children begin to recognize the same concepts recurring in different forms (Norris and Hoffman 1994). All content areas are explored in a manner that demonstrates how they are part of everything we do within or know about our physical and social world. The information is purposeful and meaningful, as children ask and answer questions, solve problems, and satisfy their natural curiosity. In this manner, children learn about the social studies, sciences, mathematics, reading, language arts, arts, and oral language as tools for thinking and learning, rather than as discrete facts learned by rote (Bickmore-Brand 1990; Britton 1982; Scott 1992).

■ Content-Area Goals

The Storybook-Centered Curriculum is integrated across content areas, so no one area is studied in isolation from the others. A single activity typically integrates learning from five, six, or more content areas. For example, an activity of researching and writing about sheep may involve the content areas of life science (sheep), geography (farms), sociology (family structure), economics (wool production), reading, language arts (writing, spelling), art (illustration), and mathematics (counting).

Meeting Social Studies Goals through the Whole Language Approach

Knowing the content areas that are introduced in the Storybook-Centered Lesson Plans will help the instructor understand the nature and value of an integrated curriculum. One content area is social studies or our knowledge of the social world. Table 1-2 summarizes the content-area knowledge related to social studies that is explored in the lesson plans. Seven areas of the social sciences are developed in the plans (Sunal 1990). The area of **history** is examined through explorations of personal and family history. Children must understand the significance of events in their own lives and experiences before they can be expected to understand the histories of other people or groups. The history of societies and cultures is explored by examining the origins of holidays, customs, and traditions, including those practiced by the children and those in other countries and social groups.

Political science introduces formal discussions of friendship, cooperation, and sharing. The class talks about or writes down rules for taking turns, contributing information, sharing materials, fair treatment, and so forth. Awareness of group needs and community coherence is emphasized. Exploring **geography** helps the children become aware of location and distance. In the process, children study the differences between rural and urban locations, with many references to their community and its characteristics. The effects of geography on clothing and other practices are discussed. Many activities incorporate the conventions of geography, including regions, maps, directions, and globes. The status of the earth as one location within the solar system also is explored.

The area of **psychology** offers opportunities to explore a wide range of emotions, moods, and life events. Early in the lesson plan series, emotions such as happiness, sadness, fear, and disappointment are examined. Later in the series, the lessons progress to more abstract concepts such as fairness, selfishness, greed, and empathy. These emotions are closely integrated with the study of **sociology**—including explorations of each child's personal family and the range of family structures, as well as neighborhoods and communities. Children learn about personal responsibilities within each level of society and the responsibilities assumed by others.

The Storybook-Centered Lesson Plans introduce children to the principles of **economics,** including buying and selling goods and services; determining personal, classroom, and community needs; and making decisions about how to use limited resources most effectively. Children become aware of the relationship between work and play as they explore a range of common occupations and what people do in the community to earn money and care for their families. They compare these aspects of the community with other communities in the study of **anthropology.** An emphasis on different cultures with varying customs, foods, music, and forms of entertainment is interwoven throughout the plans (Allen, McNeill, and Schmidt 1992; Sunal 1990). Children experience foods, games, dress, and other features of many cultures over the course of the year. They also find out about the ways in which different cultures celebrate the same holidays.

TABLE 1-2
Social Studies and Science Goals
Addressed in the Storybook-Centered Lesson Plans

SOCIAL STUDIES	SCIENCE

SOCIAL STUDIES

History
Holidays
Traditions
Personal History
Seasons

Political Science
Friendships
Sharing
Cooperation

Geography
Farm and City
Clothing
Regions and Boundaries
Maps
Direction and Space
Globe

Psychology
Moods
Self-Image
Fears
Aging and Development

Sociology
Family
Neighborhood
Community
Responsibilities
Environment

Economics
Buying and Selling
Classroom Needs
Personal Needs
Community Needs
Resources
Occupations

Anthropology
Culture
Foods
Music
Games

SCIENCE

Life Science
Plants
Animals
Development
Ecology

Physical Science
Mass
Force
Motion
Energy
Machines

Health Science
Body Parts
Body Systems
Foods
Nutrition
Growth

Earth Science
Minerals
Weather
Solar System

Observation
Collection
Comparison
Classification

Measurement
Length
Weight
Volume
Temperature

Recording Findings
Pictures
Graphs
Maps
Oral Language
Written Language

Meeting Science Goals
through the Whole Language Approach

Four areas of science—as well as the scientific principles of observation, measurement, and recording—are developed within the Storybook-Centered Lesson Plans (see Table 1-2). An in-depth study of **life science** is developed in the plans (Charlesworth and Lind 1990; Holt 1991). Rather than studying plants and animals for only one unit, such as a specific unit on "farm animals" or "plants," these important topics recur repeatedly throughout the year. Each time the children encounter the topic, they receive more specific and elaborated information and recall the background knowledge they already possess. In this manner, children are helped to understand that science is an important part of their daily experiences, rather than something to be examined once.

Many gross motor activities, as well as simple experiments with moving objects and machines, are used to explore **physical science.** Such terms as "mass," "force," and "energy" are used in the context of everyday activities such as playing at the sand table, modeling with clay, doing activities on the playground, and setting up materials. **Health science** often occurs in conjunction with activities from the social sciences. As people, their customs, and their communities are discussed, it is natural to talk about the body, its functions, and its development. Many discussions about caring for pets and animals, as well as people, help children become aware of their bodies, body functions, and needs.

Children's natural curiosity about rocks is used throughout the lesson plans to increase awareness of **earth science.** The weather is sometimes discussed casually in contexts such as Calendar time, and at other times its changes and patterns are carefully charted and monitored or discussed relative to seasonal characteristics. The relationships of the moon and the sun to the earth are discussed and their effects on day and night, seasons, and temperatures are introduced. Throughout all science explorations, the plans provide children with multiple opportunities to make scientific **observations,** including forming collections and classifying specimens; to take **measurements,** including properties of size, volume, and temperature; and to **record findings** using conventions such as graphs, maps, charts, and other representations (Charlesworth and Lind 1990; Holt 1991).

Meeting Mathematics Goals
through the Whole Language Approach

Mathematics and art are different from the content areas of social studies and sciences. Math and art function more like languages, or systems of rules and operations that can be used to symbolize meaning and accomplish purposes. Once the principles of math or art are learned, they can be applied generatively to solve an infinite number of problems or create an infinite number of designs (Bickmore-Brand 1990; Charlesworth and Lind 1990; Davidson 1983; Kamii 1988; Whitin, Mills, and O'Keefe 1990).

The first mathematical symbols are words. During the preschool years, children experiment with shape sorters, puzzles, swings, riding toys, sandbox toys, and many other things that teach them about math. They learn that pouring more juice into a cup adds more volume and that drinking the juice subtracts it. They learn that riding a tricycle faster moves you through space in a shorter amount of time. They learn that there is a match between the shape of a solid form and its corresponding hole in a shape sorter. They learn the words used to represent each of these mathematical properties, including "more," "full," "gone," "race," "first," and "last." These experiences with everyday math need to be converted to more abstract mathematical symbols and concepts during the school years (Davidson 1983).

Seven areas of mathematics are developed in the lesson plans (see Table 1-3, page 24). Calendar time provides a context for formally introducing **number concepts.** The children have many opportunities to match calendar pictures to corresponding dates, establish one-to-one correspondence between calendar squares and numbers, count the days in sequence, and identify days by their numeric dates. Additionally, number concepts should be talked about within the context of almost all activities to help children understand the functions of math as a natural part of everyday experiences. Specific suggestions are provided in this manual under the heading Teaching Mathematics beginning on page 76.

Operations are rule systems that can be used to combine, delete, or transform objects or their properties (Bickmore-Brand 1990; Kamii 1988). For example, a round ball of cookie dough can be flattened, an operation that changes its shape but conserves its mass. In contrast, eating a spoonful of the dough subtracts from the mass while conserving the basic shape. Many opportunities for cooking, working with art materials, and solving problems are included in the lesson plans. By using math language within these activities, the adult can help children to see the operations of addition, subtraction, ordering, conserving, and so forth. These activities similarly provide numerous opportunities for learning about **measurement,** including measurement of weight, volume, and time. Some of the unit plans are structured around experiments with sensory experiences, calling for many types of measurements and comparisons.

TABLE 1-3
Mathematics and Art Goals
Addressed in the Storybook-Centered Lesson Plans

MATHEMATICS

Number Concepts
  Matching Sets
  One-to-One Correspondence
  Counting to 30
  Numeral Recognition to 30
  Writing Numerals to 10

Operations
  Conservation
  Ordering
  Patterning
  Comparing
  Adding
  Subtracting
  Equivalence

Measurement
  Volume
  Weight
  Distance
  Time

Sets and Classification
  Shape
  Size
  Space
  Color
  Same
  Different

Recording
  Graphs
  Charts
  Calendar

Money
  Naming Coins
  Coin Values
  Counting Pennies
  Recognizing $ and ¢ Symbols

ART

Content
  Representation
    Body Image
    Objects
    States
    Symbolic Representations
    Abstract Expressions
  Medium
    Clay
    Cloth
    Paper
    Art Materials

Form
  Topological
    Spatial Orientation
    Spatial Relations
    Whole-to-Part Relations
  Geometric
    Shape
    Size
    Line
    Color
    Texture
    Space
  Format
    Sculpture
    Drawing
    Painting

Function
  Create
  Express
  Decorate
  Ceremony
  Symbols
  Props

Mathematics is based on understanding that objects can be grouped into **sets** and **classifications.** Classification requires viewing the properties of objects rather than the objects themselves. The differences among chips, blocks, and toy cars must be ignored while their similarity along the abstract dimension of color is used to group them together. The lesson plans provide almost daily experiences with creating sets or classifications of objects while making collages; classifying people, animals, the weather, and objects; and identifying objects that are alike along one or two dimensions. They also provide many specific opportunities for **recording** these observations using graphs, charts, and calendars (Charlesworth and Lind 1990; Davidson 1983; Kamii 1988; Whitin, Mills, and O'Keefe 1990).

The correspondence between goods or services and their numeric value to society is explored through the use of **money.** The plans provide opportunities for children to set up stores, buy airline tickets, make goods to sell, and learn in other functional ways how we exchange coins and bills for goods. The children examine the names and values of coins and experience counting and performing other operations with money (Charlesworth and Lind 1990).

Meeting Art Goals through the Whole Language Approach

Art involves **content,** the idea or ideas to be represented; **form,** the structures and patterns used to represent the ideas; and **function,** the uses and purposes for its creation (Lasky and Mukerji 1990; Mayesky 1990; Schirrmacher 1988). The Storybook-Centered Lesson Plans develop two aspects of content, three aspects of form, and a variety of functions (see Table 1-3). Within the area of content is the domain of **representation.** The lesson plans help the children develop a sense of body image as they draw, paint, and construct images of themselves and other people or characters. Similarly, they create representations of many objects and emotions or feelings that reflect story-related topics. The activities involve experimentation with both symbolic representations (that is, drawings that look like their referents) and abstract expressions (that is, use of color and form). They explore a variety of **media,** including clay, cloth, art materials, and paper.

The Storybook-Centered Lessons help children become aware of the conventional forms used to express ideas in art. **Topological** aspects of form refer to how shapes and forms are organized in relationship to one another in space. They include the spatial orientation of forms—such as an upward curve to represent happiness and a downward curve to represent sadness—and spatial relations such as the placement of eyes on the same plane separated by an approximate distance. **Geometric** aspects of form refer to the lines, curves, and points of intersection that make up the shapes and sizes of figures, as well as to color and texture.

Art may take different **formats,** including sculpture, drawing, painting, and craft. The lesson plans provide many experiences with using different formats to help children understand the many **functions** of art. These functions include providing an outlet for creativity and self-expression, a means for decorating and personalizing surroundings, and an understanding of the uses of art in ceremony; symbolizing representations of the physical and mental world; and generating props for dramatic play or other performing arts (Lasky and Mukerji 1990; Mayesky 1990; Schirrmacher 1988).

Meeting Reading Goals through the Whole Language Approach

Three areas of reading are developed within the lesson plans: **oral language,** or an exploration of the concepts and meaning of what is read; **print knowledge,** or an exploration of the conventions of printed language; and **metalanguage,** or knowledge about the structure of words and how this structure is represented in print (see Table 1-4). This content is not taught by identifying discrete oral, print, and metalanguage skills; rather it emerges from discussing books as they are transactionally read. The facilitator helps the children to notice aspects of pictures and print that readers attend to and to talk about the form and function of these properties in context.

Each day in the lesson plans, specific suggestions are given for exploring the concepts and meaning of the story by simultaneously developing (that is, "learning to talk") and using (that is, "talking to learn") **oral language** (Wells 1986; Westby 1985). A menu of language goals is provided, ranging from simply identifying and labeling concepts depicted in the picture, through talking about the concepts and events depicted at abstract levels of drawing inferences, evaluating, justifying, and explaining. Once concepts are established, the plans call for the children to combine these ideas to create stories from the pictures. Children learn narrative structure as they are assisted to include temporal, causal, and intentional links between ideas and events while telling the story depicted in the picture and communicated through the print (McCabe and Peterson 1991; Stein and Glenn 1979).

Print knowledge is acquired as children successfully read the predictable print in the narrative-centered theme books. Active involvement in reading print in meaningful contexts enables children to learn conventions of written language, including that reading occurs from left to right and from top to bottom. They establish a concept of a word—including the relationship between written words and the corresponding oral language that is read. They begin to understand the differences between oral language and written language, including more formal grammar, reading intonation, spaces between words, and punctuation marks between sentences that only indirectly relate to stress and voice in oral language, and the function of print conventions such as exclamation points and capital letters (Clay 1991; McGee and Richgels 1990; Teale and Sulzby 1986; Yaden, Smoklin, and Conlon 1989).

Table 1-4
Reading and Language Arts Goals
Addressed in the Storybook-Centered Lesson Plans

READING

Oral Language
Label Objects and Characters
Describe Actions and States
Describe by Characteristics
Interpret Meaning from Cues
Infer and Predict from Cues
Evaluate, Justify, and Explain
Tell Story with Temporal, Causal, and Intentional Links

Print Knowledge
Recognize Left-to-Right Concept
Recognize Top-to-Bottom Concept
Recognize Whole-Word Concepts
Recognize Oral-to-Written Word Correspondence
Recite Familiar Story Verbatim
Use Reading Intonation
Use Formal Grammar
Know Function of Punctuation
Know Function of Capitals
Know Title Page, Author

Metalanguage
Concept of Wordness
Identification and Production of Rhymes
Sound-Letter Correspondence
Sound-Letter-Word Matching
Phonemic Segmentation
Phoneme Substitution
Syllabic Structure
Sounds in Syllables
Association of Words with Initial Consonant Sound
Recognition of Small Written Vocabulary

Emergent Reading
Read Story Verbatim
Read Verbatim, Some Words
Attempt Word Recognition
Reading Strategies Imbalanced
Read at Preprimer Level
Read at Primer Level

LANGUAGE ARTS

Dictation
Represent Ideas in Writing
Dictate Complete Ideas
Use Written Language Style
Understand Elements of Story Grammar
Maintain a Topic
Have Purpose for Writing
Aware of Conventions
Participate in Spelling

Writing
Left-to-Right Concept
Top-to-Bottom Concept
Whole-Word Concepts
Rapidly Shifting Topic
No Sentence Patterns
No Planning, Spontaneous
No Permanence of Ideas

Spelling
Use Drawing and Writing
Use Scribbles, Lines, Shapes
Attempt to Copy Letters
Use Initial Consonants for Whole Word
Distinguish Letter Name and Sound
Use Random Letters to Capture Syllabic Structure
Vowels Spelled Perceptually
No Permanence; Much Testing and Experimentation
Small Vocabulary of Known Words

Punctuation
Include Punctuation Randomly
Emphasize Words with Punctuation
Use Punctuation at End of Sentence

Handwriting
Use Approximated Letter Forms
Use Random White Spaces
Develop Pencil Grasp
Print Many Letters
Attempt Letter Orientation
Attempt Uniform Size

Metalanguage is explored as the facilitator talks about cues that readers use to recognize words, and as children ask questions and talk about words, letters, and sounds during reading, writing, and play. Throughout reading, children are made aware of words that rhyme, the letters that begin a word, letter and sound correspondences, sequences of letters and sounds, and other aspects of metalanguage. Metalinguistic aspects of language are not thought of or taught as skills, but rather as an integral part of the story and as one layer of talk and thought that occurs when a reader makes sense of print.

Meeting Language Arts Goals through the Whole Language Approach

Five areas of language arts are explored within the lesson plans: **dictation,** or learning how a writer thinks about composition; **writing,** or exploring the conventions of printed language; **spelling,** or learning the structure of words and how this structure is represented using letters; **punctuation,** or signaling interpretations of text through specific conventions; and **handwriting,** or forming letters to represent meaning.

Dictation enables children to express complete ideas in writing while another person serves as the scribe. It is a process requiring active participation, as the children decide with the facilitator what to say, how to express the ideas in words, how to organize the ideas into discourse, how to develop the topic, and what purpose the writing will serve. As the scribe writes, the children actively participate in making decisions related to the conventions of print, such as where to start writing, what to do at the end of a line, when to leave white spaces, and what letters might be important to include in words. Dictation helps children to understand how a writer goes about the process of writing and the decisions that writers make about content, form, and function (Britton 1982; Calkins 1986; Ferreiro 1986; Gentry 1982; Temple et al. 1988).

Writing provides children with experience in all aspects of the writing process, including formulating their ideas, using letters to represent words, maintaining the conventions of print (such as left-to-right writing and providing a written word for each oral word intended), coordinating handwriting, and capturing both the phonemic structure of sounds using representative letters and the syllabic structure of words using letter sequences. Because the process is so complex and multidimensional, children begin writing from a global approach—with random marks and scribbles that reflect few of the conventions of print—and gradually refine their knowledge and skill. Developmental expectations must be appropriate; for example, recognizing that writing has no object permanence for beginning writers, so the same composition may be read to mean many different things, and that developmental spelling emerges over time (Britton 1982; Calkins 1986; Ferreiro 1986; Gentry 1982; Temple et al. 1988).

Spelling is a language process that emerges gradually, much as adult-like speech is acquired gradually from early infancy onward. Children must learn the phonemic structure of sounds and the letters that represent them, the syllabic structure of words and the ordering of letters to reflect the sound sequences, and orthographic patterns used in English spellings to signal such information as the status of vowels and irregularities of pronunciation. Children will make many discoveries about spelling as they use the knowledge they possess to write and make refinements through feedback, dictation, and reading experiences (Gentry 1982, 1989; Hoffman 1990, Hoffman and Norris 1989; Read 1986).

Through reading and dictation, children become aware of the utility of **punctuation.** They experiment with punctuation, placing it within their compositions whenever they want to emphasize a word with an exclamation point or question mark, or placing punctuation where they believe it might go. Considerable experience with writing and better coordination of the multiple processes will be required before children's punctuation begins to become more conventional. Knowledge about and skill in **handwriting** develop in much the same way, beginning with scribbles and shapes and gradually taking on more letter-like forms. Before printing letters can have any significance or meaning to children, they must know what letters do and what they are used for. Through experiences with forming letters, feedback, attention to printing during dictation, models of how adults make letters, and reading experiences, children begin to form a mental representation of letters and what they look like, how they are formed, and their relationship in orientation and size to surrounding letters (Temple et al. 1988).

Just as listening and talking take years to develop and are only gradually refined over time, reading and writing also emerge gradually as a function of becoming aware of the many layers of knowledge and skill involved, attempting to communicate in writing with existing knowledge, and refining that knowledge on the basis of feedback and new information. The teacher, speech-language pathologist, or special service provider can facilitate this learning by becoming aware of developmental stages and processes and by helping individual children to refine their own knowledge and skills according to their developmental needs.

■ Monitoring Progress

Progress in social studies, science, art, math, reading, and writing can be monitored using the Class Profile forms found in the appendix. The teacher can use a five-point rating scale to indicate the conditions that each child requires to talk about or demonstrate a skill. A score of 0 indicates that the child cannot be prompted to talk about or demonstrate knowledge of an area, such as "seasons." Or the child may know the information but be able to share it only when the situation is highly contextualized, such as when representative objects are present (a rating of 1) or when pictures are shown (a rating of 2). In a decontextualized situation, the teacher can indicate whether the child can talk about the topic with scaffolding or prompts (a rating of 3), or at the highest level of proficiency, can talk about the topic or demonstrate the behavior spontaneously (a rating of 4). The teacher can readminister the profile several times throughout the year and can monitor the class as well as individual children for change over time.

CHAPTER 2

The S-D-S Language Model

Chapter 1 introduced the concept of a language-based curriculum, consistent with principles of whole language. It examined the importance of language to all learning and the need to design a curriculum that develops language abilities (often referred to as "learning to talk") while children use language to learn about the physical and social world ("talking to learn"; Britton 1982; Wells 1986; Westby 1985). While the curriculum can be designed to support the efforts of the teacher, speech-language pathologist, or special service provider, the implementation, or the actual process, is far more critical to learning. The talk that occurs during implementation and the instructional strategies that engage the children in active involvement and problem solving are what enable them to be successful learners and language users.

The process-oriented teaching developed by the Storybook-Centered Curriculum is based on a model of language called the *Situational-Discourse-Semantic (S-D-S) model* (see Table 2-1, page 32). This model allows professionals who have not extensively studied language development, psycholinguistics, and sociolinguistics to address the language and learning needs of children with a wide range of abilities. A complete discussion of this model and its application to school-age children can be found in *Whole Language Intervention for School-Age Children* (Norris and Hoffman 1993). Becoming familiar with the principles of the model will provide guidance for facilitating transactional discussions that involve the children and that teach language and content-area information. Once the professional becomes familiar with the principles of the model, its use becomes a natural part of interactions with children. The model is designed to show that all uses of language are not equal in difficulty and function. Learning to vary the language used to accomplish different goals and purposes will empower the teacher or speech-language pathologist to maximize the effectiveness of the time spent with children in a learning environment.

The lesson plans provide specific suggestions for the levels of talk along the semantic and discourse dimensions of the S-D-S model for two situational contexts: the calendar and the thematic book reading. These suggestions are not intended as a script that must be followed verbatim or in its entirety. Rather, they demonstrate the types of ideas that are characteristic of the different levels of semantic and discourse talk. Use the levels that meet the developmental needs of the children and the purposes of the discussion. An example from the lesson plans for the thematic book *Boo-hoo* exemplifies the use of the S-D-S model. The picture for this day's plan shows an unhappy boy attempting to milk a cow. The accompanying text reads:

> My grandfather died and left me a cow.
> I wanted to milk it, but I didn't know how.

Situational
pic or object

Discourse
the way you organize
talk —
expressive

Semantic
meaning —
making

TABLE 2-1
The Levels of Situational, Discourse, and Semantic Context in the S-D-S Language Model

Situational Context

Level X *Logical* • hypothetical • mental objects • abstractions • principles	D e c o n t e x t u a l i z e d
Level IX *Symbolic* • linguistically created • possible event	
Level VIII *Relational* • relationships within event • scripts-schema	
Level VII *Decentered* • recreate event perspective of observer	
Level VI *Egocentered* • recreate event perspective of participant	
Level V *Logical* • representation • logical reason • concrete	C o n t e x t u a l i z e d
Level IV *Symbolic* • substituted objects • illustrations	
Level III *Relational* • relational actions, real functions	
Level II *Decentered* • sensorimotor exploration • discovery	
Level I *Egocentered* • sensorimotor stimulation • own body	

Discourse Context

Level VIII *Interactive Structure* • multiple plots or topics • reciprocal • integrated	T r a n s a c t i o n a l F u n c t i o n
Level VII *Complex Structure* • separate subtopics/ episodes • each complete	
Level VI *Complete Structure* • overall moral or objective • all elements	P o e t i c F u n c t i o n
Level V *Abbreviated Structure* • plans, intents • incomplete • most elements	
Level IV *Reactive Sequence* • cause-effect • no intent/plan • logical order	
Level III *Ordered Sequence* • temporal order • no causality • arbitrary	
Level II *Descriptive List* • topic-related • no unifying temporal frame	
Level I *Collection* • associations • no structure • change topics	

Expressive Function

Semantic Context

Level VII *Metalanguage* • knowledge of linguistic properties • separate form from meaning or function	E x p e r i e n t i a l
Level VI *Evaluation* • response to or reflection on event • judgment/value • significance	
Level V *Inference* • meaning beyond what's stated • meaning not present or suggested	E r u d i t e
Level IV *Interpretation* • meaning not explicit but suggested in available cues • goals, states	
Level III *Description* • unify objects, events, agents • characteristic qualities • explicit	
Level II *Labeling* • name wholes • label parts within whole • categories • sensory input	
Level I *Indication* • nonlinguistic communication • meaning known in context	

Reprinted with permission from Norris, J. A., and P. R. Hoffman. 1993. *Whole language intervention for school-age children.* San Diego, CA: Singular Publishing Group. .

■ Semantic Context

The discussion of the picture begins with the concepts and information along the semantic continuum. *Semantics* refers to the meanings or ideas talked about. At the lowest end of the continuum is nonverbal reference, accomplished through pointing, gestures, or sounds. The most concrete level of language is merely labeling objects or people. The levels become increasingly more abstract through the level of metalanguage, where language is used to talk about concepts of "wordness," letters, and sounds. Both *experiential* meanings—those that can be learned through everyday experience—and *erudite* meanings—those which are academically learned—are described along the continuum. This continuum is summarized in Table 2-2 (page 34).

The discussion of the page from *Boo-hoo* might consist of comments spontaneously produced by the children, comments elicited from children using questions or prompts, or information given by the facilitator. Directing the children's attention to the picture, the facilitator might begin by asking children to identify whole objects or parts of objects shown in the picture, thus eliciting *labels.* Experiential labels refer to people, animals, objects, or things that are visible; for example, the cow and some of her body parts, such as her horns, hooves, spots, and udder, and the boy and his stool. This establishes specific vocabulary for body parts and objects that may be unfamiliar and directs children's attention to information that may be significant to understanding the story. Erudite labels might include bovine, frontal bone, tripod, and pendulous gland.

The discussion should then be focused at a higher level, that of *description.* Descriptive language refers to qualities of objects, such as color, size, or shape, to descriptions of actions produced by characters, or to the relationship between two or more objects (Blank, Rose, and Berlin 1978; Monroe 1951). This level of language requires an analysis of the aspects or features of a situation. In this day's play, the *experiential descriptions* call for the children to carefully examine the cow and describe her in detail. They are instructed to get a good picture of the cow in their minds because they will need that information later. They describe the length of her tail, neck, legs, and horns; the location of her eyes, nostrils, hooves, udder, and spots; and the shape of her head, body, and body parts. Action descriptions include that the boy is sitting on the stool, that the boy is next to the cow, and that the cow is looking at the boy. An *erudite description* would state that Guernseys are a breed of dairy cattle.

TABLE 2-2
The Seven Levels of the Semantic Context, Reflected in Both
Experiential and Erudite Knowledge

Semantic Context

E x p e r i e n t i a l	Unconscious knowledge of the properties of language. Can use and invent metaphors, rhymes. Can state when a sentence is ungrammatical, can name letters, has concepts of wordness. Interprets metaphors by personal experience. **Level VII** *Metalanguage*	Conscious knowledge of the properties of language. Can explain metaphors, rhymes, grammatical rules, orthographic rules. Interpret metaphors, etc., through world, academic knowledge. **E r u d i t e**
	Personal evaluation of an event or situation. Indicate attitudes, likes, and beliefs. Often more closely aligned to opinion than to fact. **Level VI** *Evaluation*	Culturally valued responses, world significance or lesson considered. Value judgments, justification of behavior, moral standards, principles.
	Meaning goes beyond what is stated to include information derived from personal experience or common knowledge. Inferred information not present or suggested by context. **Level V** *Inference*	Meaning goes beyond what is stated to include information related to world, scientific, academic knowledge. Inferred meaning not present or suggested by context.
	Cues for interpretations present in context but not explicitly stated or depicted. Predicted from personal experience. Includes goals, states, qualities, changes. **Level IV** *Interpretation*	Cues for interpretations present in context but not explicitly stated or observable. Requires specific scientific, historical, or world knowledge.
	Descriptions of the relationships of action or state between two unrelated objects, agents, events; or of characteristics of objects such as color, size, shape, height, etc. **Level III** *Description*	Descriptions of historical, world, scientific events that include actions, characteristics, qualities. Information explicitly stated or observable.
	Names for concrete, observable objects or agents, including the whole object and labels for parts within the whole. Little distance from sensory perception. **Level II** *Labeling*	Names for abstract, mentally created objects or agents. Categories or classes refer to groups of objects having similar semantic properties. Distanced from perception.
	Nonlinguistic communications used to share reference to information existing external to the speaker, such as pointing to something that is noticed. **Level I** *Indication*	Nonlinguistic communication that exists or originates within the speaker. Communicates implied information, although the form is nonspecific (wink, shrug).

Reprinted with permission from Norris, J. A., and P. R. Hoffman. 1993. *Whole language intervention for school-age children.* San Diego, CA: Singular Publishing Group.

The children then should be helped to use their background knowledge and experiences to make *interpretations*. Interpretive language refers to internal states, motivations, or underlying qualities of characters, objects, or actions. These include psychological motives and plans that can only be assumed, rather than directly observed. Experiential interpretations are suggested by cues present in observable characteristics of characters or objects. In this day's plans, children are asked to examine the picture of the cow and respond to questions such as:

- "Why is the cow's mouth located at the end of her snout?"

- "What is she eating and where did she get it?"

- "Why are her nostrils on her snout along with her mouth?"

- "Where are the horns located?"

- "What would she have to do with her head if she wanted to protect her calf?"

- "What would happen to her udder if the cow had shorter legs?"

Erudite interpretations are made with respect to specific knowledge about the world. An example of an erudite interpretation would be that after the cow swallows the grass, it will be mixed and softened in the first two chambers of the stomach, and then returned to the mouth as cud, rechewed, reswallowed, and then passed through a third stomach before being digested in the fourth.

At even higher levels of semantics, children should be helped to generate predictions or *inferences*. Inferences go beyond available information to rely on the children's knowledge about a topic (Blank, Rose, and Berlin 1978; Monroe 1951). Experiential inferences rely on personal and vicarious experiences. In this day's lesson plan, the children are asked to generate predictions about the boy and the cow by asking, "Can you tell from the picture what is making him feel frustrated?" The children then test their predictions by reading the text to find out what happened. The facilitator should discuss what "left me a cow" means. What is the difference between *wanting* to do something and *knowing how* to do something? Erudite inferences are made with respect to knowledge obtained without direct experience, such as the fact that even though this boy can't get milk, dairy cows usually produce milk for five or six years, and some may give milk for twenty years or more.

The next highest semantic level is that of *evaluation*. Evaluations provide justifications for actions, evaluations of good and poor aspects of objects within an event, judgments of social and moral appropriateness, and summarizations of important aspects of events. *Experiential evaluations* are personal attitudes, beliefs, or opinions. In this day's lesson, the children might be asked, "Do you think the boy likes milking the cow? Should he have learned how first? Why?" Erudite evaluations are those that reflect cultural values, standards, or world significance. An example might be, "The ancient Egyptians valued their cattle as sacred animals and raised them in luxury."

The highest semantic level of the S-D-S model explores the metalinguistic properties of words. *Metalanguage* uses language to refer to itself (Lehr and Osborn 1994). Experiential use of metalanguage occurs when a child tells a joke, intentionally produces rhyming words, spontaneously sounds out the letters in a word that is being read aloud, or appropriately interprets figurative language. Erudite metalanguage is when a child considers language parts that have been separated from their use and meaning. Examples are discussing why two words rhyme and being able to explicitly state rules of language. In this day's plan, the metalinguistic explorations involve reading the sentences on each page again, emphasizing the words "cow" and "how." The facilitator asks the children to find the two words that rhyme and uses written words to give clues about why they rhyme: the two words are written, one above the other, and the children are asked to look at them to discover the recurring letter pattern, and then to circle the letter pattern.

The multiple levels of the semantic continuum provide opportunities for many dimensions of language to develop, including the acquisition of vocabulary, concepts, and descriptive terms; the use of cues to draw interpretations and solve problems; and the use of background knowledge to derive inferences and make predictions, evaluate the significance of events, and explore the properties of words and print metalinguistically. But concepts by themselves are only one of the dimensions of language that are important in acquiring oral and written language and using language to learn. A second dimension is the *discourse context.*

■ Discourse Context

The discussion of the picture that began with the concepts and information along the semantic continuum continues with the discourse context. Discourse refers to the organization of the talk about a topic, as described in Table 2-3 (Applebee 1978; McCabe and Peterson 1991; Stein and Glenn 1979). The organization can range from ideas strung together through free association—a discourse level termed *collections*—through highly organized discourse that develops topics according to temporal, causal, intentional, purposeful, and other relationships of meaning.

Discourse Context

(Transactional Function)		Level		(Poetic Function)
T r a n s a c t i o n a l F u n c t i o n	Many dimensions of the same scientific, cultural, political, historical, etc., topics are presented in a manner that draws comparisons and contrasts within and among them. An integrated, rather than sequential format.	**Level VIII** *Interactive Structure*	Two or more story lines develop separately within a complex story, each containing multiple problem episodes. The same set of events may be described from two or more perspectives, goals are reciprocal, and flashbacks reorder sequence.	**P o e t i c F u n c t i o n**
	Each chapter or section within a chapter addresses a separate subtopic within a main topic, with little cross-referencing to the information discussed in preceding or following sections.	**Level VII** *Complex Structure*	One story line develops but with a sequence of problems presented, each of which is resolved prior to encountering the next. The lessons learned in one episode are carried over to the next.	
	A complete and self-contained presentation of a topic is given. The information is unified by an overall objective, such as to explain a procedure, or present a problem and find a solution.	**Level VI** *Complete Structure*	Exhibits all characteristics of a complete narrative, including an overall purpose or moral, told by establishing a setting, creating an initiating event, resolved by attempts, reactions, consequences.	
	A general but incomplete presentation of a topic is made with causal links between steps in a procedure and purpose or intent guiding actions or decisions. No higher-order goals unify topic.	**Level V** *Abbreviated Structure*	Story told for its own sake, with no overall purpose or moral. But characters have plans or *intents* that precede their actions. Story has initiating event, resolved by attempts, reactions, consequences.	
	A description of a logically sequenced event based on cause-effect relationships, but no plan or intent governing this order. Reporting on "what happens" in logical order but not "why."	**Level IV** *Reactive Sequence*	Describe an event in which the actions of one character cause an unplanned effect on another in domino fashion. Order is important but not determined by intent. Has setting, problem, action, result.	
	Temporal sequences based on daily, weekly, monthly, seasonal, or yearly patterns, or spatial sequences based on actual location but not goal-directed planning. Arbitrary choice of details.	**Level III** *Ordered Sequence*	Recount the order in which events occurred, but no logic or cause-effect relationships necessitate that particular order. Order can be changed without affecting outcome. Setting, action, result.	
	Presentation of facts about a topic. All ideas relate to an overall general topic, but do not build on each other; no cause-effect or temporal relationships between them. Merely a list.	**Level II** *Descriptive List*	Some elements of stories, such as action-based events organized around a central theme. No particular order in which events occur, no time frame unifies them, no reciprocal or causal relations.	
	Loosely organized presentation of a topic, where no single object, event, or activity remains in focus. Ideas may be linked through free association or general theme.	**Level I** *Collection*	Response to immediate perceptions with no overall structure imposed. Focus of story shifts rapidly by free association. No setting, goals, attempts, consequences.	

E x p r e s s i v e   F u n c t i o n

Reprinted with permission from Norris, J. A., and P. R. Hoffman. 1993. *Whole language intervention for school-age children.* San Diego, CA: Singular Publishing Group.

In addition to defining the levels of organization of the discourse, the S-D-S model uses Britton's (1982) classifications to differentiate among three different functions of discourse. The *expressive function* refers to information that is personal or responsive. This function serves personal needs, rather than providing others with information about the world or how to interpret an event or situation. Language that is expressive in function is often informal and conversational in nature. Elements of expressive-function language are typically present in the early speech and writing of children. They can include recounting personal experiences with comments. ("I went to the circus *and I really liked the clowns.* Then the lions came out, but they were in cages *and I got kinda scared.*") Expressive-function language is often encouraged as an entry point into the writing process, when children are asked to maintain journals that include their present concerns and impressions (Staton et al. 1988).

Transactional discourse is used to accomplish a goal, such as giving information, requesting information, or requesting that some action be executed. This type of discourse is goal-directed, used to convey information for purposes of changing another person's beliefs, attitudes, or behaviors (Britton 1982). Typical types of transactional discourse encountered in a classroom include stating a sequence of procedures to be followed in completing an activity, executing a sequence of calculations in mathematics, and discussing events that happened during a historical era. Most content-area information is presented in the transactional function.

Poetic discourse refers to language that is used to create verbal objects such as differing genres of poetry, drama, and narrative. This form of discourse is used to influence the beliefs, behaviors, and attitudes of others, but through indirect example rather than direct statement. An author creates poetic discourse to elicit emotional reactions and to reflect on experience in order to discover its significance, meaning, or message (Britton 1982). Each of these forms of discourse can maintain organization at any of the eight levels of complexity along the *discourse continuum* (Labov 1972). The lesson plans provide examples of each level of discourse and the language that might be used to link the ideas through relationships of topic, time, causality, intentionality, and purpose. Chapters 3 and 4 contain methods of facilitating children's use of more complex discourse structures.

The story segment on pages 2 and 3 of *Boo-hoo* is used as an example of a lesson plan for developing the discourse context. The lesson might begin with the children providing only loosely organized *collections* of ideas. While staying within the children's range of development, referred to by Vygotsky (1962) as the "Zone of Proximal Development," the facilitator helps the children to add complexity to their story. The level above a collection—termed a *descriptive list*—organizes information by a coherent topic. The factual information discussed along the semantic continuum was an example of transactional discourse organized according to a descriptive list. A story (the poetic function of discourse) can be elicited by pointing to parts of the picture and asking, "What is he doing?" which elicits a list of topically consistent story events such as:

> The cow is eating grass. The boy is milking the cow. The cow is looking at the boy.

Children should be helped to impose greater organization on the story, beginning with the addition of a temporal order, termed an *ordered sequence.* Ordered sequences impose a temporal or spatial order on the discussion. A transactional ordered sequence might involve describing a naturally occurring sequence of events, such as the passage of the sun from east to west across the sky. An expressive ordered sequence could describe the person's changing reactions throughout the day. A poetic ordered sequence could describe a sequence of actions by a character. The example from the lesson plan suggests that five actions can be temporally ordered, as in:

> The cow was eating some grass. The boy came up to her and started trying to milk her. He kept trying, but he couldn't get any milk from the cow. Then he started to cry.

Further complexity can be imposed to create a *reactive sequence.* In reactive sequences, the order of events is determined by cause-effect relationships. A transactional reactive sequence might describe a series of events, each of which serves as the cause for the next, such as the changes in cows that occur through their life cycle. A poetic reactive sequence would specify the causal links between the events of a story. In lesson plans for this level, the facilitator helps the children to add causal language, as in:

> The cow was eating the grass when the boy saw her and decided to milk her. He tried for a long time but didn't get any milk because he didn't know how. That made him feel frustrated and he started to cry.

While causal relationships explain what happened in response to some action or event, an *abbreviated structure* imposes planned action or intentional behavior. The character's overall goal is explicitly stated at this level. A transactional abbreviated structure could describe the steps for milking a cow, starting with an explicit statement of the goal. Poetic abbreviated structures contain a statement about the character's internal emotional response to a problem and the resulting plan or intentional action taken to achieve the goal. In this day's plan, the children would be helped to include intentionality in their story, as in:

> The boy got a cow from his grandfather when his grandpa died. He decided to get some milk from the cow, so he went out to the barn and started trying to milk her. He didn't learn how to milk a cow before he tried, and so it didn't work. That made the boy feel frustrated, and so he started to cry.

A *complete structure* provides a complete presentation of a sequence of events or facts related to a topic, including an overall objective or moral that states a purpose for telling the information. Complete transactional texts include a relatively comprehensive discussion of the related facts about a single topic, such as a chapter in a science text that is devoted to the process of milk production. In the poetic function, a complete structure contains a setting that describes the typical daily lifestyle of a character. An initiating event establishes a problem, which the character reacts to by formulating a plan. The character attempts a sequence of actions dictated by the plan, with varying degrees of success. In the end, the character's motives and actions are evaluated or a moral is derived. In the lesson plans, the suggested story for this level is:

> Once there was a boy who lived in the city. His grandfather was a farmer, and when he died he left the boy a cow. The boy wanted some milk, so he went out to the barn to milk the cow. But when he tried, he couldn't make it work. That frustrated the boy and he started to cry. He gave up too easily.

Children at five years of age are capable of telling stories with a complete structure (Applebee 1978; Labov 1972; McCabe and Peterson 1991). Discourse skills continue to develop significantly throughout the school years. Older children are capable of producing texts or stories that have either complex or interactive discourse structures. *Complex structure* is characterized by the sequencing of a number of complete structures unified by an overall topic. Each component structure is presented in its entirety before the next is introduced. This level of discourse is typical of textbooks that treat different related subjects under individual subheadings within a chapter. It also appears in narratives when a sequence of episodes occurs.

Interactive structures combine multiple topics that are presented in alternation so that they interact rather than occurring in sequence (Labov 1972). This structure occurs in higher-level textbooks in which the discoveries and developments discussed in one section must be considered in relationship to previously given information. For example, an interactive discussion of the dairy industry would show the interactions among economic, geographic, and biological aspects of the topic. Novels are interactive when there are multiple subplots that affect one another. The interactive structure of events allows the narrator to reorder events with respect to time and place through the use of flashbacks and foreshadowing in order to present information when the reader needs it (Bruce 1981).

While the poetic discourse structure of the story serves to coordinate learning within a narrative-centered theme, transactional discourse is used to develop background knowledge related to the story through conducting explorations of the content areas of social studies, sciences, mathematics, art, and language arts. In each day's lesson plans, a new topic or concept important to understanding the story is explored through *topic explorations* and generalized beyond the meaning of the story through *thematic studies* (that is, community studies, cultural studies, psychological studies, or environmental studies). Each of these activities represents a different level of language use along the continuum of the situational context.

■ Situational Context

The *situational context* refers to the global characteristics of an activity or situation and how language is used within this context. Language that closely matches and talks about objects, people, and actions that are occurring in the immediate context—such as talking about the illustrations in a book—is called *contextualized language* and is represented in the lower levels of complexity along the situational continuum in Table 2-4 (page 42). Language that refers to events, people, and actions that are not present—such as talking about a historical event, making up a story, or making predictions about things that will happen in the future—is called *decontextualized language.* Decontextualized language is a much more difficult use of language, because all of the images of people, objects, and actions must be created using words alone, without any visual or other cues from the environment (Blank, Rose, and Berlin 1978; Westby 1985).

The levels of contextualized and decontextualized language along the situational continuum range from talk that is closely related to the child's own body, such as talking about a new pair of shoes the child is wearing or about the child's trip to the beach, through increasing levels of distance from the child. Talking about the illustrations in a book, for example, is more distanced because the pictures are not real, but are only symbolic representations of characters, objects, or events. The child must increasingly rely on imagining rather than experiencing (Piaget 1952, 1954). Even more distanced are discussions about logical events, such as the relationship between greater slope and faster speed of objects moving down a plane. With each increase in distance from the child's own body and sensory experience, and with increases in the requirements of language to create the important context, the activity or situation becomes more difficult for the child to understand and talk about.

TABLE 2-4
The Ten Levels of the Situational Context, Distributed along a Continuum from Contextualized to Decontextualized

Situational Context

Language refers to: objects, agents absent from immediate context past and possible actions, states, or events self-regulation, including plans primary responsibility for communication belongs to speaker	**D e c o n t e x t u a l i z e d**	**Level X** *Logical*	Language and logic are used to create a hypothetical context. The context created consists of mental objects that have no sensorimotor correlates. Topics deal with abstractions, principles.
		Level IX *Symbolic*	Factual or fictional experiences are created using language alone, as in learning about a different period in history or reading a novel. Language is not used to talk about the known world, but rather to create possible worlds.
		Level VIII *Relational*	Learning and functioning require an understanding of the overall structure of events and the relationships of the component parts. Includes scripts or schema for classroom or other conventional routines, self-monitoring to plan and complete a task.
		Level VII *Decentered*	Language is used to create an event from the perspective of an observer. The child was present for the event, but not as an active participant. Language structures what was seen or heard.
		Level VI *Egocentered*	Language is used to recreate an event from the perspective of a participant, or an experience that earlier was experienced on a sensorimotor level. The people, actions, and objects must be referenced through language.
		Level V *Logical*	Objects are present but used in abstract, representational ways. Greater focus on mental concepts and language used to refer to them. Roles different from one's own are assumed. Logical reasoning about concrete objects. Social interaction facilitates learning *about* events.
Language refers to: objects, agents present in the context ongoing actions and states social regulation of behavior of others responsibility for communication shared	**C o n t e x t u a l i z e d**	**Level IV** *Symbolic*	Language and learning are contextualized to immediately present objects, events, and people, but objects can be miniatures, replicas, substituted objects, drawings, or other representations. Includes illustrated storybooks. Social interaction involves shared participation.
		Level III *Relational*	Language and learning refer to objects used in sequences of relational actions. Actual objects are used for real functional purposes. Includes most self-help routines, such as eating, dressing, or bathing. Social interaction occurs for purposes of getting things done.
		Level II *Decentered*	Language and learning occur in relationship to the sensorimotor exploration of individual objects for purposes of discovering the relationships of the parts to the whole, or the general function of the object. Social interaction occurs for sake of interacting.
		Level I *Egocentered*	Language and learning are contextualized to immediately present sensory stimulation impacting directly on child's own body. Personal response to temperature, hunger, fatigue, as well as objects contacting child.

Reprinted with permission from Norris, J. A., and P. R. Hoffman. 1993. *Whole language intervention for school-age children.* San Diego, CA: Singular Publishing Group.

The lesson plans are designed to provide a range of activities and experiences along the situational continuum. Many activities are highly contextualized. This provides the support from the environment which some children need in order to successfully:

- talk about the event

- learn new concepts

- increase knowledge about a topic

- acquire new vocabulary, more complex sentences, and more organized discourse structures

Other activities are designed to require more decontextualized and distanced uses of language, providing the children with experiences in using language to imagine and to talk about past events, future probabilities, and hypothetical concepts, such as those explored in science and mathematics.

To exemplify the different levels of contextualization and displacement along the situational continuum, we will use an activity at each level that explores the concepts introduced on the page from *Boo-hoo*. At a *contextualized-egocentered* level, the talk would refer directly to the child's own body, sensory perceptions, and actions (Piaget 1952, 1954). The activity might include dressing the child in a striped T-shirt, shorts, and tennis shoes similar to the ones worn by the boy in the story. All of the talk would be related directly to the child, rather than to the boy in the story. The talk would include asking how the shoes felt—whether they were tight or too big, whether they felt warm or cool—and talking about wearing the shirt, including where the child's head goes and where the arms fit. The talk at this level of the continuum is about the children and their personal perceptions rather than about the clothing.

A focus on objects as entities separate from the child's own body occurs at the *contextualized-decentered* level. The body and sensory system are used to explore and manipulate objects in order to find out more about them (Piaget 1952, 1954). A sample activity might be talking about the boy's clothing. The shoes, shirt, and shorts might be identified by name and function, with questions such as, "Which ones go on your feet?" or "Which one has stripes?" The children might be helped to learn how to dress themselves. The talk at this level of the continuum requires the child to use perceptions to make sense of objects and to refer to them by name or function.

Real objects that are used in relationship to one another in order to accomplish goals are characteristic of the *contextualized-relational* level. This is the level of many everyday activities—such as eating a meal, washing the dishes, getting on a bus, preparing for bed, and so forth. The child must have an understanding of the function of the different objects encountered within these routines and how they should be used. The child must understand the relationships of the toothpaste to the toothbrush and of the toothbrush to the teeth. The child must also be able to sequence the actions within the routines.

An activity of this type would be making butter from the cow's milk by pouring a pint of whipping cream and a few drops of yellow food coloring into a jar, and then taking turns shaking it until it begins to thicken. The group should time how long it takes to turn the cream into butter. When the butter is ready, it should be spread on crackers and tasted.

Symbols such as pictures, miniature objects and figures, drawings, and artwork are examples of the *contextualized-symbolic* level. The symbols must stand in the place of real objects, and the children must know enough about real objects and their functions to impart actions, states, and behaviors to these symbolic representations (Piaget 1952, 1954). Included at this level are illustrated books in which much of the story can be derived from the pictures. An activity from this day of the lesson plans is to have the children solve the problem of not knowing how to milk a cow by making a symbolic cow and milking it. Provide materials to make a cow: a sawhorse, enough butcher paper to go around it for a body, a large paper sack turned inside out for the head, small paper sacks to cover the legs of the sawhorse forming hooves, and a large variety of colored markers, glue, tape, paper. Provide guidance, but let the children make decisions about what to put on the cow and how to affix these things. When the cow is finished, attach a rubber glove "udder" filled with milk, poke a pinhole in the end of each finger, and have children take turns sitting on a stool milking the cow and draining the milk into a pail.

Graphs, charts, and objects like blocks that are substituted for other objects (such as the cow) are characteristic of the *contextualized-logical* level. These symbols represent conceptual relationships such as comparisons of size or weight, logical principles such as conservation, logical categories such as all blue things, or logical symbols such as rectangular blocks to stand for the general properties of the cow. An example of an activity at this level is providing a variety of food cans and boxes, each of which has a note inside stating either "milk" or "no milk," indicating whether that food product is made with milk. Children should state whether they think the food contains milk, and then check by retrieving the note and reading it. The number of foods containing milk could be plotted on a bar graph and compared to the number not made with milk. Include packages for pudding, butter, cheese, ice cream, cottage cheese, cream, and sour cream, as well as cereal and several other foods that don't contain milk.

Each of the preceding levels represented contextualized activities in which the language referred to objects or events that were present and manipulable. The next five levels represent decontextualized language use. The lowest decontextualized level is *decontextualized-egocentric*, referring to the use of language to talk about the children's own experiences. The objects and other situational cues are no longer present, but the children's memories and prior sensory and motor participation in the event provide support for the discussion. This level involves telling or writing about a past experience, including dictated writing about the child's participation in a directly experienced event. An example from the lesson plans would be a journal-writing activity in which the children are asked to write about their participation in making the cow and what they learned about cows as a result.

Events that the children merely observe rather than directly participating in are characteristic of the *decontextualized-decentered* level. The memories and representations of the event are from an observer's rather than a participant's perspective. Classroom teachers often make demands at this level; an example is when they demonstrate a task or activity that the children must report about or remember at a later time or date (Cazden 1988). An activity from the lesson plans at this level would be a teacher demonstration of "how to do something" such as tying shoes, making a sandwich, using a computer program, or calling 911. The discussion would then require the children to talk about the demonstration and to make a list of things they would like to know how to do. Both of these tasks require talk about things the children have only observed others doing without direct personal participation.

At the *decontextualized-relational* level, language is used to structure events and to create knowledge. This level is characteristic of classroom rules such as, "If you are finished with your project, you may choose a learning center. But make sure all of your materials are put away first." Children are asked to follow scripts for their behavior at school that exist in the teacher's mind and perhaps in a handbook to which the child cannot refer (Creaghead 1992). The child must construct these scripts by listening to the teacher's explanations of rules. Other academic scripts include learning how to use an index to locate information in a book. Both the information being sought and the method of seeking that information are dependent on the use of language.

At the *decontextualized-symbolic* level, factual and fictional events are created using language alone. All of the people, objects, actions, cause-effect changes in location or state, and sensory perceptions must be imagined or created in the mind through the use of language without contextual supports (Golden 1990). Many oral discussions in the classroom are held at this level of complexity. An example from the lesson plans is the classroom "newsboard," where a headline from the local or national news is placed on a bulletin board and discussed. For example, the posted headline might come from a news article telling about a new breed of dairy cow that produces more milk.

The most decontextualized and decentered level is that of *decentered-logical*. At this level of the situational continuum, language is used logically to create hypothetical concepts or mental objects that cannot be seen, touched, smelled, heard, or in any way directly experienced through the senses (Piaget 1952, 1954). An example related to the lesson plans would be a discussion of how milk sours through the process of fermentation, which is the chemical decomposition of the organic substance of milk by enzymatic action in the absence of oxygen. Obviously, a discussion of sour milk with young children would need to occur at a much lower language level, as in: "When milk gets warm, enzymes in the milk cause it to get sour. Then it smells and tastes bad."

The situational context becomes an important consideration in setting goals for language, math, science, and social studies. Every learning activity will fall somewhere along the situational continuum. The higher the language demands are along the situational continuum, the lower the complexity that can be expected along the discourse and semantic continua. The language used to talk about information unsupported by the context will have to be simple and short, with vocabulary that is familiar to the child. The facilitator must continually judge by the children's responses whether they are coping with the level of situational complexity present. By lowering the situational complexity and providing more contextual support through pictures, demonstrations, and hands-on experiences, the child who is failing to comprehend at one level can be assisted in making progress along the discourse and semantic continua.

■ Use of the S-D-S Model to Guide Assessment and Establish Goals

The activities described in the Storybook-Centered Lesson Plans blend a variety of levels of situational context. New concepts are introduced through relatively supportive situational contexts, such as the manipulation of objects. During storybook activities, the children are introduced to each new page first through discussions of the concepts portrayed in the pictures and only later through discussions of the concepts referred to in print. Difficult or important concepts are explored further through a variety of activities that have different situational, discourse, and semantic demands. Over a series of days, the familiar pages are discussed with decreasing situational support and higher levels of discourse organization and semantic abstraction.

Observational Assessment

An example of the use of the model can lend insights into how one can use it to establish goals and assess progress. This example is from the *Grumpy Elephant* unit implemented in a kindergarten classroom. The main topic explored on this day was "grumpy." First, the children were shown a picture of a boy with a grumpy face during Calendar time. Most of the children's comments were situationally contextualized to the picture, as in: "He looks mad" or "He has a mean face." The children did not generate any inferences when asked the decontextualized question, "What do you think made this boy so grumpy?" until the teacher gave some possibilities. Then, all of their predictions were at the egocentered level. (For example, "I get grumpy when my brother wakes me up.") These children's responses reveal that they had great difficulty using decontextualized language in the context of a picture of an unknown character.

During Collaborative Reading, the children were able to identify that the elephant was also grumpy and to describe facial features and expressions that indicated his mood, showing good semantic interpretation of situationally contextualized symbols. When reminded of things that made them grumpy, the children were able to infer that similar things might have made the elephant grumpy.

Grumpiness was further examined in Topic Explorations. First, the class read and discussed the story *The Three Billy Goats Gruff* (contextualized-symbolic situation; complex discourse structure). Groups of children then enacted the story. The S-D-S model was used to assess the ongoing dynamics within the enactments. Analysis of the situational context revealed that the language used was primarily decontextualized in that it did not refer to objects present in the physical environment. The children had to remember the characters and what they did, said, and felt. Reference to the children, furniture, pictures on the bulletin board, or other information present in the classroom would not assist in enacting the story, but would instead be distracting and cause the children to interject inappropriate information. Furthermore, the information in the enactments did not refer to the children's own experiences, but rather to something that they had observed and heard earlier when reading and discussing the illustrated storybook. Therefore, the situational context in the enactments was described as decontextualized-decentered (Level S:VII on the S-D-S model).

Transcripts of two girls acting out the roles of the Little and Middle Billy Goats follow. These two transcripts illustrate widely differing levels of discourse ability.

Child 1: Little Billy Goat

Little Billy Goat	Other Speakers
The troll is mean. He will try to eat us. We must not go over there.	**Middle Billy Goat:** [No response] **Teacher:** Say, "But I'm . . ." What? **Middle Billy Goat:** But I'm going out to eat the green grass.
Well, we must be careful out there [begins to cross the bridge].	**Group:** Trip-trop, trip-trop. **Troll:** Who's that trip-tropping on my bridge?
It's me, the Little Billy Goat. I'm going to eat green grass on the other side.	**Troll:** No, you ain't! I'm coming up there to gobble you up.
Please don't eat me. I have another one coming, a big brother one. And he's bigger and fatter, and he'll taste much good.	**Troll:** Ok. Cross.

Analysis of the discourse context reveals that the first little girl retold the experiences of the Little Billy Goat Gruff primarily as a monologue that stayed in character, which is a poetic function of language use (see Table 2-3, page 37). She communicated her ideas in an appropriate temporal sequence and exhibited an understanding that attempting to cross the bridge could result in being eaten ("Please don't eat me.") and an ability to plan ("I have another one coming, a big brother one. And he's bigger and fatter, and he'll taste much good.") When the organization and coherence of ideas across sentences were considered, the discourse context was described as being a poetic monologue organized as an abbreviated structure (Level D:V on the S-D-S model).

Analysis of the semantic context showed that this child communicated many ideas within sentences, including labels ("It's me, the Little Billy Goat."); descriptions ("I'm going to eat green grass on the other side."); interpretations ("The troll is mean. He will try to eat us."); inferences ("And he's bigger and fatter, and he'll taste much good."); and evaluations ("We must not go over there."). She was able to use language to label and describe concrete referents and actions, as well as to go beyond the physical properties and interpret more abstract feelings, predict actions, infer outcomes, and evaluate the event. Thus, she showed evidence of being able to use language across all of the semantic levels except metalanguage under the specified situational and discourse conditions (see Table 2-2, page 34).

The second child, role playing the Middle Billy Goat Gruff, was presented with the same situational context, but analysis of the discourse context indicated substantial differences in her ability. She tromped across the bridge instead of waiting for the troll to appear, suggesting that in this decontextualized situation, where she had only observed the story events, she had not internalized the temporal sequence of the story. Furthermore, she was unable to retell her part of the story without assistance. These observations indicated an independent discourse level below that of an ordered sequence (Level D:III on Table 2-3). The discourse produced was a scaffolded dialogue ongoing among the child, the teacher, and peers who provided prompts. This interaction resulted in an overall discourse context described as a poetic dialogue organized as an abbreviated structure (Level PD:V), with the child in the responder role.

Middle Billy Goat	Other Speakers
	Group: Trip-trop, trip-trop, trip-trop (hooves on bridge).
[walks across bridge]	**Teacher:** Wait a minute, you've got to get back on the bridge. **Troll:** Who's that trip-tropping on my bridge?
[No response]	**Teacher:** Say who you are.
The Middle Billy Goat.	**Troll:** I'm gonna come gobble you up.
[No response]	**Teacher:** But I'm . . . what?
But I'm going out to eat some green grass.	**Teacher:** And wait for . . . who?
And wait for my brother.	**Teacher:** Because . . . ?
[No response]	**Teacher:** Why should the troll wait?
[No response]	**Teacher:** Because he's what?
[No response]	**Group:** Cuz he's more fatter.
Cuz he's more fatter.	**Teacher:** And he'll taste what? **Group:** Good.
[No response]	**Teacher:** Say it, Middle Billy Goat.
Good.	**Teacher:** Say the whole thing, "Wait for my . . . "
Brother cuz I'm gonna, cuz he's more fatter than me and will be good.	

Analysis of the semantic context showed that, even with prompting, the second child communicated ideas using only labels ("The Middle Billy Goat") and descriptions. ("But I'm going out to eat some green grass.") Even with prompts, she was unable to respond with information requiring higher levels of semantic abstraction, such as inferencing, until that information was provided by classmates. ("Because . . . ?" [No response] "Why should the troll wait?" [No response] "Because he's what?" [No response].) Child 2 was able to use language to label and describe concrete referents and actions, but not to go beyond the physical properties and interpret more abstract feelings, predict actions, infer outcomes, or evaluate the event. Thus, her profile of discourse and semantic use of language was very different from that of Child 1 under similar situational conditions.

Language Goals

One of the purposes of the Storybook-Centered Curriculum is to develop children's ability to understand and produce language at higher levels of semantic complexity, organized within more complex discourse structures and with increasing decontextualization of language. These are the characteristics of the literate language style that is important for success in school and academic achievement (Nelson 1992; Ripich and Griffith 1988; Westby 1985). The oral language goals of the curriculum are consistent with the S-D-S model on which the curriculum is developed. Semantically, these goals include increasing the vocabulary children use both to label and to describe concepts important to understanding the physical and social world in which they live, and increasing their understanding and use of experiential and erudite interpretations, inferences, evaluations, and metalanguage. Goals for written language include increased ability to read and write language expressing all levels of semantic complexity.

The goals in the domain of discourse include the ability to express ideas with greater semantic abstraction within higher levels of discourse complexity. The children should understand and produce expressive, poetic, and transactional discourse that is structured in more complex ways, ranging from descriptive lists through complete, complex, and interactive structures.

Situational goals include being able to understand and talk about unfamiliar, unexperienced events—including information from social studies and science content areas—when contextual support for this learning is provided. The children should be able to talk about familiar, previously experienced events or content-area knowledge at more complex levels of discourse organization and semantic abstraction with decreasing amounts of situational support. Increasing the children's ability to understand and use language changes what they can learn and the ways they can learn. As the children's language becomes more complex, greater learning can occur through the use of language at higher levels of the situational, discourse, and semantic continua. Specific goals and objectives for children at different developmental levels are provided in chapter 4.

For example, observation of which prompts were and were not effective with Child 2 in the Three Billy Goats Gruff role-play suggests that semantically she was using language effectively to code information that she could observe or experience (that is, labeling and describing), but that she had not learned to use language itself to form more mental or abstract concepts involving interpretations, inferences, and evaluations. Based on these observations, the interventionist can anticipate that this child will have difficulty with vocabulary related to internal states (worried, excited, grumpy), with nonliteral word meanings, and with the concept of wordness.

The S-D-S model also would predict that this girl might perform better semantically if visual cues were present to suggest needed information. For example, when provided with the illustrations from the storybook, she might be more successful at interpreting the troll as being mean or grumpy because of the visual cues provided in the creature's facial expression (suggesting a fairly concrete but developing understanding of these concepts).

Similarly, the discourse analysis suggested that Child 2 was unable to recall and structure the events of the story in sequence and did not refer to causality or plans in her script, although her nonverbal maintenance of the event did suggest an understanding that the discourse should be extended. Based on this, one could predict that this girl will have limited ability to impose organization on her world, manifested in difficulty finishing a task, difficulty with symbolic play involving infrequently experienced or imagined events, and difficulty following classroom rules. The model also would predict that Child 2 might show emerging abilities to sequence, refer to causality, and plan within very familiar events or when pictures or props are provided (that is, at lower levels of complexity along the situational continuum; French and Nelson 1985).

Analysis indicates that Child 2 would benefit from the use of pictures, graphs, demonstrations, and other visual materials and hands-on experiences to support the language used in the classroom. This contextualization would be important in helping this child function as a successful learner at her current level of language. The analysis also suggests that she would benefit from small-group language intervention to increase her ability to use language at higher semantic levels, to organize ideas at more complex levels of discourse, and to recreate experiences within decontextualized situational contexts.

But knowing what to talk about, how to increase complexity along the S-D-S continua to support learning, and how to establish goals within the S-D-S domains still does not address the *process* of learning (Goodman 1986; Smith 1990). The process involves what occurs in the ongoing transactions between the facilitator and the children, as well as the transactions between children, as together they explore, make discoveries, and talk about the social and physical world. How these transactions occur—including who is allowed to talk, how talk is facilitated, the strategies used to guide acquisition and development, and the attitude toward learning that is adopted—will affect the learning that takes place (Cazden 1983; Wells 1986). Chapter 3 will explore strategies for facilitating the language and learning processes within large or small groups and suggest ways to think about and teach content-area learning as a process.

Implementing the Storybook-Centered Lesson Plans

The Storybook-Centered Lesson Plans are designed to encourage use of language to create and talk about a wide range of experiences across all content areas, and to facilitate oral and written language acquisition. The goals of the curriculum are to develop active learning in children, to foster children's curiosity and understanding about their physical and social world, and to provide rich experiences with oral and written language. The plans can be used flexibly to meet the needs of a wide range of children across a continuum of regular and special education settings. There is no one way to implement the plans; rather models of implementation are given that can be modified to fit the needs, objectives, and circumstances of a classroom or intervention program.

The models of implementation include use of the curriculum (1) in the regular classroom, (2) for the provision of special services within the classroom, and (3) by special service providers in other intervention contexts. Suggestions are presented for implementing activities in large groups, researching information in small groups, and independently exploring topics in learning centers within these three different models. Large and small groups and independent learning centers provide different means for exploring topics.

The model for regular classroom implementation views the classroom much like any other community. Sometimes all community members meet together in large groups to share information and learn about a topic. Strategies for maximizing learning for all group members within these large groups are discussed. At other times, community members meet in small groups. Heterogeneous groups allow for active problem solving and cooperative learning among peers. Homogeneous groups allow for individualized instruction and high levels of feedback to the group members.

Communities also provide opportunities for independent learning and self-directed exploration. A variety of both permanent and temporary learning centers can be established to explore the topics within the Storybook-Centered Curriculum.

The teacher or special service provider can maximize the learning that occurs within all these settings by understanding learning as a process. In this chapter, we discuss the difference between a transmission model versus a transactional model of teaching and learning. We present methods for facilitating process learning in the domains of art, reading, mathematics, writing, and spelling, while emphasizing the importance of viewing these domains from a perspective of meaning and communication. We examine the developmental nature of these symbolic abilities and the stages of increasing knowledge and refinement.

These principles are appropriate for teaching and learning for children in regular education as well as children with special needs. Children with special needs will require smaller groups, more scaffolding, more frequent feedback, and other modifications in order to meet both language-acquisition and content-learning goals. These modifications are introduced here and elaborated on in chapter 4.

■ The Regular Classroom

The regular classroom must meet the needs of a broad range of children. The large number of children in a classroom results in a heterogeneous group of individuals with different backgrounds, personalities, interests, strengths, and needs. Increasingly, children with special needs, including those with physical and learning disabilities, those for whom English is not a first language, and those who are highly gifted, are integrated into the regular classroom program for the majority of their school day. Any curriculum implemented must be flexible and multidimensional in order to provide both challenges and supports that meet the educational needs of all of the group's members.

The classroom is a community and functions best when it maintains the properties of a good community. These properties include:

- an attitude of caring and support for others

- participation in the decision-making process to find solutions to group problems

- active involvement in building the community

- a broad base of knowledge from which to make informed decisions and to foster the continued development of the individual and the classroom community

A good community develops because of good leadership. Whatever the teacher models, provides opportunities for, and supports will develop in the community (Short, Burke, and Harste 1991). Whatever is not nurtured will diminish. Therefore, much more important than "what" is implemented in the lesson plans is "how" it is implemented.

Large-Group Activities

Large-group activities provide the classroom community members with shared information and experiences. They build a sense of cohesiveness and identity with the community, including all of its members. They teach members attitudes and behaviors that must be adopted for the good of the group and respect for the rights of individuals within the group. Each of these is important to children's success in the community of the school, and they provide early experiences with the types of group dynamics that adults encounter in the workplace, community groups, and other group-oriented democratic institutions. The classroom is the first experience that many children have with participation in a large group. It will take time, patience, and support to build effective large-group dynamics in the classroom community (Short, Burke, and Harste 1991).

Many of the components in the Storybook-Centered Lesson Plans, including Calendar time, Collaborative Reading, Topic Exploration, and Thematic Studies (specifically, Community Studies, Cultural Studies, Psychological Studies, and Environmental Studies) may be conducted in a large group. These general activities are designed to introduce new topics, to add new episodes to the unfolding thematic story, and to provide a rich background of knowledge for interpreting the story and making generalizations to other contexts or experiences. During these times, the children are provided opportunities to learn about a topic with maximum adult guidance, preparing them to explore the topic more independently in small groups or centers with an understanding of why the topic is important and what their own discoveries might mean. Large groups provide opportunities to be exposed to the ideas and opinions that other community members share about a topic and a forum for learning how to express one's own views.

Several principles are important in implementing large-group activities effectively:

1. **Discussions should involve talking *with* children, rather than talking *at* children.** Very often, books are read to children, the calendar is explained to children, demonstrations are done for children, and information about a topic is given to children. The adult thus usurps all of the real opportunities to use language, derive insights from pictures or materials, regulate the behavior of the group, create a story, and all of the other benefits of community participation and learning. Children learn to be passive and quiet, and to expect that learning will be transmitted by others. However, the purpose of a discussion is to help children learn how to attend to relevant information and to ask and talk about it with increasing complexity and abstraction. The teacher's role is to refer to important information and to guide children to talk about these concepts and events (Morrow and Smith 1990; Norris 1989b, 1991; Straw 1990).

2. **Discuss the same information at multiple semantic levels,** beginning at the most concrete level and progressing to the most abstract (Blank, Rose, and Berlin 1978). Very often, an important concept is discussed at only one level of meaning, with the assumption that the information is accessible to all of the children in the group. In fact, the information is often too abstract for many of the class members and too basic for others; as a result, nearly half of the children do not learn from the experience. Spending more time covering less information results in better learning than does presenting a lot of information at a superficial level. The children who are unfamiliar with the information can be helped to name the concept and discover some features about it, while the children who understand the concept can be challenged to make evaluations, predictions, or associations.

   Addressing different levels of questions to children at different levels of understanding enables each child to actively participate in the discussion. The children with the least understanding of the concept can talk about it at the most concrete semantic levels and can be helped to add greater complexity and detail using scaffolding strategies (see chapter 4). They also benefit from hearing more elaborated or abstract information contributed by other group members, which exposes them to information that they may be able to use and talk about at a later time (Sinatra 1990).

3. **Respond frequently to the children who DON'T know an answer,** instead of accepting a correct response from the child who does know. The role of a teacher is to *teach,* not to test what children already know. When children are asked questions that they cannot answer, if the teacher moves on to other classmates, then the first children have been taught that they are not capable of answering the questions and their self-worth is diminished. Those children are less likely to risk giving an answer in the future, instead assuming that their answer is wrong without ever offering it. By failing to answer correctly, children are showing the teacher that they do not know what is important to attend to in a situation or how to make sense out of it. This indicates that they need more information and assistance in order to organize and learn from the situation (Norris and Damico 1990; Norris and Hoffman 1990). Furthermore, if one child does not know an answer, then it is highly likely that several other children also do not know it. A wrong answer is therefore a signal that the teacher should take time at that moment to teach the information or provide the children with salient cues and guide them to derive the answer.

   If a child *does* answer the question correctly, then the same question should be repeated to a second child who is less likely to know the answer. Even though the second child has heard the answer, if the information doesn't make sense to that child, it will not be processed. If the second child cannot answer the question, this indicates a need to teach that information. Too often, the children who most need to be taught are the ones forgotten or neglected in a classroom. It is human nature to avoid asking questions of children if one anticipates that they will not know the answer. The result, however, is that the distance between these children's knowledge and that of their classmates widens because they have fewer opportunities to express information and are provided less feedback (Miller 1991).

4. **The very boisterous and the very quiet children both require frequent turns to respond.** Boisterous children by nature require attention and involvement. They need to know that they will have frequent opportunities to contribute and to be noticed, or they will create nonproductive ways to gain this attention. Placing these children in the role of assistant or helper who holds materials or points to information in a picture as others talk about it often will help them learn how to allow others to take an uninterrupted turn and make them more aware of the group's needs.

The very quiet child often wants to contribute but lacks the self-confidence or the strategies to volunteer. Some of these children experience stress or panic when asked to respond and therefore avoid being called on. One can often enhance the self-confidence and comfort level of these children by including them as active group members. The teacher might begin by attributing contributions to the child without requiring verbal responses through comments such as: "I noticed Sally looking at the bull, and that's a good idea. The lamb might be asking the bull to be his mother." Gestures and single-word answers may be interpreted in a similar manner, until the child feels sufficiently comfortable to contribute more. Frequent, short interactions that do not place pressure on the child provide the needed experiences with group interaction. Often, teachers fail to notice the very quiet child because so many others are demanding attention. The child may become progressively more disenfranchised from the group or even from school unless the teacher offers extra patience and support.

5. **Elaborate and clarify information provided by the children to add meaning and refinement to their ideas.** By beginning with the information that they provide, and then adding world knowledge, personal reactions, related information, details, or attributes, one helps children build on the knowledge they already possess (Vygotsky 1962). For example, if a child says, "It's a bus," an elaboration could be, "You're right. It's a bus that looks big enough for everyone in this room to ride on at the same time." Elaboration and clarification indicate to children that the adult is interested in what they have to say, because these comments reinforce their ideas. Such comments are a natural means of teaching through attributing greater meaning to the children's ideas than they are able to express independently (Nelson 1985).

6. **Engage children in problem solving rather than focusing on teaching facts or skills.** The purpose of teaching is to help children make developmentally appropriate discoveries, beginning with their current level of understanding, and then refining or building on this knowledge base (Hill and Hill 1990; Smith 1990). This strategy teaches children to seek answers or information for themselves, rather than to expect adults to provide the right answers. The children's errors or mistakes give insights into what they understand and what guidance the instructor needs to provide in order to help them modify their hypotheses.

7. **Provide communicative assistance by helping children who cannot immediately formulate an answer or a comment to generate one.** Often a child who cannot think of the answer or put the information into words can respond if the difficulty of the request is reduced (Norris and Damico 1990; Norris and Hoffman 1990). One strategy is to ask the question in a semantically less complex way. For example, if the child does not respond to an interpretive question ("Why was the bear unhappy?"), then reduce the semantic complexity to the level of a descriptive question ("What happened to the bear?"). If the child requires assistance knowing what to talk about, provide suggestions ("Do you want to tell us its color?") or offer choices ("Is it red or blue?"). If the child requires assistance coding the information into words, the interventionist can parse the ideas into sequences of information ("First tell us what he has. . . . Now tell us what he's doing with it.") or take some of the responsibility for constructing the sentence ("It's a _____ with a big red _____.").

8. **Provide visual cues and salient information to attend** to when introducing new concepts or helping children to solve problems or clarify misinterpretations. Visual cues create a situational context in which the language is contextualized and easier to grasp. Visual cues may take the form of models, reenactments, exemplars, or pictures (Blank, Rose, and Berlin 1978). By pointing to or demonstrating something very specific while briefly talking about its significance, one helps children to focus on the salient aspects of the object or event. After showing the object or event, give the children an opportunity to talk about it. This provides them with more time to think about the concept before the discussion moves on, the redundancy of hearing the same information a second time, the opportunity to receive feedback or clarification about their interpretation of the new information, and the experience of putting their observations into words.

9. **Act out or model the meaning of a difficult word or phrase,** such as "He *warned* the goat not to cross the bridge," or "The giant *roared* at Jack." The concrete visual, motor, and whole-body participation inherent in acting out events or information facilitates children's understanding of information that they may not fully understand through the

words alone (Piaget 1952, 1954; Vygotsky 1962). Acting angry or bossy enables children to understand the intent and underlying feelings associated with a warning or a roar. Walking onto a "bridge" and being stopped before reaching the other side establishes the meaning of the phrase "*not* to cross," in which the most important word to attend to is not a noun or a verb, but the function word "not." Vocal intonation, changes in pitch, exaggerated expression, gestures, facial expressions, slower speech rate, and sound effects all can enhance the meaning and intention of words and phrases.

Large-group instruction exposes children to information under the guidance of a facilitative adult. Guided discussions establish the background knowledge necessary to contextualize more independent hands-on experimentation. The background knowledge creates (1) a meaningful context from which to view the independent explorations and (2) a purpose for conducting such experimentation. The groups provide a context in which the majority of the children can derive an understanding of the concepts and the procedures involved in completing an independent or small-group project. When the group disperses, these children have sufficient information to proceed on their own, while the instructor assists those who are less able to organize extended sequences of actions.

Small-Group Activities

Small-group activities provide the class members with opportunities to work collectively as cooperative groups. Interdependent learning is fostered as small groups of children work together and share the responsibility for a group project or participate in joint construction of a topic during a small-group discussion. Small groups have many advantages: they provide more opportunities for members to talk and make significant contributions; the discourse style in a small group is less formal and may be less threatening to children who are reluctant to contribute in a large group; and children receive more individualized feedback on the content and relevance of their ideas. Several children can offer suggestions regarding how to solve a problem or approach a project, resulting in opportunities for the group to negotiate and consider options logically. The group can consider potential outcomes of different plans before implementing one, thereby using language to plan, predict, and reason (Hill and Hill 1990; Reid, Forrestal, and Cook 1990).

Any of the activities in the lesson plans can be implemented in a small-group setting. For example, Calendar time, Collaborative Reading, Topic Explorations, and Thematic Studies may take place in small groups within a self-contained classroom for children with special needs or in small-group intervention outside of the classroom or in small groups within the regular classroom. (See chapter 4 for ways to use the curriculum with children who have special needs.)

If the intervention setting is the regular classroom, many of the activities in the lesson plans, including activities listed under Additional Suggestions, are ideal for small-group dynamics. For many Topic Explorations and Thematic Studies activities, a large-group discussion may be used to establish the needed background information or procedural steps for a project, but the implementation takes place in small cooperative groups. For example, after discussing the process of milking a cow, examining pictures of cows, and discussing where a cow's body parts are located and how these locations are adapted to a cow's needs, children construct various parts of a cow in small cooperative groups. Some children are given an inverted paper sack and asked to create the head, while others are assigned to cover the sawhorse with butcher paper, and others must design hooves. The facilitator makes available materials—including construction paper, glue, scissors, tape, and markers—and provides guidance, but leaves the problem solving and decision making to the group. In one of our groups, the children found cat's-eye marbles in the science center and used them for the eyes of their cow, determining after several rejected solutions how to attach the marbles using clear tape.

Several principles are important when implementing cooperative small-group activities:

1. **Establish needed information prior to forming the small groups.** Doing so provides children with the knowledge they need to understand the nature of the problem, the purpose of the project, and the procedures or expectations for implementing it. Establish the information by engaging the children in active problem solving and giving them information they can use in deduction, rather than by giving them step-by-step procedures or predetermined information (Hill and Hill 1990). Information or instructions given in rote format must be remembered as a nonmeaningful sequence of actions which the children perform to achieve someone else's goals or purposes. Anything that is forgotten cannot be reconstructed because the children have no meaningful way to think about the information. Hence, instead of showing children where the eyes, nose, and mouth belong on a cow, ask them to describe where, for example, the mouth is located and why that location would help the cow eat grass. The problems, as understood and negotiated by the children, guide the sequence of steps taken to complete the project.

2. **Maintain a facilitative role** rather than directive control. During small-group cooperative activities, the adult moves among groups and facilitates problem solving. Facilitation might take many forms:

   - reminding children of information that they need to consider (For example: "Your cow can eat, but she'll have trouble breathing. What else could you put on the cow so she can breathe?")

   - giving individual help (for example, showing a child who is struggling how to measure and cut paper)

- helping to clarify issues for the group (For example, "Do you remember why we are making the cow? If she is going to give milk, she has to eat, so what do we need to do?")

- guiding decision making (for example, helping the children to decide on the sequence of steps they will perform or the materials they will use)

- answering questions about content, procedures, or goals,

- providing feedback or prompting refinements (For example, "The cat's-eye marbles make great eyes, but the cow can't see because her eyes are covered up with the brown tape. I wonder what else you could use.")

- giving reassurance and encouragement (For example, "That looks like a good way to get the paper all the way around the sawhorse. Keep trying; it should work.")

These forms of facilitation continue to place the responsibility for making decisions and solving problems with the children and teach critical thinking. They also provide children with models for cooperative interactions in which group members help one another (Reid, Forrestal, and Cook 1990).

3. **Encourage peer teaching and cooperative learning** rather than individual achievement and competition. Achieving the goal, rather than performing better than others, is the desired outcome in cooperative learning. Focusing on the goal directs the group's attention toward how best to achieve the desired outcome using the strengths and abilities of all group members. Peer teaching becomes a natural part of such small-group interactions, as the contributions of all individuals become important to achieving the goal (Hill and Hill 1990; Reid, Forrestal, and Cook 1990). The children who are the recipients of peer teaching benefit because they have access to information when they need it, rather than having to wait for the teacher. Children also learn to use language to initiate questions and determine what information is needed to solve their problem. But the children in the teaching role also benefit from peer teaching. Whenever one individual teaches another, the act of explaining results in as much or more learning for the teacher. Explaining requires the child to decide what information is important to convey, how much information to provide, how to sequence or organize the information, and how to judge whether the information is understood. Explaining also requires the child to choose the most appropriate language to convey the ideas (Blank, Rose, and Berlin 1978). It requires the child to consider the information at a metacognitive level and, in the process, to become more aware of his or her own knowledge. All group members therefore benefit from peer teaching and cooperative learning.

4. **Organize heterogeneous groups** containing some children with good language and problem-solving skills and others who need more assistance in learning but who might contribute good fine motor abilities, creativity, or other assets. Groups should range in size from three to six members, depending on the activity and the group dynamics. Heterogeneous groups enable all groups to work productively on their projects, because each group has members who can function as peer teachers in their respective areas of strength (Reid, Forrestal, and Cook 1990; Short, Burke, and Harste 1991). Groupings can accommodate in a single class a great heterogeneity of membership, including children with special needs who have mild, moderate, or even severe disabilities. In large groups, the teacher may not be able to provide children who have low language abilities or special needs with frequent opportunities to contribute or even to examine materials at close range or to give them enough contextualized support along the situational continuum for learning to occur. Small groups provide for more frequent opportunities to make comments or ask questions, and to see, touch, and manipulate materials. These opportunities improve the learning of all children.

   Aides, speech-language pathologists, and other special service providers who may be in the classroom to assist the children with special needs should interact with the entire group, thus providing additional resources for all learners. In heterogeneous groups, each child can at different times be assigned the leadership role or the responsibility for ensuring the completion of a project. Children also can be given the responsibility of ensuring that all group members know designated information and can work with one another until everyone can count, name body parts, read the assigned page of the story, or meet some other goal. Heterogeneous groups thus promote a sense of belonging, inclusion, and cooperation for all children functioning within the small-group community and the community of the classroom.

5. **Work toward specific goals with small homogeneous groups** to provide information or experiences specific to the needs of group members. The teacher can work with children who have similar needs during times when others are in small cooperative learning groups or in individual center activities. During these small homogeneous group activities, concentrated experiences with difficult or challenging information can be provided at the level needed by those group members, rather than addressing the entire range of information normally presented in large groups (Norris 1989b; Reid, Forrestal, and Cook 1990). In a large group, for example, the facilitator cannot talk for extended periods about a picture from the thematic story at the level of labeling and describing without losing the attention of children for whom this is already known information, or talk only at higher levels of interpretation and inference without losing the attention of children who cannot easily process higher-level language. Small homogeneous groups provide children with

the extended time, frequent opportunities to comment and ask questions, and almost instant and continuous feedback needed to refine their own levels of understanding.

Encountering information in small homogeneous groups prior to talking about that information in the large-group setting will enable children who are at risk for learning because of language differences (as in children for whom English is a second language or children with oral language styles) or because of language disabilities (as in children with identified disabilities) to understand, benefit from, and contribute to the large-group discussion (Hill and Hill 1990). Similarly, for children who are gifted in their language and learning abilities, small homogeneous groups provide opportunities to interact with peers who can challenge their thinking and add a broad range of knowledge and new perspectives to the discussion. Special service providers who are available for consultation or who are in the classroom to support children with special needs can provide valuable information, assistance, or small-group instruction for group members with special needs (see chapter 4 for specific strategies and suggestions).

Small homogeneous groups enable teachers to interact with children on an individualized and personal level not possible within large-group activities. The specific strengths and needs, likes and dislikes, experiences and desires, learning styles, and personality traits of individual children can become known in small-group interactions. This knowledge enables the teacher to better provide for the needs of all the children in the classroom community and to gain insights into how each child learns and uses language. The short but concentrated instruction children receive in small groups allows the teacher or special service provider to organize experiences for children, teach them strategies for learning more independently, enhance their language abilities, and assist them to talk at greater levels of complexity than they could independently achieve (Norris and Hoffman 1993).

Independent Learning Centers

Independent learning centers are environments set up in the classroom to allow for independent explorations of books, materials, topics, interests, or skills. They provide children with opportunities to explore independently information that was introduced within a large or small group (for example, individually looking at the pictures in books used during Topic Explorations, or continuing to work on a collage), to expand knowledge about the daily topic by interacting with books and materials that add new information and experiences (for example, setting up a dairy store and selling milk products), or to pursue other interest areas (for example, exploring math manipulatives, creating an art project, or listening to books on tape). Independent learning center activities involve materials that children can use with little or no teacher guidance and which can be used to meet children's individual goals, including to practice, explore, or create (Fisher 1991).

Independent learning centers may be used at any time during the school day. A child with limited language may not be able to learn from a highly decontextualized discussion at the symbolic level of the situational context. During this large-group time, this child might be provided with manipulative materials that allow exploration of the same general topic at a more contextualized level. Or when a small-group activity requires teacher guidance—such as learning to dye and comb raw wool—most of the children can work in independent learning centers while small groups take turns exploring the wool. Children also may work in independent learning centers during times when small homogeneous groups are meeting with the teacher or special service provider. These centers also may be available during transition times, such as after lunch or outdoor play, when classmates are washing hands, hanging up coats, and so forth. Or the entire class may be involved in independent learning time at once.

The physical composition of an independent learning center can be anything from a box of materials that children can take to any part of the room for exploration, to a table where a temporary center is set up to elaborate on that day's topic, to a permanent center set up for a specific purpose, such as a table holding science equipment and supplies or a book reading center with bookshelves, comfortable chairs, and floor pillows. Children may be free to choose centers, or they may be assigned to a center in order to explore materials or content that they are unlikely to try on their own. Some centers, such as the computer center, may have rules regarding the use and sharing of materials, so that everyone has opportunities to use the equipment. Some centers may be present for the entire year with few changes in available materials, while other centers are permanent but with regular changes in the specific activities they contain, and still others are short-term and specific to a topic or event (Fisher 1991). Suggestions for independent learning centers include:

- book reading center
- writing center (writing materials, magnetic letters and board)
- listening center with recorded books and music
- math manipulative center
- puzzle and pattern center (pegboards, lighted pegboard games)
- dramatic play center (clothing, props, child-size kitchen equipment)
- creative play center (farm animals, people, and other symbolic toys)
- art center
- science center
- sports center
- cultural learning center

■ Facilitating Developmental Learning

A teacher or special service provider must develop an understanding of development and the whole language learning process in order to implement the Storybook-Centered Curriculum. One important aspect of a whole language learning environment involves the establishment of large-group, small-group, and independent learning opportunities to meet the different goals and needs of all the children in the classroom community. Equally important are the beliefs held by the teacher or special service provider regarding what constitutes learning and how that learning is best facilitated. Many interventionists view the acquisition of "products" as learning. Products are specific skills or facts—such as naming alphabet letters, writing numerals, identifying colors, labeling body parts, defining the characteristics of a farm compared to a city, or any of the many goals profiled on Tables 1-2 through 1-4. The emphasis on products leads to the use of strategies to teach specific skills or information—for example, drills, worksheets, and other product-based methods.

Whole language views the goals profiled on these tables as *outcomes* of learning, rather than as learning itself. The important aspect of learning is refining the *process;* that is, learning how:

- to identify a problem
- to apply known information to the problem
- to search for new or additional information
- to analyze cues found in pictures or stated in language for insights and generalizations
- to make associations
- to reorganize information in new ways
- to gain information from observations and manipulations of physical and mental objects
- to use language to understand, create, and transform knowledge (Goodman 1986; Smith 1990)

As the process of learning is refined, it can be applied to any content area and used to build complex networks of knowledge. The acquisition of knowledge is the outcome of the learning process. The network of knowledge, in turn, can be used to interpret experience and support new learning (Norris and Hoffman 1994).

Traditional product-focused teaching practices are based on the belief that children learn best when learning is carefully controlled and error-free, with the goal of producing a conventionally correct and adult-like product. It is feared that if children are free to draw, write, spell, talk, or read "their way," they will establish and practice incorrect skills that will be difficult to correct later on. These fears are based on a lack of understanding of child development and the acquisition of symbolic abilities. Research has clearly shown that development is not a process of systematic acquisition of progressively more difficult but fully formed products or skills. Rather, development occurs as a dynamic process in which children engage in meaningful, purposeful use of their current level of knowledge or symbolic ability to explore, solve, express, create, and share (Applebee 1978; Brown 1973; Calkins 1986; Ferreiro 1986; Ferreiro and Teberosky 1982; Gentry 1982; McCabe and Peterson 1991; Nelson 1985, 1991; Piaget 1952, 1954; Read 1986; Teale and Sulzby 1986).

The manner in which the teacher or special service provider presents an activity, talks about the concepts, guides learning, and provides feedback will dictate how the children perceive learning and how they will approach a project or situation. By adopting a belief that children know how to learn, that it is the nature of the mind to refine and change through experience, and that changes will move in the direction of conventionality because of the need to adapt to the physical and social environment, the instructor allows the children to engage in a learning experience at their own levels of understanding. The teacher or special service provider who understands development can guide the children to add complexity and to fine tune their understanding about how to write, draw, read, and so forth in accord with developmental stages or principles (Applebee 1991).

Teaching Art

Art is a wonderful medium for facilitating many aspects of development, including cognition, imagination, content-area knowledge, math, fine motor skills, perception, and speech and language development. It is frequently used within the Storybook-Centered Lesson Plans to explore concepts and content-area knowledge as part of Topic Explorations and Community Studies, as well as in many of the Additional Suggestions.

Three important principles must be understood and followed in using art. First, art begins with ideas that the *child* brings to the project, rather than with adult-made models of completed projects. Second, there is an interaction between art and language at all levels, both developmentally and in its use, from initial planning to an oral presentation of the final product. Third, an art project should be meaningful and purposeful, embedded within a larger context of exploration.

ESTABLISHING IDEAS

Art does not begin with a finished product that children are asked to copy. Rather, art begins from within the children, embedded in the knowledge and ideas that they possess for the subject of their art (Piaget 1952, 1954; Schirrmacher 1988). Any art project should begin with sufficient exposure to information about the subject so that the children can create from within. For example, in a thematic unit in which ants are under study, examine real ants in an ant farm using a magnifying glass. Talk about how long their legs are and why that length is perfect for an ant. Study their hooked feet and deduce how those feet might help an ant move through the tunnels within anthills. Ask whether ants always walk right side up.

Examine the shape of the ant's body and watch ants moving through their tunnels. Ask questions that focus children on these features: How does their body shape help them to do this? Focus on the ant's head, particularly the jaws. What can ants carry and how does the position and shape of the jaws help them to carry things? How well do you think they see, and how do their eyes meet their needs? How are they like and different from people in their appearance and behaviors? What colors are they, and why might those colors be useful to an ant? Help the children to locate and read the answers to some of these questions in reference books. Then have the children design and make an ant from available materials, including egg cartons, pipe cleaners, paper, tape, hole punchers, glue, and bits of clay.

The preparatory discussion provides opportunities to talk about quantity concepts such as size, shape, length, number, distance, directionality, strength, weight, speed, and so forth. It provides instances where language is needed to establish cause-effect, if-then and if-when, either-or, but, except, compared to, and many other relationships between ideas. It requires children to coordinate temporal relationships between what they think will occur compared to the events that actually occur. The same concepts are examined and talked about at many levels of abstraction, from concretely describing the ants through abstract evaluations of why things are the way they are, thus developing vocabulary across a range of difficulty. This helps the children to develop strategies and skills such as using reference material to answer questions. It also serves to develop pragmatic skills, such as taking turns, asking relevant questions, and maintaining a topic. And it immerses the children in critical thinking about the world and its properties (Blank, Rose, and Berlin 1978).

The discussion also enables the child to bring ideas *to* art, so that the artwork becomes an expression of the child's knowledge rather than an empty reproduction of someone else's ideas. The actual construction of the ant provides further opportunities for language and problem solving—for example, deciding how to represent important features of the ant, which characteristics to include, the proportional length and dimensions of the body parts, spatial locations, color choices, and how to physically attach parts of the ant to the main body. It also provides many pragmatic opportunities for using language to cooperate with others, make requests for materials, request information, make statements, explain decisions, and so forth (Lasky and Mukerji 1990; Mayesky 1990).

LANGUAGE AND ART

If the first principle involves helping children to establish ideas to represent in art, then the second principle involves helping them to communicate their ideas. To help children translate between oral language and art, the adult must treat the children as successful communicators, attributing more meaning to their utterances than they actually provide and assisting them to expand on their ideas. For example, instead of asking all of the questions during the discussion, the adult might impose that role on the children by asking, "Rachel, what do you want to ask about the legs?" If Rachel asks, "Do ants have legs?" the adult might extend the question by saying, "She's asking you to notice the length and shape of the legs. Do ants have legs that are useful to ants?"

The adult should also assist the responders by helping them to notice relevant clues and to put them into words, as illustrated in the following example (Norris and Damico 1990; Norris and Hoffman 1990):

Child: They have six legs.

Adult: (expands this sentence by adding): that are not very . . . (gestures a short height with fingers)

Child: tall

Adult: because . . . (points to the tunnel where the ant moves)

Child: because they have to walk through tunnels.

Adult: They sure do, very narrow tunnels, so their short, bent legs let them crawl through without scraping their knees!

The shared responsibility for linking several ideas into one grammatically complex sentence enables the children to participate in generating and expressing ideas with greater complexity than their independent language abilities can support. By participating in the use of complex language, children begin to think in terms of more complex ideas, and thus have both the need for longer, more complex utterances and the models for creating these sentence types (Bruner 1983).

Similarly, if some children experience difficulty representing the ant in art, the adult can help them through active problem solving. For example, if the child sticks a pipe cleaner through the top of an egg carton, the adult might say, "It will be difficult for your ant to walk because its legs won't reach the ground or bend when it is in the tunnel. I wonder where a leg could go that would be more useful to the ant?" Or if the child feels that the project is complete after adding one body part, the adult might say, "But your ant won't be able to help the colony—it has no way to carry food or pieces of dirt." These suggestions provide feedback the child can use to direct his or her thinking or to reevaluate a problem. It also provides many opportunities for meaningful language to be used in negotiating a change.

ART IN CONTEXT

The third principle is that an art project should be embedded within some larger topic that extends across many weeks of intervention so that the art has a purpose other than "just to do it," and so that the language learned becomes networked with a wide variety of other concepts and skills (Nelson 1985, 1991; Norris and Hoffman 1994). For example, the ant project might be part of a larger exploration of the concept of community and how it is expressed in the children's own families, the creatures found in their own backyards, and the persons in the larger community with whom they interact. This thematic focus allows for the same language to be used in many contexts, across many intervention sessions, and interrelated with many concepts. Thus the child develops well-established, flexibly used language that is already generalized in content, form, and function. Art thus becomes part of the children's lives, a method for simultaneously representing ideas in words and visual media, and a tool for thinking critically about the world.

Teaching Reading

Reading is a complex process that involves far more than mastering the alphabet, sound-symbol relationships, sound segmentation, rhyming, and other aspects of the alphabetic code. These abilities are the products or outcomes of reading and serve as evidence of an underlying understanding of the form of written language. But learning to read requires more than mastering the form. The content and function of reading also must be known. The content, form, and function of reading work together as a system that parallels the processes of listening and speaking (Goodman 1986; Smith 1985; Sulzby and Zecker 1991). Like learning to speak, learning to read is a meaning-making process in which children merge their own understanding about the world and print with the information provided by the author through the illustrations and text (Clay 1991). During reading, each word encountered in print is simultaneously met with:

- the reader's expectations and knowledge about the topic
- the meaning and abstractness of concepts referred to by the words (the semantic context)
- the relationships of meaning among the words, expressed through grammar
- the background established by previously read text or discussion
- the overall organization of the information (the discourse context)
- knowledge of the written symbols and orthographic patterns of printed words
- the degree of support provided for the printed words by the illustrations (the situational context)

A fluent reader with good comprehension must simultaneously coordinate these multiple aspects of the reading process. This coordination is too complex to be mastered one discrete skill at a time, causing many children to fail to master fluent, meaningful reading. These principles are important to understand and follow in order to facilitate children's acquisition of fluent, meaningful reading:

1. Reading must be meaningful and make sense to the child, beginning with ideas and whole stories rather than isolated letters.

2. Fluent and accurate reading is integrally related to language, both in its development and use. It emerges across time developmentally from experiences with reading.

3. Reading must be purposeful, embedded within a broad context of environmental uses of print.

Fluent reading requires experiences with text that is easy to read so that attention can be focused on various aspects of written content, form, and function (Goodman 1986; Smith 1985). For example, one page in the book *The Grumpy Elephant* shows an angry-looking elephant standing in the jungle accompanied by the text: "'I feel grumpy,' said Elephant." This page could be discussed for content ("What does 'grumpy' mean?"), form ("Which word says 'grumpy'? What letters tell a reader that the word says grumpy?"), or function ("Is this a story about an elephant that really exists, or is this fiction? Can we learn anything from fiction?")

READING FOR MEANING

Experiences with meaningful text are critical for all children who are learning to read and who must coordinate the many aspects of content, form, and function. Meaningful experiences are especially important for children who are at-risk because of limited experience with or acquisition of the more complex and abstract levels of language. For fluent reading to occur, these children simultaneously must learn language that their peers already possess and must use language to acquire fluent reading (Gibbs and Cooper 1989; Merritt and Liles 1987; Ripich and Griffith 1988). It is important for teachers and special service providers to use instructional strategies that assist children to interpret and process all levels of language simultaneously (Norris 1988, 1991). This can be accomplished only through the exploration of whole, meaningful, and purposeful uses of written language (Goodman 1986, 1993).

COLLABORATIVE READING

The teacher or special service provider can maintain the wholeness of written language through reading and discussing a story as described in the Storybook-Centered Lesson Plans. This type of reading is called *collaborative reading* because the information needed to learn how to read is not transmitted from the teacher to the children through direct instruction. Rather, the teacher and the children work together—*in collaboration*—to read the text and discover the cues that readers use to recognize words and interpret meaning. Collaborative reading is a process involving both reading and discussion (Teale and Sulzby 1986). Reading and discussion help children to learn how they can use the multiple levels of language in unison to construct meaning from print.

Repeated reading of the thematic book is an important part of this learning. The first time an episode of a story is read, the pictures, the print, the concepts, the words and word order, the background knowledge, and the events in the story all are unfamiliar (Roser and Martinez 1985; Sulzby 1985; Teale and Sulzby 1986, Yaden, Smoklin, and Conlon 1989). Each of these aspects must be considered and understood before the episode can be read with fluency, word recognition, and comprehension. During the first reading, many children may process and understand only the most concrete and simple information—such as learning the names for objects or characters in the pictures (labeling) and recognizing the actions (descriptions) without understanding how these actions relate to previous events or states (thus comprehending the discourse structure of the story only at the level of a descriptive list of actions).

During the second reading, the characters, objects, and actions are known information, having been established through the initial book reading and through Topic Explorations and Community Studies. This familiar information forms a foundation that can be built on and expanded. Because the children no longer have to direct attention and processing efforts to this basic information, they are able to listen to and understand more abstract and complex ideas. For example, they may be able to attend to the shape and orientation of the elephant's eyes, instead of the whole elephant, and begin to interpret that expression as representing "grumpy." Similarly, they may be able to locate the printed word for "Elephant" by its capital "E" once the meaning and word order of the sentence are familiar.

During the third reading, the children may be able to link the page introducing the grumpy elephant with succeeding pages to tell a story at an ordered sequence level on the discourse continuum. They may be able to recognize the quotation marks enclosing "I feel grumpy" by name and function, to identify the first and last letters of the word "Elephant," and to draw inferences concerning possible reasons for the elephant's bad mood. Repeated readings provide children with the time and the information they need to refine their understanding of the many levels of language content, form, and function involved in the reading process (Clay 1991; Sulzby 1985). The teacher or special service provider can facilitate this growth by being sensitive to different children's levels of understanding across time and by providing appropriate information when it is needed.

CYCLES OF EXPLORATION AND ATTENTION

The Storybook-Centered Lesson Plans provide examples of things to talk about and to help children notice at different levels of semantic and discourse complexity during collaborative reading of the thematic story. All these levels would not be discussed every day. Rather, the plans provide a menu of suggestions that the instructor can use to meet the needs of the group or individual children at different points of the thematic unit. Studies conducted using the Storybook-Centered Curriculum showed that the most effective teachers spent a greater portion of the Collaborative Reading time discussing information that closely referred to the meaning of the story during the early days of a thematic unit (Taylor 1993; Waters 1993). They made sure that the children knew information about the elephant, the jungle, the animals encountered by the elephant, what it means to feel grumpy and how a grumpy person acts, and what events would cause an individual to feel grumpy.

As the unit continued, the teachers began to emphasize an understanding of the continuity of the story (the discourse context). Teachers helped children to link the pages and events, using words like "when," "next," "because," "so," "wanted," and so forth to build sequence, causality, and intentional planning into the narrative structure. Toward the end of the unit, a greater percentage of the Collaborative Reading time was spent reading the text and talking about the print, including the words, letters, and punctuation. This does not mean that the instructors did not talk about print until the end of the unit. All levels were addressed throughout the unit, but the emphasis, expectations, and amount of time devoted to concepts, story structure, and print changed across the duration of the unit.

These teachers recognized that learning occurs through cycles of attention that are directed at different aspects of the reading process, including (1) the topic, (2) individual concepts and words, (3) grammatical relationships, (4) background knowledge, (5) information present in illustrations, (6) orthographic features of words, (7) knowledge of letters and their relationships to words and word meaning, and (8) conventions of writing. These cycles of exploration and attention enabled children to discover how patterns of letters, word structure, concepts, word ordering, punctuation, and text structure recur within and across pages, across books, and within other sources of written language. They helped children to gradually attend to more of these aspects of reading, giving children the time and the repeated exposure necessary to internalize these patterns.

The cycles of exploration and attention characteristic of whole language differ from the direct instructional practice of identifying a specific skill, directly teaching that skill, and assessing whether the skill has been learned. Whole language practices are based on the premise that multiple aspects of development and learning will emerge simultaneously when children are presented with meaningful, whole information and are helped to discover the important features of it (Goodman 1986; Straw 1990; Teale and Sulzby 1986). From these collaborative transactions, closer approximations to adult-like understanding and mastery will be demonstrated across time. Rather than viewing learning as a series of skills existing along a linear continuum in which the easier skills are mastered before more advanced skills are introduced, all of the aspects of reading are seen as interactive. Insights or developments at one level of knowledge allow for refinements at other levels and are, in turn, refined by the developments in those other levels of language and knowledge. Change occurs in the entire system of knowledge and language as the child internally constructs an understanding of the reading process (McGee and Richgels 1990).

EMERGENT LITERACY

The developmental view of reading has been examined by researchers studying *emergent literacy*. Their work reveals changes across time in what children know about reading and what they focus attention on as their reading attempts increase in sophistication. Elizabeth Sulzby has shown that reading behaviors in young children change according to a predictable sequence of stages. The eleven stages identified by Sulzby (1985) are described in Table 3-1 (page 74), beginning with early collaborative storybook reading and progressing through independent reading.

Children who have had minimal literacy experiences during the preschool years or who have language and learning disorders will evidence more behaviors characteristic of the lower stages of storybook reading (Adams 1990). They will use pictures to derive meaning without expecting information also to be provided by the print and will respond to the pictures by labeling the objects or characters depicted without attributing many actions to them. The actions that are interpreted will be viewed as isolated events, with little story continuity or structure governing them. These children need opportunities to explore both the pictures and the print at a level that is developmentally consistent with their present levels of language and literacy and that assists them to discover more abstract and literate properties of oral and written language (Clay 1991; Lehr and Osborn 1994; Norris 1988).

Other children in the classroom will have considerable knowledge about reading, and some may already be proficient readers. They will be able to coordinate information from the multiple levels of language required for fluent reading with good comprehension. They will be able to tell detailed and well-structured stories, and will know a considerable amount about the conventions of print and orthographic patterns (Sulzby 1985). These children benefit from opportunities to explore concepts in depth and to make generalizations and associations with a wide range of related concepts and topics. Much of this exploration can occur in small groups and independent learning centers.

TABLE 3-1
Sulzby's Stages of Emergent Literacy That Develop through Storybook Reading Experiences

Attempts Governed by Pictures, Stories Not Formed

I. Labeling and Commenting

Stage I is characterized by the child pointing to or giving the name of objects or people in the story. The child directs little attention toward the actions represented and does not interrelate the pictures in any way to tell even a primitive story. Each picture is talked about as a discrete event, with little attention to an overall topic or theme.

II. Following the Action

Stage II involves a focus on the actions, rather than the objects, in the pictures. The child refers to the action as if it is occurring at that moment. The child's speech may be paired with an indicating finger that traces the action. The child also uses conversational intonation as opposed to storytelling intonation. Reenacting actions, sound effects, and words that fit the context of the picture are also characteristic of this stage.

Attempts Governed by Pictures, Stories Formed

III. Dialogic Storytelling

Stage III is still governed by pictures, but stories begin to take form. In dialogic storytelling, an overall story-like structure can be inferred, even though the story lacks cohesion. The child depends on oral language techniques such as using "voices" to distinguish the dialogue. The child's attempts are contextualized to the pictures.

IV. Monologic Storytelling

In Stage IV, monologic storytelling, the stories begin to take on characteristics of literate language, including use of storytelling intonation. The child's comments are still context dependent in that the child assumes that the listener can see the pictures. Such comments as, "I'm done" or "That's all" may be used to end the story.

Attempts Governed by Pictures, Reading Attempts

V. Reading and Storytelling Mixed

In Stage V, a child begins to demonstrate greater use of written language conventions. The storybook reading begins to sound like written language, including use of written language intonation or wording.

VI. Reading Similar to the Original Story

In Stage VI, the child creates patterns of wording or language similar to that of the chosen book, and the language is decontextualized from pictures. The intonation becomes more reading-like.

VII. Reading Verbatim-Like Story

In Stage VII, the stories are recited almost verbatim and the child begins to use self-correction behaviors when trying to recall the actual story.

Attempts Governed by Print

VIII. Refusing to Read Based on Print

In Stage VIII, children initially may refuse to read based on their developing print awareness. They realize that they are not able to read word for word and abandon their "pretend" reading. This change seems attributable to exposure to formalized reading instruction in school.

IX. Reading Aspectually

In Stage IX, reading becomes tied to print or aspectual elements such as a few known words or letters. Reading development at this stage is characterized by holistic attempts. This implies that the child is beginning to integrate the different aspects of reading and is reading from the print.

X. Reading with Strategies Imbalanced

The tenth stage is described as reading with strategies imbalanced because the child is more independent, but still does not integrate the process. Reading is characterized by omitting, substituting, or sounding out words.

XI. Reading Independently

The final stage is reading independently. In this stage, a child is able to read and comprehend text and to self-correct miscues.

Teachers and special service providers must be aware of the entire continuum of developmental reading stages outlined in Table 3-1 in order to help children progress toward higher stages. The S-D-S model was used to develop the suggested interactions during Collaborative Reading. It also can be used to aid in planning and implementing reading instruction that is appropriate for children at different stages of development. Interactions for children at the earliest stages of reading development (Labeling and Commenting, and Following the Action) can emphasize levels of language ranging along the semantic continuum from labeling to interpretations and inferences (Norris 1992). Interactions for children in the middle stages (Dialogic and Monologic Storytelling) can emphasize talking about the story with more complexity along the discourse continuum. Children who are emergent readers and are paying attention to the print (Reading and Storytelling Mixed, Reading Similar to the Original Story, and Reading Verbatim-Like Story) can be helped to focus on the metalanguage level of the semantic continuum.

Having different goals and developmental expectations for children at different stages of emergent reading enables the teacher to appreciate and understand the progress made by each child. Children are encouraged to think, make choices, problem solve, and make discoveries about reading that are consistent with their current levels of understanding and development. Teachers and special service providers can facilitate each child's growth by becoming good listeners. As children talk during Collaborative Reading, the teacher can ascertain what information children possess about a topic, and then add to or expand existing knowledge (see chapter 4 for specific strategies). Children may collaborate with peers during these interactions. In our classrooms, we found that peer conversations during Collaborative Reading were almost always book-related, even though the specific topic might have been different from the one pursued by the teacher and the majority of the group (Taylor 1993; Waters 1993). These peer conversations often involved elaborations of a topic, predictions about the story, or related personal experiences. These conversations were often "leaked" to the whole group and became part of the discussion.

READING IN CONTEXT

In the Storybook-Centered Lesson Plans, the Collaborative Reading time is followed by a Topic Explorations activity and a Thematic Studies activity that elaborate on important concepts from the story. These activities frequently include reading an entire piece of children's literature—for example, reading the story *The Three Billy Goats Gruff* to explore the concept of being grumpy. Reading this story to the children and discussing it allows them to listen to stories written at a level of language and discourse structure far more complex than they could read themselves and to experience an important concept from the story in a new context. Exploring the concept in a new context helps children to understand that reading is done for a purpose. Listening to complex stories enables children to learn the language and structure of the stories on an oral level, laying the foundation for what they will later read themselves.

Similarly, reading and discussing factual information from books written in the transactional mode, such as a book about elephants, is a regular feature of Topic Explorations and Thematic Studies. Children learn that when people have questions or are interested in a topic, they can find information in books. Other contextual uses of books include reading and following recipes to make modeling clay, paint, or food. These experiences with print provide children with an understanding of how to find information in books and of the discourse patterns in different types of transactional text, from the descriptive lists of recipes to the more complex organization of history or science books.

The books used in Topic Explorations and Thematic Studies are placed in the reading center for children to reread independently. Thus, children are able to read each book at their own level, from looking at the pictures while labeling and commenting, through stages of reading verbatim-like stories or higher. Environmental print—such as the calendar, charts listing classroom rules, and signs—is also read when it is appropriate to the context. The reading experiences provided in the Storybook-Centered Curriculum—attending to environmental print, reading predictable books written at an emergent level of text difficulty, listening to more complex stories as they are read, and independently reading these stories and others—expose children to a wide range of literacy experiences. In this manner, reading becomes part of the children's lives and a tool for making discoveries about themselves and their world.

Teaching Mathematics

Often we think of mathematics as an abstract and difficult subject that is first learned in school. In reality, the world from birth onward is mathematical. Children are immersed in operations such as addition and subtraction, principles of geometry, and concepts of number and mass throughout the early childhood years. By making children aware of the existence of mathematics in everyday experiences and by using math language during these events, one can help them become comfortable and competent with mathematics in its written and oral forms.

Mathematics learning is governed by the same principles of acquisition as art or reading:

1. Mathematics should be approached from the perspective of meaning, or how it makes sense to a child.

2. Mathematics is integrally linked to language at all stages of development and use. It emerges developmentally, beginning with sensorimotor experiences with objects and only gradually evolving toward abstract, internal operations (Piaget 1952, 1954).

3. Mathematics is found in everything we do, embedded in a wide range of purposeful contexts. Language principles can be seen in all domains of mathematics, including geometry, addition, subtraction, number concepts, and other mathematical concepts.

GEOMETRY

Children visually explore the world, and vision is ideally suited to organizing experience according to mathematical principles. The visual system responds to horizontal and vertical lines, curves, and other geometric perceptions. From infancy, children interpret a world made up of shapes, sizes, and spatial directions according to geometric shape and orientation, beginning with the faces of their mothers and extending to the wide range of objects used in eating, dressing, and other daily routines. Sorting and classifying are a natural part of early childhood, as children learn to call a range of objects that differ somewhat in size, shape, color, or other features by the same name, such as "cup" or "dog." (Davidson 1983). The child uses geometric properties to form mathematical relationships between objects by matching shapes within puzzles or shape sorters, stacking blocks to various heights, and nesting smaller cups within bigger cups.

Experiences with geometric objects establish the foundation for mathematical concepts such as same, different, bigger than, smaller than, and equal to. These concepts, in turn, are the precursors to all mathematic operations, such as addition and subtraction. Children need extensive experience with objects such as these and the language used to talk about their properties in order to understand mathematics at more abstract levels. Oral language is the first symbol system for math. Adults talk to children about finding the biggest block, having a cup that is smaller than another, wanting more raisins, having a full glass, or establishing recurrence as in emptying a pail of sand and refilling it. This talk focuses attention on the mathematical properties of objects, rather than on the object itself. Children begin to notice and talk about mathematic properties as they acquire more mathematics vocabulary and translate experience and action into language (Bickmore-Brand 1990; Davidson 1983; Whitin, Mills, and O'Keefe 1990).

ADDITION

The language of math then may be translated into mathematical symbols, including numbers and the equations that establish the relationships among them, such as $X + Y = Z$. When children have the requisite experiences and can express these experiences in language, then they can understand the mathematical symbols. They can remember and manipulate the symbols in relationship to concrete objects and familiar actions, such as knowing that adding two shoes and two socks results in four items (Bickmore-Brand 1990; Kamii 1988). Mathematical symbols are too often introduced in the abstract, outside of a context that is meaningful and familiar to children. They are required to learn mathematic facts, symbols, and equations by rote without knowing what their purpose is.

Many experiences throughout the day can be used to introduce children to mathematical equations in meaningful contexts. For example, when reading the theme book *One Cold, Wet Night,* one can talk about the story using mathematic terms. In this story, a farmer gets out of bed and goes outside. One by one, animals jump into his warm bed and refuse to get out.

One can present the empty bed as having no animals in it and write a 0 on the chalkboard to represent the concept of none. As you read each page, represent the increasing number of animals in an equation. As the first animal climbs into the bed, add 1 to the 0 to form the equation $0 + 1 = 1$. Toys can also be used as props to demonstrate the actions and the results. Help the children to translate the equation into words; for example:

> The bed was empty (pointing to the 0) but in went (pointing to the + sign) one animal (pointing to the 1) and now there is (pointing to the = sign) one animal in the bed (pointing to the 1).

On the next page, help the children to develop the equation with statements and questions such as the following:

> How many animals are already in the bed? So is the bed still empty? Then when we write the math story, we need to tell the reader that there is 1 animal instead of 0 animals in the bed. So we would write the number _____. Then another animal jumped in bed, so how many animals are in the bed now?

Write the resulting equation $(1 + 1 = 2)$ on the chalkboard, and then point to the symbols while saying: "One horse jumped in the bed" (1) and then in jumped (+) one cow (1) so now there are (=) two animals in the bed (2). Recalling the familiar story whenever they see the mathematical equation helps children understand and remember what the symbols communicate and how they function to express meaning.

SUBTRACTION

Conservation, knowing that something is constant, is a precursor to subtraction (Kamii 1988; Piaget 1954). Children have a myriad of experiences with this principle, including repeating actions or playing games which teach that something which is gone or completed can be repeated (that is, conserved). They learn through swinging that they can leave and return to the same space as the swing moves back and forth. They learn by climbing up the ladder to a slide that the number of steps to reach the top is always the same and that when they reach the high point, they can immediately return to the beginning point by sliding down. Knowing that the whole is conserved after transformation is a prerequisite to understanding subtraction (Davidson 1983). Many experiences in the child's world can be talked about in terms of subtraction. For example, when walking down a set of stairs, the adult can ask, "We had six steps, and we walked down two steps. How many steps do we have left?"

The relationship between addition and subtraction can be shown and these equations written. For example, in the theme book *The Red Rose,* a series of animals enters a garden. The caterpillar enters because he is attracted to a rose; a bird spots him and enters, and is herself spotted by a cat, who enters the garden, and so on. You could write a series of addition equations to represent these actions and talk about them in the manner of the preceding example. But then a man walks into the garden and picks the rose, which causes the caterpillar to leave. You would now write a subtraction equation to represent the changing actions in the story ($4 - 1 = 3$). Have the children put the equation into words: "There were four animals in the garden (point to the 4), but then one animal went home (point to $- 1$), so there are 3 animals left in the garden (point to $= 3$). Modify the equation as each animal leaves until there are 0 animals in the garden.

Reinforce the words "addition" and "subtraction" throughout the day in the context of a wide range of activities. For example, as children are playing at the sand table, you could say, "You are adding scoops of sand to your pail. Let's see how many you add." Count as the child scoops sand into the container. Similarly, as the child pours the sand out, comment, "You are subtracting sand from your pail, and it will be empty. It will have zero sand in it." Talk about adding and subtracting as children find the appropriate number of plates for their snack groups and then pass out the plates until they have zero left. Talk about adding as the child builds a tower from blocks and about subtracting as the tower gets too high and some blocks topple off. By hearing math language used to refer to everyday experiences, children learn the content and function of operations like addition and subtraction, as well as the words that refer to them. Then when the children see the written equations, they have the understanding needed to make sense of them.

NUMBER CONCEPTS

Children are immersed in experiences with number concepts from the earliest stages of their development. Talking about the world using numbers helps children establish the ability to count, recognize the relationship between objects and numbers, seriate, locate position by number concepts such as first, second, and fifth, and associate numbers with numerals (Kamii 1988). Numbers are part of everyday talk, such as saying "We have only one shoe. We need both before we can go" or "You can take two cookies." Using number words during routine events, such as counting while walking up steps, or counting the number of times batter is stirred with a spoon, or counting shoes and socks as they are put on helps to make children aware of numbers and how they function to solve problems or mark attempts at and completions of a task.

Many experiences with literature, rhyme, and music establish number concepts. Classic fairy tales such as *Goldilocks and the Three Bears, The Three Little Pigs* or *The Three Billy Goats Gruff* repeat similar sequences of events three times. They also provide multiple opportunities for children to learn about ordinal counting as the stories talk about the characteristics and actions of the first little bear, pig, or billy goat, followed by the second, and then the third. Number sequences and one-to-one correspondence are modeled in games such as "This Little Piggy" or "Ten Little Indians," as a different predictable number is associated with each toe or finger as it is touched in order.

Play and daily routines provide a wide range of opportunities for children to establish one-to-one correspondence (Whitin, Mills, and O'Keefe 1990). For example, distributing materials for art, writing, or snack activities provides repeated opportunities to count the number of children in a group, count an equivalent number of plates, napkins, cups, pieces of paper, pens, and so forth, and then to match each object to a child in one-to-one correspondence. Too many or too few objects for the number of peers provide the children with immediate feedback on the accuracy of their counting. Children who are having difficulty establishing correspondence can be assisted to learn this through play. For example, they can act out a tea party with small toy figures and dishes. At first, the child can seat a small number of toy people or figures at a table and count them. The child might then be asked simply to match the number of plates to the number of figures "so that everyone has a plate." Extra plates can be "put away in the cupboard."

The task can be made one level more difficult by having the child count the people, and then select the needed plates by counting them while the people remain in sight. The accuracy of the child's matching can be tested by setting the table using the number of plates the child selected. Too many or too few plates will result in feedback that the child can use to rethink the problem and try again. Multiple opportunities to use this emerging knowledge are created as the child passes out cups, spoons, forks, and napkins, each object providing a repeated experience with using the same new strategy to solve a similar problem. The number of people seated at the table can be changed to establish the same strategy for different numbers. Once the child can establish correspondence, the people can be counted but then removed "until dinner is ready." The child must now use just the number of needed plates and the memory of the people to select the correct number of objects.

Once the child has selected what he or she believes to be the correct number of objects, the accuracy can be checked by calling the people in for dinner and matching the selected number of plates to guests in one-to-one correspondence. This step focuses the child's attention on establishing correspondence to the total number of objects in a set, rather than on correspondence for matching. A more abstract mathematical correspondence can then be established by telling the child that a given number of people will be present for dinner and an equivalent number of plates must be placed on the table. To do this task, the child must be able to count with one-to-one correspondence and understand when the number of objects and the number of people have equivalence. This equivalence is necessary for understanding operations such as addition and subtraction.

Many opportunities for counting, one-to-one correspondence, and equivalence are present while reading a story, talking about the calendar, preparing for an art project, giving instructions, playing circle games or finger plays, solving problems in science or social studies, organizing class members into groups for a special event, and almost any other event during the day. Teachers and special service providers need to become aware of the math that is used functionally in these contexts. For example, one can use opportunities such as breaking the class into groups to engage the children in dividing into groups and deciding how many need to go in each group to reach equivalence. Take the time during reading to count the characters, objects, number of actions, or other relevant things depicted. Children who are made aware of the content and function of counting and other math concepts in many contexts throughout the day view math as a natural part of experience. They become comfortable using mathematical vocabulary and concepts and can translate between language and math symbols (Davidson 1983).

Similarly, many of these experiences can be written down using math symbols and equations, as described previously. These representations provide children with opportunities to learn to recognize and write numerals and to associate numerals with meaning and function. Children also can be given opportunities to learn about and experiment with numerals during independent center activities involving puzzles, magnetic numbers, games, and toys that incorporate counting and numerals. Children also learn how numbers are organized into patterns and how the patterns make meaningful differences (Charlesworth and Lind 1990; Whitin, Mills, and O'Keefe 1990). A number 2 written alone, for example, communicates something very different than the number 2 written in the context of 12 or 231. Routine activities such as Calendar are especially useful for guiding these discoveries because the children have multiple exposures to the concepts across days, weeks, and months.

MATHEMATICAL CONCEPTS

Experience is filled with mathematical concepts, including size, texture, dimension, distance, speed, position, direction, weight, balance, and time. Many of these math concepts maintain a contrastive relationship with their polar dimension, such as big versus little, thin versus thick, heavy versus light, long versus short, before versus after, more versus less, tall versus short, rough versus smooth, and so forth. All of the child's visual, tactile, and other sensory experiences are composed of these concepts and contrasts. Everything that is touched, smelled, heard, viewed, and manipulated has these properties in differing levels of magnitude and intensity (Charlesworth and Lind 1990). Talk about perceptual experiences using mathematical vocabulary and help children to see the significance of these concepts in both meaning and function.

Talking about these concepts during play enables children to become aware of the relationships between them in naturally occurring and interesting ways (Bickmore-Brand 1990). Activities such as running races teach them that the same distance can be covered in different amounts of time—that is, the concept of speed. Using this vocabulary and having children measure the distance of the course and time the race with a stopwatch, instead of having them merely run the race, helps them to understand the mathematical principles involved. Racing with tricycles and other riding toys adds the concept of force, as children are helped to understand that whoever pushes on the pedals with the greatest force will win the race. Running toy cars down a slope that they can vary in steepness helps the children to understand the relationship between angle, distance, and speed, especially when these concepts are phrased in mathematical terms.

Gross motor activities are especially useful in enabling children to experience concepts related to location and distance. Climbing, walking planks, swinging and other activities help them to see transformations in location and distance which they can talk about using opposites such as up/down, near/far, or forward/backward. Pushing the swing and observing the consequence of a higher and longer range of motion helps to establish concepts of force. Too often, we fail to talk about these experiences while they are happening, or we talk about them only during math, and as a consequence children do not see the natural applications of math in their worlds or understand abstract math concepts. Swings, teeter-totters, and merry-go-rounds foster an understanding of weight, motion, speed, force, height, and distance. Going through a tunnel establishes concepts of changes in position over time, resulting in the emergence of complex prepositions such as through, across, around, over, and so forth.

Talking about objects comparatively using explicit mathematical language within the context of activities across the curriculum helps children to understand the relative nature of opposite terms (Charlesworth and Lind 1990; Davidson 1983). For example, a Topic Exploration within the theme unit *The Grumpy Elephant* has children design a happy-or-angry-mood indicator from a paper plate attached to a craft stick. While talking about how they might make the mood indicator, ask where the glue should be put on the stick—at the top, in the middle, or at the bottom—and discuss what would happen if the glue were placed in the opposite location. Similarly, the children can decide where the stick should attach to the plate, where to locate body parts, what shapes to use, and the opposites of each of these decisions.

The lesson plans also provide for specific explorations of these mathematical concepts. The theme unit *Obadiah* provides for exploration of a different sensory system each day for all of the different concepts and contrasts, including those associated with vision, movement, taste, touch, sound, and smell. Children are asked to judge, discriminate, categorize, and imitate a wide range of mathematical and scientific contrasts as they experiment and play.

Math is a part of every experience in a child's world, and in this curriculum it is intended to be a part of every activity, rather than a discrete subject taught outside of a context of meaningful and functional use. Some activities, such as Calendar, are largely mathematical by their nature and provide for a wide range of mathematical concepts to be explored. Suggestions for reinforcing some of these concepts are specified on the lesson plans. Some activities, such as those from *Obadiah,* are specifically designed to focus on math and science concepts. Other activities provide multiple opportunities for the incidental teaching of math. Be alert to the many daily opportunities to talk about math and to use mathematical vocabulary to describe actions and observations. Playground, snack, cleanup, and other routine times of the day provide some of the best opportunities to sort, classify, measure, perceive, add, subtract, count, and transform experience mathematically.

Teaching Writing

When children discover the medium of writing, they have a new and powerful method of communication. They discover that they can write down and save an idea for another day. They can take home the written idea and share it with someone in a place different from where it was created. They can give a written message to a friend, who can write back. Notes can be taken when interesting topics are discussed (Temple et al. 1988). Communication can occur with the principal, cafeteria workers, or other people in the school community for purposes such as lunch counts, needed supplies, or other important classroom business. The class can make lists of materials needed for projects or procedural steps that must be taken. People of interest in the community, such as fire fighters or zoo keepers, can be written to with questions about their occupations, fire safety, or zoo animals. The power to communicate across time and distance with unmet people and to save information in a form that can be revisited adds new possibilities to the child's communicative world.

To become writers, children must know what people do when they write, including what they write about, the purposes for writing, and how writing is done (Calkins 1986; Ferreiro 1986; Ferreiro and Teberosky 1982). They acquire this knowledge from a wide range of sources, including watching other people write; dictating ideas while others write; writing stories, letters, or reports; and experimenting with print by practicing letter and word formation for fun rather than to communicate meaningful information. They also learn about writing by reading books, environmental print, and other things that have been written. As children begin to learn about writing and its form, content, and functions, they become more aware of written materials and attend to them with greater curiosity and interest. This interest and self-generated desire to know more about writing prompts children to discover and refine their writing skills. Soon children's writing changes from scribbles and random lines produced for fun into progressively more letter-like sequences produced as communications (Gentry 1982, 1989; Hoffman 1990; Read 1986). The teacher or special service provider can easily facilitate this process, but often they unintentionally inhibit learning to write.

By understanding and following the three basic principles of learning as they are manifested in writing, educators can help children fearlessly enter the community of writers:

1. Writing begins with whole ideas, not with isolated letters or skills.

2. Writing at all stages of development and use is integrally related to language and emerges developmentally in accord with principles of language learning.

3. Writing is conducted in a context of meaningful purposes and uses.

These principles should be maintained whether children are observing the writing of others (including dictated writing), planning and rehearsing their own compositions, or engaging in independent or facilitated writing experiences.

MAKING SENSE OF WRITING

Early writing experiences should be whole, maintaining the interconnections between content, form, and function (Calkins 1986, 1991; Temple et al. 1988). Too often, educators separate written form from its meaning and purpose by having children copy letters or letter sequences in the mistaken belief that children cannot be writers until they have mastered the alphabet, sound-letter associations, punctuation marks, the fine motor skills needed to make well-formed letters, and some rudimentary spelling skills. Acquiring all of this knowledge requires that any experiences with real writing are postponed for many months or even years. This paradigm teaches children that they are not writers and that writers don't make mistakes. When children finally have attained sufficient "prerequisite" writing skills, they still have no idea how to put all these subskills together and have only vague ideas of what kinds of texts people write or why. The children are then accused of showing no creativity in their writing, as they carefully choose only words that they can spell and minimize what they write in order to maintain neatness and correct letter and word formation.

Whole language experiences with writing teach children that they can be competent writers using whatever knowledge and skills they currently possess, even if they have limited language abilities or are able only to make random marks on a page with a marker (McGee and Richgels 1990). Teachers and special service providers can help children understand that random marks on a page, when shared with other people, can communicate to and be read by others. Adults then can help children add greater complexity and refinement to their attempts. One method for accomplishing this is the use of dictated writing experiences.

DICTATED WRITING

Writing begins with ideas that children want to communicate. Ideas evolve from information and experiences. Writer's block occurs when children cannot think of anything to write, do not know what types of things people might write about, or do not feel comfortable putting their ideas into words (McGee and Richgels 1990; Temple et al. 1988). One way to help children learn to communicate ideas easily in writing is to use dictated writing experiences. In such an experience, the teacher or special service provider writes down the ideas that the children dictate to him or her. While writing, the adult helps the children to discover the ways that writers think as they are writing and how these thoughts translate into words, punctuation, and print.

Writing should be a natural continuation of whatever topic or activity children are already exploring. For example, after reading about a lamb whose mother has died in *Who Will Be My Mother?*, one might pursue the topic by researching the life cycle of sheep using illustrated books from the library. This exploration might reveal where sheep live, what they eat, how they communicate, their life cycle, their family unit, their wool or fleece, and why they are raised on farms. The educator can use the illustrations to prompt children in generating their own ideas about these issues and ask them questions that help them derive interpretations. (For example, "Look at the fences and the large grassy areas. Where do you think sheep live?") One might use elaborations to add information and details to the children's observations. While reading parts of the text, the adult might comment, "We can find out interesting facts by reading about sheep."

Following the discussion, introduce the children to a purpose for writing using statements such as, "We can remember what we learned from our research by writing reports. Then tomorrow or the next day, we can look at our reports to help us remember what we learned." Then have children take turns dictating information about sheep that they think the group should remember. For example, one child might suggest, "The mama is a ewe and the baby is a lamb."

The adult will want to begin by planning the text, helping the children to be active decision makers in the writing process. For example, one might say, "We have some decisions to make. The research books that we read had illustrations and words. Should we have illustrations in our report?" If the children decide to include illustrations, then another decision is elicited: "We have to leave room for our illustration at the top of the page (showing an example from the library book). Where should we start writing the words?" If the children say, "The bottom," this leads to another observation. For example, "We have a lot of words to write, so we have to leave enough space on our paper. If we start at the bottom, we may have room for just a few words. Should we start at the bottom or in the middle?" If the children still believe the bottom is the appropriate starting point, the adult begins the writing there to show children the consequences of that decision.

Similarly, one can involve children in the decision to write from left to right by saying, "We want our audience to be able to read our report, so where should we start writing—on the right (pointing) or left (pointing) side of the page?" If the children are unsure, help them check the theme book to determine the answer. Tell them, "watch carefully as we start to read," and then point to the words "Who Will Be My Mother" one by one while reading the words in unison with the children. Then place the writing paper over the book page while explaining to the children that readers expect to see the words that we write in the same order. One child can indicate by pointing where the writing should begin and in which direction it should continue on the writing page (McGee and Richgels 1990). When children listen passively as the adult tells them conventions such as where to begin writing and in which direction to write, they have to recall this information through rote memory because they have no way to deduce the information logically. The children's potential confusions and incorrect hypotheses are never addressed, so the children have no basis for revising them. In contrast, participating as an active decision maker enables children to try out a range of hypotheses and to attempt to reason out the potential problems and solutions during the discussion. Actively exploring information requires making associations with other known information, reasoning by analogy from similar problems, following logical processes, or learning at a more elaborated level of processing than rote memory.

The children can be asked to make the same types of decisions throughout the actual writing process. The instructor might tell the children which word needs to be written next and invite suggestions concerning which letter might represent the first sound, the last sound, or other parts of words the children might know. Or one can talk about how a writer makes such decisions; for example:

> I want to write "mama," so I need a sound that will make the reader's lips close together to make a /mmm/. I'll use the letter "m" because that tells my mouth to say /mmm/.

Then demonstrate and talk about how to form the letters (Norris and Hoffman 1993):

> When I make an "m," I start in the middle of the line space, because "m" is a short letter. Then I print a straight line going down to the line. Then I go to the top of my line and I make a hump like this (demonstrating), and then another one (demonstrating). Now it looks like an

"m." Next I'm going to make an "a," so I start in the middle of the line space again and make a half circle. Then I go to the top of the half circle and print a straight line down. Now it says "ma." How could I get it to say "mama?" What do I need to do next, and what letter should I use?

After a word has been written, help the children become more aware of the concept of wordness in print. For example:

We wrote the word "mama," and now we can tell the reader to look at the next word by leaving a space before we start writing the word "is." So I'm leaving a space (demonstrate) and now I'm going to write the word "is" by printing "i" and "s" like this.

After writing a few words, the adult can elicit the cue to leave the white space from the children, as in, "I'm done with that word, so what should I do?" This provides children with an opportunity to indicate what they have discovered about the conventions of written words and to get feedback on the accuracy of their hypotheses. It also allows the adult to discover which children are making inferences about print from the discussion and which ones might need more individualized instruction.

Other decisions can be made with the group, including where to start writing the next word when the end of a line is reached, when to capitalize a letter and why those words are special or important to signal to the reader, and how to punctuate the sentence at the end of the idea. Help the children to decide whether the sentence should be read with excitement or anger and therefore highlighted with an exclamation point ("This tells our readers that he said it really loudly!"), as a question signaled by a question mark, or as a comment ending with a period. The function of quotation marks can be discussed in a similar way, by asking the children to pick out the words that a speaker actually said.

As the dictation continues, one might comment on which letters are used to spell each word and why. Simply name the letter or read the word while writing it, talk about what procedures are used to print a letter, or invite the children to give suggestions and actively participate in any of these decisions. What is talked about and in what depth will depend on the children's interest and level of existing knowledge. For children who already know and use conventions such as spaces between words or left-to-right printing, it may be unnecessary to explicitly direct their attention to this practice and you will spend little time during dictation addressing these conventions. Conversely, as children know more about orthography and letter-sound correspondences, they may be interested in helping to choose more of the letters to represent parts of words in a dictated sentence, and more time and attention can be devoted to collaborative spelling (Hoffman 1990). Some children might be invited to suggest a spelling for an entire word as an adult takes dictation, while others may be challenged by being asked to provide the first sound and its corresponding letter. The collaborative writing during dictation thus can be individualized to meet the needs of group members at a variety of levels of understanding about the writing process.

Including the children in the decision-making process during dictation teaches them how to think like writers and what things a writer must know and include in order to communicate successfully with a reader. It provides children with opportunities to see and hear how a writer coordinates ideas; words; word order; knowledge about letters, sounds, and orthographic principles; conventions such as spaces between words and left-to-right writing; punctuation; and letter formation in order to print capital and lower-case letters as a whole language process. The dictated experiences provide opportunities for a writer to make explicit and public what is usually unnoticed and private when the writing process is merely observed without metacognitive reflection and talk. It includes children in the process of writing before they are able to coordinate all of the levels of language and skill needed for independent conventional writing. And it helps them refine their own knowledge about writing and how it is done, which they can then incorporate into their own independent developmental writing.

After the sentence has been written, the children can illustrate it. Then they can dictate additional ideas until they begin to understand how they might go about writing their own research reports (Calkins 1986). Armed with ideas and new information about writing, the group then disperses and children are given the opportunity to independently write and illustrate a research report telling something about sheep that they want to communicate. The teacher can combine these reports into a book with a cover page and page numbers. Creating classroom books lets children know that their work is valued by others and contains information that they and other people can read and reexamine at a later time.

Research reports are not the only type of writing that can be dictated. Other dictated writing experiences include these:

- Discussing a picture, identifying the characters, their actions, the consequences of their actions, and their dialogue, followed by writing a story

- Writing about an experience, such as a field trip, a visitor to the classroom, or a special event in the school

- Writing a thank-you note from the class to a visitor or someone who helped the class accomplish a goal

- Writing letters of inquiry to request information on a topic from some person or agency

- Drawing an illustration, followed by writing about the topic it suggests

- Dictating a personal experience related to a topic of interest

PLANNING AND REHEARSAL

Even very young children can be helped to recognize that writers plan and rehearse their ideas before writing them down (Calkins 1986). Organizing ideas before writing and saying the sentences to oneself are both means of planning and rehearsing that allow children to dictate or write their best ideas. A *semantic map* is one method of organizing ideas prior to writing. Semantic maps are used to organize ideas into categories, such as "places," "animals," "products," and "food" on a farm.

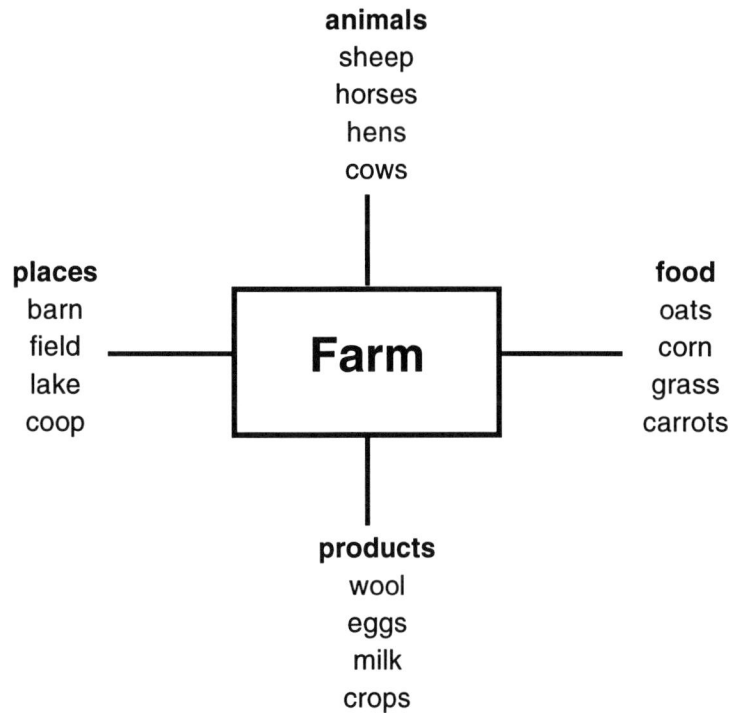

animals
sheep
horses
hens
cows

places
barn
field
lake
coop

Farm

food
oats
corn
grass
carrots

products
wool
eggs
milk
crops

Children can use information from the semantic map to plan their thoughts prior to dictating sentences. They can use words from the map in their sentences, the map providing a model for spelling and letter formation, as well as assisting them with idea formation. They also can rehearse the ideas they want to write using the words in the semantic map. Some of the concepts from the semantic map can be further organized into a flow chart that establishes the relationships among them. These relationships help children form sentences and generate more complex ideas (Norris and Hoffman 1993). The interventionist can help them rehearse their ideas orally by pointing to words on the flow chart as the children create related sentences such as, "A farm has animals like sheep and cows," or "Sheep eat grass and play in the fields."

Farm

```
              Farm
         /            \
     animals          places
     /     \          /      \
  sheep    cow     field     barn
  /    \           /    \
wool  shear     grass   play
```

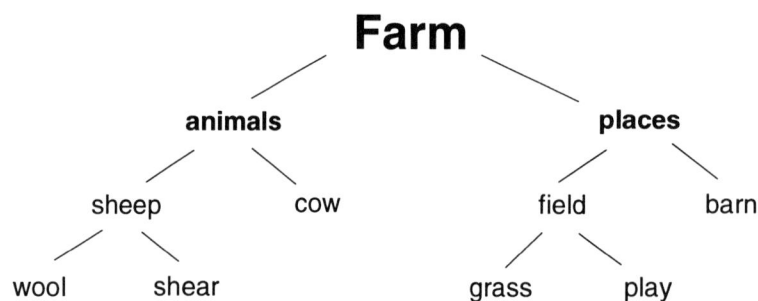

INDEPENDENT WRITING

Collaborative writing experiences, including dictation and rehearsal, help children to understand what people write and how they go about the writing process. They provide children with sources of information and models for coordinating the many levels of language and skill involved in the writing process. But children also need opportunities to write independently, expressing their ideas using their current level of knowledge and incorporating new insights and discoveries. Children must be fearless about engaging in independent writing. They should not be encumbered by worries about correct spelling, correct letter formation, or grammatical sentences (McGee and Richgels 1990; Temple et al. 1988). Independent writing for young children must be viewed developmentally rather than conventionally. Understanding how beginning writers think helps the teacher or special service provider establish developmentally appropriate expectations.

Children use a variety of symbol systems to represent writing in the initial stages: pictures, scribbles, shapes, letters or letter approximations, numbers, and anything else they consider to be writing. At this stage, writing exists as a process, and its purpose is for children to create and enjoy making marks on paper rather than to produce a written product for purposes of communication across distances of time and space. The functions of writing are to have fun and to write for personal enjoyment and one's own purposes rather than to communicate with others. It would not be unusual for children at this level to leave a dictated writing experience ready to write independently about the day's topic, only to change the topic and function to something else they are interested in at that moment. The topic and function may change several times while they are in the process of writing (Ferreiro 1986; Ferreiro and Teberosky 1982).

Because the process of writing and reading is most important at this stage, the meaning and function of the product can change even after it is written. The written product lacks object permanence, and thus it means whatever the child wants it to mean at that moment. The child may read the same selection of writing as, "The sheep is the lamb's mother" when asked for a report, and then immediately read the same selection as, "I have new shoes" when reading the note to a friend or as, "My sweater is made of wool" after hearing a classmate read that his sweater is made of wool. Similarly, others can read the child's note and ascribe to it any meaning that they choose. For example, a child who states, "I don't know how to write" can be encouraged to make marks, copy letters from environmental print found in the room, or helped to form letters, with the assurance that others will be able to read the result. Any writing that the child does attempt should be "read," and the child should be encouraged to "read" it also. Many experiences with repeated readings of the same storybooks, recognition of environmental print, and opportunities to write and dictate will be required before children understand the permanent nature of a written message.

Independent writing for children, like that of adults, requires time and quiet reflection. Journal writing is one means of providing this quiet time. Journal writing is a time when children can write (or draw or copy) anything they choose (Staton et al. 1988). The entries may include personal experiences or feelings, comments or observations, stories, poems, or other text. Journal entries may not be read by others unless the writer wishes to share them. Dialogue journals, on the other hand, are specifically designed for communicating with another person. The journal is passed back and forth between those involved in the dialogue, so that each person may read it and add comments. The teacher and the child, two classmates, or children in other classrooms can be paired as dialogue partners. In some cases, dialogue partners may not know each other (for example, children in morning and afternoon sections of kindergarten) until a special party is arranged for correspondents to meet each other after months of journal exchanges.

A journal may consist of a spiral notebook, several pieces of paper stapled together, or more elaborate versions such as bound books or pages cut in a shape such as a barn to reflect the theme unit explored during that period of journal writing. Journals also may be used as a method of sharing information between home and school. Children can take their journals home and read them to parents, who then can add comments by writing a response in the journal. Children may choose to dictate information for teachers or parents to write in the journal. If a correspondent cannot read a child's message, this is an opportunity to talk about the need to provide the reader with conventional words and spellings, as described below. The desire to communicate with others is the most powerful motivation for making changes toward more conventional writing and spelling (Staton et al. 1988).

In addition to formal writing experiences, writing can become a natural part of all activities throughout the day. For example, rather than privately and silently writing notes to the main office, you can make the children aware of the function of writing by saying, "I'm going to write a note to the office so they will know what we need." Or while introducing an activity such as drawing a sheep and covering it with wool, take the opportunity to write the words "sheep" and "wool" with the children. Drawing children's attention to everyday print and making use of incidental writing opportunities help children to understand that writing is a natural mode of communication which people use to accomplish a variety of useful functions, including both achieving goals and entertaining. Being part of a community of writers enables children to become writers themselves and, in the process, to master many of its conventions, including spelling.

Teaching Spelling

For many years, it was thought that children learned to spell by mastering the correct spellings of individual words and the orthographic rules that commonly apply to English words. Learning to spell was viewed as an exact process in which no errors were allowed. A word either was correctly spelled or it wasn't. Research in emergent literacy has shown, however, that spelling is a language process and, like learning to talk, learning to spell emerges creatively in stages that reflect a progressively more sophisticated understanding of the sound and syllable structure of words and their representation in spelling. Like art, reading, mathematics, and writing, spelling emerges developmentally as a meaningful language process within purposeful contexts of use. Teachers and special service providers who understand developmental spelling can direct their instruction toward encouraging children to spell using their current level of knowledge—with the long-term goal of facilitating further refinement—rather than toward teaching correct adult spelling.

SPELLING AND WRITING

Spelling in the context of writing is very similar to speech in the context of talking. They both represent modes of outwardly communicating the thoughts and ideas that the speaker/writer has formed into language. Both are based on what the child understands about the structure of language and how it is conventionally organized and represented. Just as correct speech emerges gradually during the preschool years in the context of meaningful talk, correct spelling emerges gradually in the context of meaningful writing (Hoffman 1990; Hoffman and Norris 1989). Therefore, any writing experience should begin with a reason or purpose for writing and with interesting ideas to write about. For example, in the thematic unit *Mrs. Wishy-washy,* the manner in which animals clean themselves is studied. Interactive reading of the book *Do You Know What I Think?* familiarizes children with the pattern "I think giraffes [or other animal name] should have to clean their necks [or other body part]."

One can then present pictures of different animals, and the children can decide what body part the animal should clean and how to write about this. Help the children to examine and think about the manner in which these words are spelled:

> How does the author spell "think"? What sound does he want our mouths to say at the beginning of the word? What letters does he use to tell us that? What sound is at the end of the word? What letter

makes that sound? As a writer, those would be important clues to give to my reader, so I would include those in my spelling (for example, THK).

Provide several examples of how to think like a speller before the children engage in independent writing about the pictured animals cleaning themselves (Norris and Hoffman 1993).

A meaningful writing context provides a framework within which the principles of writing and spelling emerge simultaneously as a written language process. Spelling emerges attached to meaning and purpose, rather than as isolated alphabetical knowledge that the children then must generalize to a context of use. All aspects of spelling and metalanguage, including sound awareness, sound discrimination, syllabic structure, letter-sound correspondences, and metalinguistic awareness, are taught as a dynamic, problem-solving process within the same experience.

SPELLING AS COMMUNICATION

Communicative success is a strong motivator for change and refinement in both oral and written language. In each child, development proceeds both creatively—as an expression of that child's unique way of viewing and organizing the world—and conventionally, that is, similar enough in pattern and form to that used by other people in the culture to be communicative (Ferreiro 1986; Ferreiro and Teberosky 1982; Gentry 1989). By treating spelling as one integral aspect of the writing process conducted in order to share insights, feelings, and information with an interested reader, one can immerse children in a context where there is opportunity and motivation to be more communicative. The need to be more communicative motivates children to develop both creatively and conventionally.

To create a communicative context for spelling development, writing experiences should involve real communicative situations—stories that are read, letters that are mailed and answered, research that is shared, messages that are sent to parents and peers, plays that are enacted, recipes that are followed, and so forth. For example, an author's chair can be established in the classroom (Calkins 1986). Following a writing experience, children can take turns sitting in the author's chair and collaboratively reading their compositions with an adult or peers. In the context of these interactions, the adult could make comments such as, "I know that you're talking about the dog because your letters tell my mouth to say /d/ at the beginning and /g/ at the end of the word," or "What letter could you write that would let me know what animal you were talking about?" In this context, children learn that they must provide cues to the reader about the words and meaning that they intend to communicate. Successes serve to confirm their hypotheses about sound and word structure. Requests for clarification motivate changes and refinements.

BEGIN WITH CHILDREN'S KNOWLEDGE

Shared compositions enable the adult to gain insights into a child's level of spelling knowledge and to monitor changes (or lack of changes) in the child's knowledge about the sounds and structure of words and their spelling representations. Spelling progresses through predictable stages as children experiment with its form and function, and adults can observe these changes in children's spelling attempts and problem-solving strategies. At the earliest stages, children do not have a concept of wordness, and writing is not differentiated from drawing. They consider pictures to be the medium for communicating a message and, when asked to write, they may scribble or draw. The first discovery children need to make is that print is different from illustrations. The adult can guide them toward this discovery by examining a book such as *Mrs. Wishy-washy* and distinguishing between the pictures and the print. For example, point to the picture and say:

> This is a picture of a duck, and because it's a picture, I can talk about it. I can say, "The duck is white," "The duck has a beak," or "The duck is quacking." But as a reader, what I really pay attention to is the print.

Then point to and read the print with exaggerated reading intonation. Now ask the children to write something. If they draw, respond:

> Well, I can talk about your picture. I can say, "I see a duck and I see his feet" (spoken using conversational intonation). But I can't read unless you write some letters.

Point to and read the letters in the book again, using exaggerated reading intonation (Norris 1989a). Direct children's attention toward individual letters by isolating one from the context of a word and talking about how a writer might make that letter:

> If I want my reader to know that I'm talking about the duck, I would write a "d." First, I would draw a straight line (doing so), and then I would put a circle at the bottom of it. Let's see, I want my circle to be on this side (pointing to the left of the line) so it looks like a "d."

Then help the child to print the letter. The goal is not to spell the word "duck." Rather, this word is used as a forum for helping the child discover the difference between pictures and print.

Another important developmental discovery children make relates to the form of print. During this stage of spelling, termed *prephonemic,* children experiment with a wide range of symbols in their word representations, including letters, shapes, numbers, punctuation marks, and letter-like scribbles (see Table 3-2). These symbols often are interspersed with pictures and scribbling. There is no object permanence to any of these words. They exist as word representations only at the moment the child writes them, and their intended meaning can change in the next moment (Gentry 1982, 1989). The child does not attempt to represent specific sounds with specific letters or to represent the syllabic shape of a word with letter sequences. The association of symbols to words is purely arbitrary and fleeting. The goal for this level is to establish an understanding of the nature of symbols.

TABLE 3-2
Stages of Developmental Spelling

Prephonemic: Phonetic principle is lacking.

    Letter strings may have numbers or random letters:

    P k n n o r s t 5 e w 3 1

Early phonemic: Phonetic principle is applied to initial letter(s). Beginning letters may be followed by random letters:

    POLSAT A BO LA = Pinocchio told a big lie

Letter name: The letter name is used to spell syllables:

    LFNT = elephant; DP = deep

Semiphonetic: Incomplete syllable/phonemic representations are used:

    ag = edge; parches = purchase

Transitional: More orthographic principles are incorporated:

    reech = reach; nachure = nature

Conventional: Orthographically correct spelling appears

    reach; nature; kitchen

Sources: Chomsky 1980; Ferreiro 1986; Gentry 1982, 1989; Hoffman and Norris 1989; Read 1986.

Adults can facilitate progress toward this level of spelling by helping the child to become aware of the form of print. Placing environmental print at eye level in the classroom or therapy setting—for example, calendars, books, alphabet strips, dictated writing, maps, or other materials with print—is one method of providing children with needed models. After establishing ideas and a purpose for writing, the children can be encouraged to look around their environment for help with writing their stories. For example, one might say:

> As you try to write about your animal, you could look at the alphabet strip or the calendar for ideas about how you can make letters. You could put a "b" or a "t" or any letters that you would like to make.

In this manner, children are free to experiment with print and to make discoveries about how letters are formed. The adult can ask for refinements by saying, for example:

> As a reader, I expect to see the circle touching the line at the bottom—that tells me the letter is a "b."

Once children have a knowledge of printed symbols, the goal changes to one of establishing the phonemic principles of sound-letter correspondences. The first stage in this process is termed *early phonemic*. The child must learn to coordinate two aspects of word structure during this stage: (1) the relationship of a specific sound to a specific letter and (2) the order of sounds used within a syllable to represent the consonant and vowel patterns of the word (Ferreiro 1986; Gentry 1982, 1989; Read 1986). Much experimentation takes place during this stage, and it must be allowed to occur freely and without risk. Until children have sufficient experience, they will shift their focus from one dimension of word structure to the next as they think about word generation. Their spelling of a word is unstable, created anew with each attempt. Many of their attempts will capture the first or last sound with a corresponding letter but contain other random letters included in an attempt to represent the syllable shape, with more letters representing a long word (for example, PKOVR for "picture") and fewer letters, a short word (for example, PG for "pig").

To help children progress toward this stage, the adult can point to a pre-phonemically spelled word and say:

> That word (TGM) tells my mouth to say "tig" because of the "T." The letter "p" tells my mouth to say p-p-pig. Let's look at the name in the book and check. (Look at the reading book and verify that the author did, in fact, use a "p" to spell "pig.")

Contrast "pig" with a few other words in the same text to establish a contrast between "p" in "pig" and other letters in other words. As the child begins to spontaneously represent initial sounds, begin to focus on ending sounds, and finally on medial consonants and vowels. Similarly, in the context of reading books, one can highlight important words and talk about the manner in which they are spelled and the relationship between the letters and what occurs in the reader's mouth ("That letter tells me to pop my lips to make a /p/ sound.") and ear. ("This letter tells me to listen for a /p/ sound.") In this manner, the child is guided to discover principles of both the sound and syllable structure of words and how they are represented in print.

During this stage, children are learning the names for letters as well as their sounds. Many instances of *letter name* spelling can be seen in their writing. This occurs as children use the name of the letter to represent a sound sequence (for example, the letter L is pronounced "el"); thus they spell a word such as "Ellen" as LN. They are quite convinced that no other letters need to be included in the word because they are clearly represented in the letter names (Gentry 1982, 1989). With more experience, children begin to sort out the difference between the name of the letter and its sound without a concerted effort on the educator's part. Clarifications such as, "But as a reader I pay attention to the sound, and it tells my mouth to say /l/," cue children to the need to modify their hypotheses.

Semiphonetic spellings increasingly appear in children's attempts as they move toward more conventional spelling, keeping in balance both sound and syllable representation. Children spell in ways that simplify either the phonetic features or syllable features of words that are too difficult for them or for which they do not have the conventional rule (Hoffman and Norris 1989). For example, the child might spell the word "truck" as CHUK. The letters "ch" are used for "tr" because truck is pronounced not with a /tr/ sequence (as in "t-er-uck") but rather with a gliding tongue movement more like that of /tʃ/. The letter "k" is used for "ck" because the child has not yet discovered the more conventional "ck" pattern. Similarly, if the word has more than one syllable, the child might represent only the stressed syllable or syllables in the spelling (as in ELFUNT for "elephant").

Progressively more and more words appear that have all of the sound and syllable features correctly represented, but the word may not contain the correct vowels or phonic principles. Such spellings are termed *phonetic.* As children experiment with orthographic patterns, they begin to incorporate them into their spellings and make many incorrect hypotheses about which patterns belong in what words, resulting in *transitional* spellings. It takes many years for children to gain enough experience with writing and word representation to build a large vocabulary of *conventional* spellings. But even at the kindergarten level, children can spell, using conventional spelling, many simple words that they read frequently (Gentry 1982, 1989).

Understanding the developmental emergence of spelling enables the adult to analyze the stage of discovery that each child has reached and to accept that stage as the entry level of writing and spelling for that child. It also enables one to establish a sequence of goals that guide the information and the feedback given to various children, predicated on what will help each child make the next necessary refinement or modification. Progress can be monitored, not by measuring the number of correctly spelled words or letters of the alphabet, but rather by determining the percentage of words spelled at more sophisticated levels during writing and spelling (Norris and Hoffman 1993).

■ Summary and Conclusions

The Storybook-Centered Curriculum and Lesson Plans are designed to provide early childhood teachers, special education teachers, speech-language pathologists, and special service providers with a comprehensive, integrated curriculum that simultaneously facilitates language development and the acquisition of content-area knowledge. The lesson plans are based on the S-D-S model and provide specific suggestions for developing language along the semantic, discourse, and situational dimensions as children explore reading, writing, mathematics, art, social studies, and the sciences. The lessons have been proven to work with children who are at risk for academic failure, as well as with children who need a challenging and comprehensive exposure to the physical and social world in which we live. The Storybook-Centered Curriculum is ideal for schools implementing the full inclusion of children with special needs into the regular classroom.

Chapter 4 will discuss adaptations and strategies that can be used to meet the special needs of children with language disorders and other learning disabilities. These adaptations and strategies allow the curriculum to be used to address the needs of children with special needs either in the regular classroom or in other settings, such as self-contained classrooms or small-group intervention sessions. The plans are to be used flexibly, so that any part of them (for example, Collaborative Reading) might be used without implementing the entire curriculum. A different activity could be substituted for any of the Topic Explorations or Thematic Studies in order to meet the specific needs of a particular group of students. Only the discussions that are at appropriate levels of semantic and discourse might be presented to the group—as opposed to presenting the entire continuum.

The Storybook-Centered Curriculum is designed to meet the needs of a wide range of children in regular and special education. It is a language-based curriculum in which the process of learning—how the learning is facilitated—is more important than the product—what is taught or learned. The products emerge from the process and, therefore, learning how to be an active learner is valued. When children have the strategies and language skills to be active learners, they are capable of learning content-area knowledge more independently and with greater depth of understanding.

CHAPTER 4

Using the Storybook-Centered Curriculum for Children with Special Needs

Children with language delays, learning disabilities, or other special needs will learn and progress while participating in a classroom where the Storybook-Centered Curriculum is used. A study by Hoffman and Norris (1994) using the curriculum showed that the children who represented the lowest achievers in the kindergarten classrooms (below the 25th percentile at the beginning of the year) made greater gains in alphabetical knowledge and deriving meaning from print than did children who were systematically taught readiness skills. However, children with special needs require more opportunities for facilitated learning than can be provided by classroom interactions alone. Modifications may be needed to enable these children to succeed in the classroom while at the same time acquiring speech and language skills that their peers have already mastered without intervention. These special services may involve modifications in the learning environment, modifications in the facilitative interactions provided within activities, or both.

■ Providing Special Services

The special services provided for children with language and learning delays or disorders may be delivered along multidimensional continua of options as detailed on Table 4-1 (page 100) and profiled in Figure 4-1 (page 101). All or parts of the Storybook-Centered Curriculum can be adapted within these various options for use with children who present special needs. The service-delivery modes and the aspects of the curriculum that are implemented for any child will result from a combination of the child's needs, the time and personnel resources available, the level of involvement of teachers and special service providers in the child's program, the curriculum and teaching methods used in the primary classroom, and the degree of integration of the regular and special education curricula.

TABLE 4-1
Multidimensional Continua of Service-Delivery Options for
Using the Storybook-Centered Curriculum with Children with Special Needs

1. *The child's special needs are primarily:*

◄──►

| Monitoring for continued progress and periodic reevaluation or intervention | Ongoing intervention to increase oral and written speech and language abilities and to support classroom learning | Intensive intervention to increase ability to function in school setting |

2. *The most appropriate use of the Storybook-Centered Curriculum is:*

◄──►

| Collaboratively, as the regular early childhood curriculum in the classroom supported by intervention based on the S-D-S model | Collaboratively, with all special service providers using parts of the curriculum to achieve complementary goals | Independently, with service providers using parts of the curriculum to meet specific group objectives |

3. *The most appropriate model of service delivery is:*

◄──►

| Providing intervention within the regular classroom | Providing intervention within a self-contained special education classroom | Providing intervention in a pull-out program |

4. *The most appropriate group structure is:*

◄──►

| Small groups including children with special needs and peers | Small groups of children with special needs | Individual intervention directed specifically to the child's needs |

5. *The most appropriate role for the special service provider in service delivery is:*

◄──►

| Consulting with and modeling for classroom teachers and others | Team teaching with regular or special education teachers | Providing direct services independent of other teachers |

6. *The most appropriate time schedule for service delivery is:*

◄──►

| Intensive intervention in blocks of time over six to eight weeks | Short periods of intervention provided several times weekly | Support provided for most of the school day |

7. *The most appropriate use of the curriculum is:*

◄──►

| Primary focus on development of oral language abilities | Simultaneous focus on development of oral and written language | Primary focus on development of written language abilities |

FIGURE 4-1
Service-Delivery Options with the Storybook-Centered Curriculum

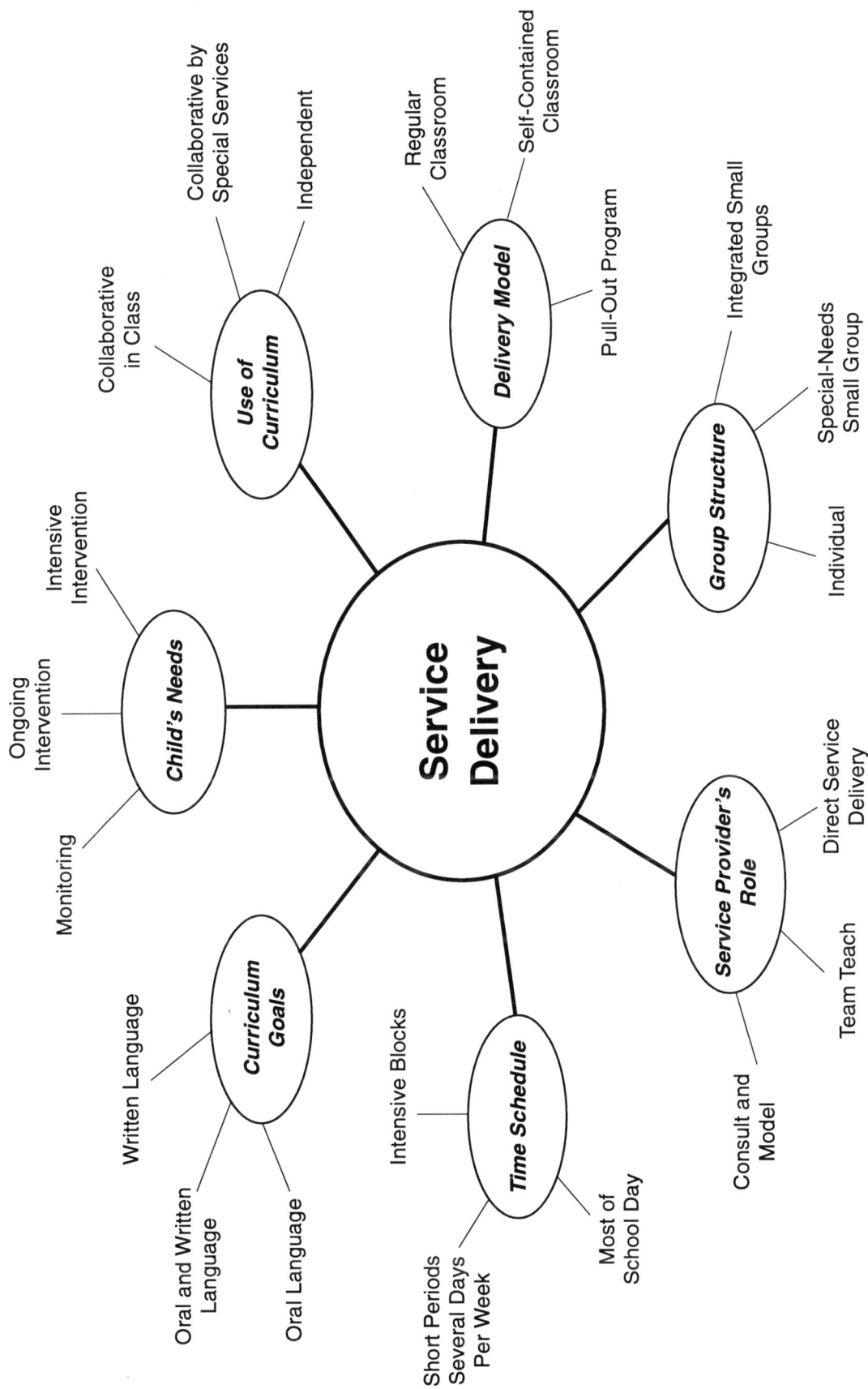

Considering the Child's Needs

The child's needs may be minimal, consisting primarily of monitoring and periodic reevaluation or intervention for specific problems or concerns. The teacher using the Storybook-Centered Curriculum may be able to address the child's language and learning needs in the regular classroom with consultation and monitoring from the speech-language pathologist (Phillips and McCullough 1990; Secord and Wiig 1991). When problems arise, the teacher and speech-language pathologist may jointly decide on modifications in the activities or their manner of implementation to foster more successful inclusion of the child with special needs. At a higher level along the needs continuum, the child may have a sufficiently serious delay or disorder in language acquisition to warrant intervention by the speech-language pathologist, other special service providers, or both. The child who is significantly delayed in language development on school entry will fall progressively further behind without specialized intervention (see chapter 1). Early intervention can help to prevent or lessen years of academic failure and other language-based problems and will enable the child to participate more successfully in the regular classroom program of which he or she is presently a member. Children with concomitant problems, such as a physical disability or a behavioral disorder, may require intensive intervention and assistance from an aide for most of the school day (Westby 1994).

Appropriate Uses of the Storybook-Centered Approach

Many preschool and kindergarten classroom teachers may use the Storybook-Centered Curriculum as the curriculum for the entire class. Similarly, the curriculum may be used in many self-contained classrooms for children with special needs because of its flexibility in implementation and its relevance to prereaders, emergent readers, and older children with poor oral and written language skills. When the Storybook-Centered Curriculum is used in the child's regular classroom, the speech-language pathologist or other special service provider can use the same activities to achieve specific oral and written language objectives. For example, the thematic story may be explored with small groups of children immediately prior to its use in the classroom. The speech-language pathologist can introduce the vocabulary and the details in the picture which are needed to derive descriptions and interpretations of the actions, states, and consequences of the actions. These interactions teach children how to look beyond superficial perceptions and seek information and how to use background knowledge and experiences to construct meaning from the pictures. Similarly, children can be assisted to generate inferences, to organize the individual events into progressively more complex stories along the discourse continuum, to read the text and engage in metalinguistic analysis, or to articulate correctly (see Specific Intervention Strategies for Facilitating Language Learning beginning on page 139 in this chapter for specific information on achieving these goals).

In addition to teaching language, collaborative use of the Storybook-Centered Curriculum enables the children to participate more actively in and learn from the classroom discussion, because they have the prerequisite vocabulary and information to understand and contribute to the interaction. The prior exploration in small groups enables children with language and learning disorders to remain active learners rather than becoming frustrated and engaging in off-task behaviors because the classroom discussion does not make sense. The children will have legitimate contributions to make and will be more able to benefit from and process the ideas provided by others. As the children's language skills improve and their backgrounds of concepts and knowledge expand, they will be able to function more independently within the group and will require less time in small-group explorations. The children begin to internalize the language skills and strategies for examining and organizing experience that they learn in small groups and thus become able to independently think and talk about the social and physical world.

If the Storybook-Centered Curriculum is not used in the child's regular classroom, parts of it are ideal for use in speech-language intervention to develop a wide range of speech and language abilities and for use with older children who demonstrate poor reading, writing, spelling, and academic achievement. For example, each intervention session may consist of Collaborative Reading, either a Topic Explorations or Thematic Studies activity, and some writing. If the objectives focus primarily on oral language development, use the suggestions for discussion along the semantic and discourse continua, emphasizing the discussions that are appropriate to the developmental levels of the group (see Specific Intervention Strategies on page 139 in this chapter). If the objectives are primarily related to written language, then emphasize the meta-linguistic levels of the semantic continuum for word analysis, and employ communicative reading strategies (CRS) (Norris 1988, 1989a, 1989b, 1991; Norris and Hoffman 1993) to establish fluent reading and comprehension (see page 150). Emphasizing higher levels of discussion along the semantic and discourse continua will develop good comprehension abilities.

One might then use an activity from Topic Explorations or Thematic Studies to establish background knowledge needed for good comprehension and to allow the children to explore the patterns of organization and information found in expository text. In this context, the Topic Explorations or Thematic Studies can be adapted to help older children learn how to ask questions and find answers using reference materials, tables of contents, indexes, chapter headings and subheadings, main ideas stated in topic sentences, and other strategies important for academic success. You might use the library books listed under Suggested Books for these explorations or select slightly more advanced ones, depending on the needs of the group members.

This topical research can be followed by a writing activity. For young children, the writing activity might be taken directly from the Storybook-Centered Lesson Plans or adapted. For example, the children might draw a picture to represent information presented in the Topic Explorations then write about it. (Procedures for facilitating art and writing are discussed in chapter 3.) The older child might write a research summary or topical report in order to learn how to organize information logically and to present it in writing. For example, the children might generate three questions about a topic, find relevant information to answer those questions, and present them in an expository text. They may then be asked to construct a flow chart to organize that information into logical main points and supporting details, as described in chapter 3. They can use the flow chart to plan the information they will include in each paragraph and how to use relational terms such as "when," "because," "if-then," "next," "although," and so forth to express their ideas logically. Active participation in oral discussion, generation of questions, location of answers to specific questions, reading of the written information in reference materials, construction of the flow chart, and oral planning and rehearsal for communicating the information help to prepare children to write well-structured and informative compositions, far more complex than what they could produce independently. As children engage in meaningful writing and all of the preparatory steps, they begin to internalize the process and become better writers with increasingly less assistance. (See Norris and Hoffman 1993 for an in-depth discussion of reading and writing intervention for school-age children.)

Service-Delivery Models

Schools are increasingly enacting policies or practices that call for the full inclusion of all students—including those with physical, cognitive, and language and learning disabilities—within regular education classrooms in their home schools. Many programs are implementing inclusion successfully for the majority of students. Organizations such as the American Speech-Language-Hearing Association (ASHA) and the Learning Disabilities Association of America (LDA) have taken a strong position against any policy that mandates the same placement, instruction, or treatment for all children with special needs, however. These policies state that the regular education classroom is not an appropriate placement for all students and that decisions regarding educational placement must be based on the needs of the individual student, rather than on administrative or budgetary considerations. Furthermore, placement decisions are to result from a cooperative effort involving the educators, parents and, when appropriate, the student. A continuum of alternative placements must be available to meet the needs of all students.

The Storybook-Centered Curriculum is designed to be implemented flexibly within a continuum of educational environments and service-delivery models. The original curriculum resulted from a collaborative effort between classroom teachers in regular kindergarten classrooms and speech-language pathologists to create a comprehensive language-based curriculum that would serve the needs of all children in the classroom. Practices such as using parts of the curriculum during small-group intervention sessions enabled children who entered kindergarten with two curricular needs—(1) to acquire the oral language skills already achieved by their peers, and (2) to acquire content-area knowledge and advanced language abilities—to achieve both goals using one curriculum. In this manner, the efforts of all individuals working with a child were coordinated and directed toward different aspects of the same goals. Communication among professionals was enhanced because all worked from the same theoretical base, as outlined by the S-D-S model, and all were aware of the range of academic and oral and written language learning needs presented by the children and addressed by the curriculum.

The Storybook-Centered Curriculum also has been used successfully in other placement settings—such as small-group pull-out therapy and individual speech-language therapy. Many classrooms are not structured in a manner that is conducive to oral and written language learning. Many classrooms are full of quiet children who sit in rows separated from their peers and complete worksheets and other individual work. In these classrooms, fewer than two minutes of talking may be afforded to a child during an entire school day. It might be viewed as disruptive or inappropriate to have small groups of children engaged in active problem solving, predicting, restructuring of a story at progressively higher levels of discourse complexity, engaging in collaborative research, and so forth in such a classroom. Pull-out service delivery might be a more appropriate alternative for children in such classrooms.

Children with similar speech, language, and learning needs are often placed in different classrooms or at different grade levels. A limited number of special service providers and limited contact time may require that small groups be drawn from several classrooms. This situation might require that children be pulled out of their classrooms or that they all meet in one classroom rather than in each child's own classroom. Some children with severe attention deficits or behavioral problems may be unable to focus on very specific details or to hear nuances of speech and language when intervention is provided in a classroom with numerous distractions and background noises. For these children, intervention might be more effective in a small group meeting in a smaller, quieter room.

Group Structure

When the Storybook-Centered Curriculum is used in the regular education classroom, children with special needs have the opportunity to participate in a number of different groups and group structures (see chapter 2). During some parts of the day, they are members of large-group activities where they meet with peers to acquire and share information and experiences (Hill and Hill 1990). In these groups, they build a sense of cohesiveness and identity with the classroom community and all of its members. Speech-language pathologists and other special service providers can help to make large-group experiences successful for children with special needs. They can help children understand and learn the "hidden agenda," the social rules and classroom expectations for participation in the group (Creaghead 1992). Using discussion, pictured examples, role playing, flow charts, and other strategies can help children become aware of and learn how to follow these rules and scripts. Special service providers can sit with children in large groups, modeling and prompting a variety of language functions in this setting, including asking a question, initiating a comment, responding to a question, acknowledging a comment, and making a prediction. They can help the child discover when it is permitted to talk in unison or spontaneously, versus when a turn must be solicited by raising a hand.

They can also help children to learn phrases that the teacher typically uses, such as "If you are in the red group, line up at the door" to enhance orderly transitions; "Excuse me" to signal too much noise; or "Are you in the learning center?" to indicate that the child is in the wrong place. Children with language disorders may take such conditional language and indirect speech acts literally and move toward the door on hearing the command to "line up" or answer "yes" when asked whether they are in the learning center. Teachers often perceive such responses as noncompliance or poor listening, when in fact they represent misunderstanding of the language. Speech-language pathologists can help children to understand that there are different contingencies for different teachers and different activities and can teach children how to watch peers or listen for instructions that provide clues about expectations in a given setting. Children can learn to tell teachers when they don't understand the instructions or are uncertain of the rules and procedures. At the same time as speech-language pathologists are helping children to understand classroom agendas and rules, they can collaborate with teachers to make them aware of how easily children with language delays and disorders can misinterpret instructions or understand only the most concrete component of them ("line up") while missing the conditional contingencies (membership in the "red group" and the "if-then" logical relationship).

Speech-language pathologists and other special service providers also can prepare children for the content encountered in large groups by introducing the vocabulary, concepts, relationships, discourse, inferences, print, and so forth prior to the large-group discussion. Discussing this information first in a small group provides children who have special needs with the special circumstances that they need for learning: additional time, multiple trials, immediate feedback, individualized clarifications or elaborations, multiple opportunities to put the concepts into words, and more detailed explorations with smaller steps and more explicitly stated inferences. Familiarizing children with these concepts in a small group gives them the appropriate background to understand and follow the classroom discussion and establishes information at lower levels of the semantic continuum (such as labels and descriptions), enabling them to understand the interpretations, inferences, or evaluations generated in the large group, and allowing them to provide meaningful and relevant contributions to the large-group discussion. The second encounter with the concepts in the large group provides them with the repeated exposure and redundancy they need to internalize and generalize the concepts.

Small-group intervention using the theme books also allows for the development of the story at a more advanced level along the discourse continuum than the children can independently generate. With the assistance of scaffolding strategies, the children can engage in telling the story with greater complexity and elaboration (Norris and Hoffman 1990). They can understand and use a greater number of relational connections among agents, objects, actions, and events including temporal, spatial, causal, conditional, intentional, and adversarial relations. Becoming more familiar with relational connections gives the children the appropriate frame, not only for interpreting what is happening when the information is presented in the large group, but also for understanding when, how, and why.

Use of the Storybook-Centered Curriculum in the regular classroom provides opportunities for speech-language pathologists and other special service providers to meet with children in small groups for these purposes, or to collaborate with the classroom teacher so the teacher can achieve these goals in small-group time with these students. Other opportunities for small-group interactions are present in the regular classroom. For example, heterogeneous cooperative learning groups provide opportunities for members to work collectively in cooperation (Hill and Hill 1990). They foster interdependent learning and inclusion of all members (see chapter 2). The speech-language pathologist can help children with special needs function more effectively in these groups by teaching the social and classroom rules and agendas for collaborative interactions. Knowing what peers expect and how they express various communicative functions in that community can help children with language disorders to interpret and use the same language, slang, and jargon as their classmates, and to maintain the same goals and expectations as their peers.

The speech-language pathologist can maintain a facilitative role for all of the children in the group. This may involve reminding children of information they need to consider, giving individual help, helping to clarify issues, guiding decision making, demonstrating where to locate information or how to find answers to questions, or giving encouragement and assurance. This facilitation thus becomes part of the assistance that the adult provides to all group members, so that the child with special needs is not singled out, while at the same time it provides the support that certain children need to function within the group. Speech-language pathologists can use a collaborative model to teach aides, parents, or other classroom personnel to perform these functions (Phillips and McCullough 1990; Secord and Wiig 1991). They also can assist peers to understand the needs of children with language and learning disorders and show the peers how to provide peer teaching. Much of this can be done through modeling or by giving suggestions; for example, "Jenny, why don't you show Stephen how to measure exactly six inches?" or "Ask Maria what the cow might eat. Tell her to look carefully at the bottom of the picture"; or "I know I learn better when people show me. Can you show Phan and me what you mean?"

Speech-language pathologists must keep in focus that their role is to help children to learn the language and pragmatic skills they need to function in the classroom, not to become tutors or aides within the classroom. Children who are identified as speech and language delayed or disordered must learn two curricula: language acquisition and content-area knowledge. Speech-language pathologists are responsible for coordinating the formulation of speech and language goals and objectives and for assuring that the program outlined on the child's special educational program is implemented. Given the limited time speech-language pathologists have for interactions with any one child, their efforts must be directed at accelerating the child's rate of language acquisition, flexibility of language use, comprehension and expression of complex discourse, and proficiency along the Situational-Discourse-Semantic dimensions of language use.

Use of the Storybook-Centered Curriculum in regular classrooms also provides opportunities to interact with children on an individualized basis. Independent learning centers provide a wide range of activities, from play to art to reading to content-area materials that can be explored individually or in loosely organized groups. Speech-language pathologists can use these contexts for providing language facilitation, especially for children with very limited verbal abilities. The toys or materials that the child selects can be talked about, manipulated, and used in more complex ways than the child could achieve in independent play or exploration. A variety of scaffolding strategies (described under Specific Intervention Strategies on page 140) can be used to accomplish these language and learning goals. Similarly, in the book reading center, the interactions described in the lesson plans for facilitating language acquisition in groups can be implemented individually.

When pull-out models are used, the special service provider must make the same types of decisions about individual versus group intervention, homogeneous versus heterogeneous groups, and so forth. The best solutions will depend on the child's current learning characteristics, the learning environment within the classroom, and the time and personnel available for individual instruction. Children's placements may need to change as they increase their language abilities and as classroom teachers modify their instruction to accommodate children with special needs.

Service-Delivery Role

Speech-language pathologists and other special service personnel have traditionally provided direct services to children individually or in small groups. The intervention occurred in isolation from the classroom and independent of the classroom curricula or the goals and objectives established by other special service providers. This service-delivery role evolved from the medical model of speech-language pathology (hence the terminology "pathology," "clinical practicum," "differential diagnosis," "speech clinician") rather than from an educational model. Theories of language focused on language form—the underlying syntactic rules and semantic features thought to govern language acquisition—rather than on meaningful and communicative uses of language. Written language problems have been considered a separate disorder from oral language delays, with the result that new labels are given to children with language disorders at school age; for example, "learning disabled" or "dyslexic" (Aram, Ekelman, and Nation 1984; Gibbs and Cooper 1989; Maxwell and Wallach 1984).

Twenty-five years of research have changed many of these beliefs about spoken language, how it is learned, its relationship to written language, and the relationship between oral and written language disorders (Miller 1991). The medical model has slowly diminished in influence while the education model has increased in practice for school-age children, and goals and objectives have become more educationally relevant (Nelson 1992; Ripich and Griffith 1988; Scott and Erwin 1992). Methods of intervention are consistent with newer theories that recognize language acquisition as a meaning-making process occurring in social contexts with the assistance of parents, teachers, and others who provide a scaffold for the child's learning. Reading disabilities are recognized as language-based disorders, with longitudinal studies demonstrating that the language learning difficulties displayed by preschoolers are later manifested as written language disabilities at school age (Aram, Ekelman, and Nation 1984; Gibbs and Cooper 1989; Maxwell and Wallach 1984).

These changes in theory, focus, goals, and attitudes have resulted in the evolution of different roles for speech-language pathologists and other special service providers in schools. Just as collaboration and peer teaching are encouraged for children in the classroom, professionals are adopting these approaches (Phillips and McCullough 1990; Secord and Wiig 1991). Many of the barriers between disciplines are being eliminated and professional roles are being seen as overlapping and complementary rather than as separate and unrelated. Professionals are evaluating the resources that they have available, working together to design the best possible program for a child using one curriculum and one long-term plan, and sharing the responsibility for implementing that curriculum. The special needs of the child are addressed within the curriculum, so that, for example, language learning is used as the foundation for the entire curriculum and a range of language levels and abilities can be accommodated through flexible use of the curriculum. Different individuals working with the child through the curriculum can focus on different aspects of the child's needs according to their own skills and knowledge. Speech-language pathologists, other special service personnel, and regular education teachers can support one another by providing inservices to parents and teachers, consultation regarding curriculum modifications or learning techniques, and collaborative intervention.

Concepts such as the inclusion of children with special needs in the regular education classroom, collaboration among all school personnel in curriculum development and service delivery, and consultation between personnel with special training and teachers are good practices, but time must be allotted for them in daily and weekly schedules, and administrative support and commitment must be present if they are to work. Most teacher training programs do not require coursework on normal language development, language disorders, learning disabilities, or other problems for which teachers are increasingly asked to take primary responsibility in the classroom. Consequently, teachers are frustrated because they are not trained to facilitate learning for children with special needs, children are penalized for not following rules and procedures that are presented using language they do not understand, content is taught at a level that is too decontextualized and abstract, and children with the lowest achievement levels spend the most time doing worksheets and other individualized activities that isolate them socially and academically from contexts of real language learning and use.

Inclusion, collaboration, and consultation models of service delivery for children with language and learning disorders must include these features:

- Frequent inservices for teachers, aides, administrators, and others who directly and indirectly serve children with special needs

- Understanding of the characteristics and needs of children with language and learning disabilities or disorders (see Table 4-2)

- Time in daily and weekly schedules for professionals to collaborate and plan who, what, where, and how regular and special educational goals will be addressed that week

- Frequent reevaluation of each student's performance, goals and objectives, and educational program

- Development of long-term plans (goals for the school year, transition to the next school year, five-year plan, and beyond)

- Suggestions for classroom modifications (see Table 4-3, page 112)

- Sufficient personnel to adequately support learners with special needs in the designated service-delivery model

- Agreement among professionals to support, accept, or tolerate whatever philosophy of providing services for children with special needs is adopted by the school, and to avoid behaviors that will sabotage its effectiveness or success

- Commitment to providing the best educational program possible for all children

TABLE 4-2
Characteristics of Children with Language and Learning Disabilities

Facts about Language and Learning Disabilities

- 3-15% of school-age population affected
- Academic delay leads to identification
- Uneven pattern of development, with academic strengths and weaknesses
- CNS dysfunction suspected cause
- Environmental disadvantage not a cause
- Mental retardation, emotional disturbance not causes
- Phonemic processing of language implicated
- Language deficits most prevalent (Gibbs and Cooper 1989)
  > 90.5% language problem
  > 23.5% articulation problem
  > 12% voice problem
  > 1.2% fluency problem
  > only 6% received SLP services that focused on articulation or fluency
  > rather than educationally relevant language

Soft Signs

- Sensory and motor hyperactivity
- Dissociation (facts but no relationships)
- Auditory and visual figure-ground reversals
- Perseveration
- Motor immaturity
- Attention deficit disorder (ADD; inattentive, hyperactive or hypoactive, impulsive, distractible, insatiable)
- Minimal brain dysfunction (MBD): some parts of brain more integrated than others
- Genetic component strong, especially in males
- Mixed laterality
- Problems with temporal serial organization

Learned Components

- Learned helplessness
- Poor self-concept
- Depression
- Acting out, aggression, boredom
- Delinquency: 89% are poor achievers
- Poor auditory processing

Areas Affected

- Academic performance
- School behavior
- Peer relations
- Interpersonal relationships at home
- Use of leisure time

Indicators of High Risk

- Delays in acquiring language forms
- Deficits in word finding and fluency of expression, frequent use of fillers
- Poor coherence, organizational content
- Difficulty with metaphoric language, defining words, idioms, indirect speech acts
- Poor social interaction, social perception, and perspective
- Difficulty with code switching, politeness, situational appropriateness
- Difficulty establishing referents, clarity
- Failure to request clarification
- Less assertive and effective
- Poor expression and elicitation of opinions
- Poor vocabulary, word retrieval, lack of morphology
- Simple sentences, frequent grammatical errors

Sources: ASHA (1989); Bryan (1986); Simon (1985)

TABLE 4-3
Suggested Classroom Modifications to Accommodate
Children with Special Needs

Content Strategies

- Contextualize difficult concepts using familiar experiences and examples.
- Provide pictures, graphs, charts, objects, and other visual supports.
- Point to details and examples in pictures to help clarify concepts.
- Provide hands-on experiences and demonstrations.
- Discuss important concepts at multiple levels along the semantic continuum.
- Organize ideas at increasingly more complex levels along the discourse continuum.
- When children do not respond or know an answer, provide more information, clarification, guidance to respond, assistance to communicate the information, or other teaching.
- Provide opportunities for children to work with others who have more skill or knowledge.
- Individualize goals, expectations, instruction, and evaluation procedures for children based on their developmental needs and abilities.
- Encourage collaborative learning and peer teaching.
- Provide opportunities for special service providers to collaborate in curriculum development and classroom instruction.

Instructional Strategies

- Engage children in active problem solving.
- Reduce reliance on rote memorization.
- Write rules and procedures on charts displayed in the classroom and frequently discuss and refer to them.
- Model metacognitive strategies children can use to plan, implement, and evaluate classroom assignments and skills.
- Reword abstract or difficult concepts in concrete terms.
- Use calendars, daily planners, maps, and task charts to help children understand what steps, activities, and procedures they need to complete an assignment and to organize their day.
- Recognize the continuum of performance between doing things for children and expecting them to do things for themselves.
- Help children to use oral language in negotiating conflicts.
- Use flow charts and other graphic organizers during discussions or activities.
- Provide opportunities for small-group and individualized learning.

Scheduling Special Services

Perhaps one of the greatest challenges speech-language pathologists and other special service providers encounter is scheduling. The number of children requiring special services continues to increase while funds to support these programs decrease. Many current practices—such as providing intervention for 20 minutes two or three times weekly—in reality result in very little actual instruction by the time group members are located, walk to the therapy room, and set up the activity. Children who are distractible or hyperactive, have short attention spans, or have poor language processing abilities will require nearly the entire session to begin to focus and attend to the task and will just be starting to learn by the time the group is to return to the regular classroom. Better alternatives must be sought if early intervention is to effectively facilitate language acquisition and prevent or reduce future language-based academic problems.

One scheduling alternative is intensive, short-term cycles of intervention, also called block scheduling. Short-term cycles provide longer periods of intervention (up to one hour) intensively (three to five times per week) for short blocks of time (four to eight weeks). Children may receive between two and four cycles of intervention during the school year, depending on the severity of their language and learning delays and their ability to function within the classroom environment (Neidecker 1980). When these children are not receiving intervention, the special service provider consults with the classroom teacher and others who interact with the children on a regular basis. During an intensive cycle, considerable language acquisition and learning can occur. With greater language skills, children are able to function more independently in the classroom.

If services are provided within the classroom, the speech-language pathologist can work for an intensive block of time with a heterogeneous group of children, including children with identified needs and higher-achieving peers. When children are in a collaborative setting, providing assistance to others becomes a natural part of the group dynamics. Therefore, group members are likely to continue to provide scaffolding for the child after the concentrated block of intervention has ended. If services are provided outside the classroom, the disruption can be minimized by carefully discussing and planning the goals of the intervention with the child's classroom teacher. Understanding the long-term benefits of oral and written language development and its implications for improved performance in the classroom encourages the teacher and special service providers to work cooperatively to set goals, objectives, and curriculum expectations for the duration of the block. Neidecker (1980) reviewed studies indicating that most classroom teachers preferred this model to intermittent intervention schedules because it fit better with other aspects of their daily schedules.

Another scheduling alternative is to provide speech and language support to children in the regular classroom for most of the school day. In this model, classroom aides, teachers, and other special service providers work in collaboration with the speech-language pathologist to teach language as a part of all interactions with the child. These professionals are provided with explicit information regarding the child's language-learning needs and with specific strategies they can use in the context of content-area learning. In this situation, the speech-language pathologist is one team member working to implement the program and is responsible for prescribing the objectives and language facilitation procedures and for monitoring progress.

■ Conducting Assessments Using the S-D-S Language Model

The Storybook-Centered Curriculum is a language-based program founded on the S-D-S language model. Individualized assessment, goal selection, long- and short-term planning, intervention, and program evaluation can all be conducted using the S-D-S model, resulting in continuity of a child's speech, language, and educational program. Speech and language intervention can be conducted within a classroom that is using this curriculum in its broad scope, allowing for total inclusion of children with special needs in the regular classroom, or it can be used independent of the classroom curriculum in small-group or even individual therapy. The assessment of children, whether they participate in the regular education classroom or receive support services, should begin with an individualized assessment based on the S-D-S language model.

Three types of individualized assessment can be conducted using the S-D-S language model:

1. Classroom-based or environment-based assessment

2. Language sampling

3. Task sampling

Each provides different information about the child that can be used to determine the nature and extent of the child's language-learning and communication difficulties and to plan the most effective intervention program.

Classroom-Based or Environment-Based Assessment

Classroom-based or environment-based assessment is conducted to determine how well the child functions and communicates within a natural communicative situation. This assessment involves observing the child in the classroom, on the playground, with a parent, or in other naturally occurring contexts. The S-D-S model allows for systematic evaluation and interpretation of these observations. Interpreting the observations goes beyond recording "what" was observed, to gain insights into "how" and "why" a child learns language and uses language and other communication to function within the environment. The assessment is based on evaluating the transactions occurring between the child and the people and objects encountered in the interaction so that judgments can be made regarding factors that facilitate or inhibit the child's learning and communication. Thus, these evaluations examine the dynamics within the language process, rather than the acquired products of language.

The assessment can be guided by the S-D-S Profile of Communication in Context form. The first step is to describe the context of the language use, focusing on the relationship of the language to the participants and the environment (the situational context). The second is to describe the characteristics of the discourse used to verbally organize and interpret the event (the discourse context). The third is to examine the quality of the ideas to gain insights into the dynamics that contribute to communicative difficulties and successes for the observed children (the semantic context).

PROFILING THE SITUATIONAL CONTEXT

Defining the situational context means designating how language is used in relationship to (1) the participants, and (2) the information referred to by the language. The examiner should describe the participants by designating the peers and adults participating in the interaction and whether they are unfamiliar, somewhat familiar, or very familiar to the observed child. Individuals who are very familiar with one another have many common experiences and share a background of common knowledge. When they interact, speakers need to provide less information and use less explicit language because they can assume that listeners already possess much of the information needed to share the intended meaning. The familiarity of the topic should be indicated as well, because less information needs to be explicitly exchanged when it can be assumed that participants possess an elaborated body of shared knowledge about the topic.

After describing the participants, the next step is to examine the language for references to contextualized and decontextualized information. The examiner decides whether the language refers primarily to objects, events, or other sensory information present within the environment (contextualized language) or to events or ideas that must be mentally created from the words alone (decontextualized language). Visual or other sensory cues can be used to clarify and interpret the intended meaning of contextualized language. Pointing to a picture while saying, "It's big enough for all five" is a clear statement if the speaker is pointing to a small boat and five people who are standing on the dock (contextualized language). But this statement is not sufficiently specific to share meaning without the support of the context (decontextualized language).

Many factors interact to determine how well a child will understand and use language within contextualized and decontextualized contexts. They include the familiarity of the topic, the familiarity of the participants, and how related the topic is to the child's experience. Therefore, it is important to indicate on the form how related the language is to the child. It is easier for children to understand information that relates to their own bodies or their own experiences. Comprehension becomes increasingly more difficult as language begins to refer to objects or events merely observed; to events created through symbols such as pictures, toys, and words; and to events that are logical rather than concrete. Chapter 2 contains detailed descriptions of these levels.

S-D-S Profile of Communication in Context

Name _____ Age _____ Date _____

Situational Context
Describe the general context of the communicative setting.

Participants

1. *Number of Participants*

   Child + _____ peers and _____ adults

2. *Familiarity of Participants*

   _____ Unfamiliar _____ Somewhat familiar _____ Very familiar

Language Characteristics

1. *Contextualization of Language*

   _____ Contextualized (refers to objects, action, events, people, present in the environment)
   _____ Decontextualized (refers to objects, action, events, people not present in the environment)

2. *Language Refers To*

   _____ Logical events, mental objects   _____ Objects, people, observed events
   _____ Symbolic objects, unobserved events   _____ Child, child's own experiences
   _____ Routine events, scripts

Discourse Context
Describe one representative topic of discussion.

1. *Discourse Participation*

   _____ Child produces monologue.   _____ Child is prompted, answers questions.
   _____ Child leads dialogue.   _____ Child primarily listens.
   _____ Child and other speakers are equal participants.

2. *Duration of Topic*

   _____ Brief (1-10 utterances)   _____ Long (41-99 utterances)
   _____ Moderate (11-40 utterances)   _____ Exhaustive (100+ utterances)

3. *Discourse Mode*

   _____ Oral   _____ Written   _____ Both oral and written

4. *Discourse Type*

   _____ Expressive (expressing personal feelings, chatter)
   _____ Transactional (giving information or instructions)
   _____ Poetic (recounting or reflecting through narration, poetry, or other literate form)

S-D-S Profile of Communication in Context (Continued)

5. *Discourse Organization*

_____ Interactive (overlapping topics)

_____ Complex (series of topics)

_____ Complete (includes a moral)

_____ Abbreviated (includes a goal)

_____ Reactive (includes a cause)

_____ Ordered (temporal sequence)

_____ Descriptive (list of facts, ideas)

_____ Collection (free association)

Semantic Context

Describe the quality of ideas responded to across communicative turns.

1. *Concreteness of Information*

_____ Experiential (learned through world or scientific exploration)

_____ Erudite (learned through academic or sensory experience)

2. *Complexity of Information Comprehended*

Rate the child's responses on a scale from 0 through 5:

  0 = not observed 1 = almost never appropriate 5 = almost always appropriate

Child answers or responds to ideas that are:

_____ Metalanguage (letters, sounds, rhymes, word concepts)

_____ Evaluative (judgments, evaluations, significance)

_____ Inferential (meaning beyond what is stated or suggested)

_____ Interpretive (meaning suggested, not explicitly stated)

_____ Descriptive (qualities, scenes, properties described)

_____ Labeling (whole objects, parts of objects named)

_____ Indicating (nonverbal communication, gestures)

3. *Complexity of Information Produced*

Rate the following items on a scale from 0 through 5:

  0 = not observed 1 = almost never appropriate 5 = almost always appropriate

Child answers or responds to ideas that are:

_____ Metalanguage (letters, sounds, rhymes, word concepts)

_____ Evaluative (judgments, evaluations, significance)

_____ Inferential (meaning beyond what is stated or suggested)

_____ Interpretive (meaning suggested, not explicitly stated)

_____ Descriptive (qualities, scenes, properties described)

_____ Labeling (whole objects, parts of objects named)

_____ Indicating (nonverbal communication, gestures)

Explanatory Notes and Interpretations

PROFILING THE DISCOURSE CONTEXT

The characteristics of the language used to verbally organize and interpret the event are described according to the length, mode, turns, discourse type, and complexity of its discourse organization. To evaluate the discourse context, select from the total event or conversation several sentences that comprise a representative topic. First, indicate the general characteristics of the discourse used to present the topic by designating whether the discourse was primarily a child-generated monologue or a dialogue involving some degree of shared responsibility along the continuum listed on the S-D-S Profile, or whether the child was primarily in the listener's role. Also describe the duration of the discourse on the topic, ranging from a brief discussion of the topic to a long, exhaustive coverage. Finally, indicate whether the language mode used in the communication was oral (including conversations, telling a story, or lecturing), written (including reading a book or writing a composition), or both (including interactively discussing a book as it is read or referring to notes or other graphics).

Designate the function of the discourse as expressive, transactional, or poetic. *Expressive discourse* is casual talk not intended to cause someone else to perform an action, change an attitude or belief, or give information to be used for a purpose, but rather to express or maintain social interaction. In contrast, *transactional discourse* is intended to change beliefs, attitudes, behaviors, or knowledge through the presentation of facts, commands, opinions, or questions. *Poetic* discourse is intended to influence beliefs, attitudes, behaviors, or knowledge through the use of narration, poetry, song, or other cultural forms of teaching.

Finally, specify the complexity of the organization to indicate whether information is merely listed, or whether temporal, causal, intentional, moral, or interactive links are used to organize the information. (See chapter 2 for a complete discussion of these levels.)

PROFILING THE SEMANTIC CONTEXT

The ideas that are responded to and expressed within the discourse are examined within the semantic context. The first judgment is whether the quality of the ideas is *experiential;* that is, whether they can be understood or learned through everyday world or sensory experience; or *erudite,* ideas that are accessible only through academic or scientific exploration. An experiential comment would be, "The leaves are green and healthy," while the erudite equivalent would be, "The leaves contain chlorophyll that plants use to make their own food by changing minerals from air and water into sugar."

The next step is to evaluate the abstractness of the ideas the child expresses and responds to. Low levels of abstraction include *naming* or *labeling* objects or their parts ("a plant," "a leaf") or *describing* actions or characteristics. ("The leaf is green." "The boy stepped on the plant.") Higher levels of abstraction are *interpreting* meaning from available perceptions ("The plant is healthy"), generating *inferences* ("The plant must have been watered and fertilized on a regular schedule"), and producing *evaluations* ("It is important to take care of plants and animals"). The highest level of abstraction is that of *metalanguage,* in which words themselves are analyzed and talked about. ("When 'leaf' is pluralized, the 'f' is changed to its voiced cognate 'v' and 'es' is added.") Metaphors and other types of figurative language are also examples of metalanguage. Rate the child's ability to respond to and produce these levels of language along a scale from 0 (not observed), 1 (almost never appropriate) through 5 (almost always appropriate).

EXPLANATORY NOTES AND INTERPRETATIONS

For any child, several S-D-S Profiles should be completed across different activities, different conversational participants, different topic explorations, and different settings to obtain a representative sampling of the child's understanding and use of language. A different profile form is completed for each observation. The S-D-S Profile is not completed merely to describe the characteristics of the interactions. Rather, these observations and descriptions provide insights into what the child knows about language and how the child uses language to communicate and learn. The *interactions* among the situational, discourse, and semantic contexts are important to understanding the child's language and learning. The following questions can help to guide these interpretations:

1. When the language used in the situational context is contextualized to ongoing objects, actions, and events

    a. are there positive effects on the maintenance, duration, and complexity of talk within the discourse context?

    b. are there positive effects on the response to and production of ideas at higher levels of abstraction along the semantic continuum?

2. When the language used in the situational context is decontextualized, are there more behaviors such as inattention, distractibility, motor activity, or other indicators that the child is having difficulty processing the discourse and the semantic information?

3. When the language refers to the child's own experiences, are the child's sentences longer, more fluent, organized into higher discourse structures, and more purposeful, and do they include more instances of higher-level ideas on the semantic continuum?

4. When the topic is familiar, does the child produce longer, more fluent, and more purposeful sentences that are organized into higher discourse structures and include more instances of higher-level semantic ideas?

5. Does the child tell a story with higher levels of discourse organization and greater abstraction along the semantic continuum when storytelling is supported by pictures (contextualized) as opposed to being spontaneously produced (decontextualized), even though the story is the same?

6. Does the child include more detail and organization along the discourse and semantic continua when prompts and other assistance are provided to result in a dialogue than when the child produces a monologue?

7. Does the child understand information better when participation is elicited during a lecture or classroom discussion as opposed to when the child primarily listens?

8. When sentences are complex and the duration of the topic is long to exhaustive, does the child exhibit greater inattention, distractibility, motor activity, or other indicators of difficulty processing the discourse and the semantic information?

9. When the discourse is written rather than oral, does the child's ability to process the discourse and semantic information increase or decrease?

10. Does the child's ability to read fluently with good word recognition, expression, and comprehension increase when the text is contextualized to pictures (compared to the same text without pictures), or when the story or topic are very familiar (compared to an equivalent level of readability but an unfamiliar story)?

11. How do expressive, transactional, and poetic discourse functions affect the child's ability

    a. to produce longer and more organized discourse?

    b. to respond to and express more abstract ideas along the semantic continuum?

12. Can the child respond to comprehension questions better

    a. when the same information is reworded at a lower level of organization along the discourse continuum?

    b. when concepts are restated more concretely along the semantic continuum?

    c. when more contextualized support is provided along the situational continuum?

13. What factors are characteristic of the child's best context of language understanding and use?

14. What factors are characteristic of the child's worst context of language understanding and use?

Answering these questions can lead to insights into how the child uses language to learn and to communicate, when language is above the child's current level of development, how the environment can be modified to enable the child to learn, and what factors interact within the environment and either cause the child to perform at his or her own maximum potential or inhibit the child's learning. These factors then lead to recommendations for modifying the child's environment to maximize learning at the child's present level of language development and for helping the child to acquire greater language proficiency along the situational, discourse, and semantic continua.

Language Sampling

Language sampling provides a means of analyzing the child's language and communicative abilities for both the contextual dynamics—the contexts profiled in the S-D-S model—and the specific properties of language structure produced—the syntax, morphology, pragmatic functions, conversational devices, vocabulary, and phonology. Each of these specific properties of language may vary depending on the amount of support provided for the language by the situational context, the amount of discourse organization required by the task, the degree of support provided by other participants, and the level of abstraction at which the interaction is maintained along the semantic continuum.

Language samples may be selected from naturally occurring interactions within the classroom or during small-group or independent learning center peer interactions, or they may be elicited under more controlled conditions. For example, the speech-language pathologist might choose to compare the language produced under some of the following conditions:

1. Telling a story in response to a picture or sequence of pictures that suggests a story. For example, wordless storyboards from the *Story Starters* series published by the Wright Group show a sequence of pictures that establish a setting, an initiating event, a problem, and a conclusion for interesting topics such as "Witch's Brew," "Puppy Trouble," or "Firemen."

2. Telling a *familiar* story in response to a picture or sequence of pictures, such as the wordless storyboard "The Hare and the Tortoise" from the *Story Starters* series.

3. Telling a story about a personal experience with no support from pictures or other context cues.

4. Retelling a story that was read or told to the child immediately prior to eliciting the sample.

5. Talking about a topic in response to a picture or sequence of pictures that suggests factual information, such as the wordless storyboard "A Pet for You."

6. Explaining the rules and procedures for playing a familiar game.

The speech-language pathologist might choose first to analyze the sample for the characteristics of the situational context under which it was elicited. Then one would designate the discourse structure of the individual episodes and analyze the structure of the overall story for the types of relationships held between episodes. Finally, the range and frequency of ideas along the semantic continuum is specified.

LANGUAGE SAMPLE ELICITED FROM A STORYBOARD

Episode A
1. Once there was a little puppy and his mother.

2. They were sitting on a thing, a circle thing, a rug.

Episode B
3. Then the puppy got a bath.

4. He splashed all around and got water on the floor.

Episode C
5. Then the puppy is in the mud and then he is dirty.

Episode D
6. And the puppy went in the garden.

7. He was digging and the dirt is going everywhere cuz he is digging.

8. The puppy looked, he was digging the dirt and he looked at the dirt and the dirt was goin' everywhere.

Situational context: contextualized-symbolic; language refers to information symbolized in the pictures.

Somewhat familiar topic; puppies, baths, and digging in the dirt are common experiences, even though the storyboard pictures and story are new to the child.

Discourse context: *Episode A:* descriptive list; lists characters, one action, one object

Episode B: reactive sequence; the child includes reference to time and suggests causality through the use of "got water," implying that the puppy's splashing got the water on the floor (as opposed to saying "and there is water on the floor," which only states the presence of water).

Episode C: ordered sequence; the order of utterances indicates that getting in the mud preceded getting dirty, but no causal connection is explicitly stated.

Episode D: reactive sequence; child specifies a cause for the dirt going everywhere and a temporal understanding of the relationship between digging and looking, as indicated by revising the sentence to specify that the digging occurred before looking. No goal or purpose for digging is specified or implied.

Overall story structure: ordered sequence; the individual episodes are linked only by the temporal order in which they occur. No causal relationships between them are given, and the order of the episodes could be changed without changing the story. No connections are drawn between the bath and getting dirty, going from inside the house to outside, or finding a stick and deciding to bury it.

Semantic context: The majority of the ideas expressed are at the level of description, including actions (60%; sentences 2, 3, 4, 5, 6, 7, and 8), and characteristics (20%; sentences 1, 2, 5). The remaining 20% are interpretations, including that the big dog was the mother of the puppy, splashing caused the puddle on the floor, and the flying dirt was caused by digging. The child makes no inferences that go beyond explicitly pictured cues.

Structural analysis: When false starts are eliminated and sentences are divided between conjunctions that link two complete sentences, the MLU is 8.18 morphemes per utterance (7.45 words). The majority of the sentences are simple sentences, with frequent inclusion of prepositional phrases and coordinating conjunctions. The child produced one subordinating conjunction, and this was the most complex syntactic structure in the sample. No instances of infinitive clauses, noun phrase complementary clauses, relative clauses, compound noun phrases, or other complex structures were elicited. Three instances of false starts were noted, all of them used to repair or clarify an idea.

ESTABLISHING LOCAL NORMS

The most effective method of determining whether the language observations and language samples reflect adequate language performance versus language delay is to establish local norms or criteria. For example, a sample of ten stories from poor, average, and high-functioning students at each grade level can be used to establish prototypes of typical stories produced by each population and descriptors of different aspects of the stories including discourse, semantic, and structural variables, as well as creativity and overall coherence of the story. Once prototypes and descriptors are established, the performance of individual children can be examined relative to their own peers. Local norms eliminate problems encountered when children from differing socioeconomic, cultural, regional, or dialectical groups are compared to national norms. The child's performance also can be compared to norms that are established for narrative structure and syntactic forms, such as those provided in Loban's (1976) *Language Development: Kindergarten through Grade Twelve,* published by the National Council of Teachers of English.

Task Sampling

Task sampling involves the use of a task, such as a worksheet, standardized test, or other task to examine some specific language-related skill. In these tasks, children are not asked to use language in ways consistent with meaningful and purposeful language. Rather, they are asked to respond to the grammatical accuracy of a series of sentences that are unrelated to one another in meaning or function, to pronounce words organized by speech sounds or reading level, or to explain the meaning of metaphors or other metalanguage in isolation from a context of use. A better understanding of the task performance can be derived by interpreting the tasks and the child's response according to the S-D-S model.

For example, vocabulary tests commonly present a set of four pictures from which the child must choose the one that best represents the meaning of a vocabulary word provided by the examiner. An analysis of the task would reveal the following profile:

Situational context: contextualized-symbolic; the vocabulary words correspond to information symbolized in the pictures.

Discourse context: transactional-collection; the information is factual and is merely a collection of words unrelated by topic, temporal sequence, or any other association.

Semantic context: Each word presented to the child should be analyzed to determine whether the information reflects experiential or erudite knowledge and for the degree of abstraction along the semantic continuum that a correct response would require. For example, responding to the word "ball" when the pictures show four common objects requires a response at the level of labeling. A response to the word "dangerous" when the target picture shows a fire fighter battling a blaze requires an interpretation. A response to the word "triceratops" is at the level of labeling, but to erudite knowledge.

Examining the child's profile of answers can give insight into the patterns of response. It could be that what superficially appears to be poor vocabulary development is instead an inability to examine aspects of objects or events, to describe their properties, or to derive interpretations. The implications for intervention would be very different if the problem was identified as poor vocabulary development (remediated by teaching the definitions of words) versus one of using language to displace meaning from concrete perception (remediated by talking about the same event at increasing levels along the semantic continuum in a meaningful context such as Collaborative Reading).

■ Goals and Objectives for Speech-Language Intervention

The goals and objectives established for each child, and the corresponding activities and levels of discussion selected from the Storybook-Centered Lesson Plans, will depend on the developmental level of the child and his or her language and learning needs. The goals are organized along a continuum of developmental language levels, ranging from an emergent oral language level through an advanced literate language level.

Goal Selection

Language has been described as existing along an "oral-to-literate language continuum." The oral language pole of the continuum refers to development focusing on learning to talk (Tannen 1982; Westby 1985). Oral language is characterized by topic-associated, nonspecifically worded talk expressed in simple, often incomplete, sentences or phrases. The meaning is contextualized to objects or events present within the situation, so that much of the meaning is derived from the nonverbal context. Semantically, the ideas are concrete and learned through experience.

The literate language pole of the continuum refers to development focusing on using language to learn about literacy and content-area knowledge—that is, talking to learn. This language is topic-centered, explicitly worded, and expressed using formal grammatical structures. Literate language is decontextualized, referring to events or aspects of situations that are not present in the immediate environment, and thus requires the listener to derive the appropriate inferences and meaning from the words without visual or sensory support. Children's ability to use a literate style of language correlates positively with high academic achievement.

The Storybook-Centered Curriculum can be used to address the needs of children exhibiting a continuum of language abilities. Sample goals and objectives are provided for four different developmental levels along the oral-to-literate language continuum. The four developmental levels and corresponding goals for children are as follows.

EMERGENT ORAL LANGUAGE LEVEL

Goal: To use language to label and describe experientially acquired information (semantic context); topically and temporally organized in discourse that is supported through a dialogue with others (discourse context); to refer to meaning that is contextualized to objects or events present within the situational context

Emergent Oral Language Level

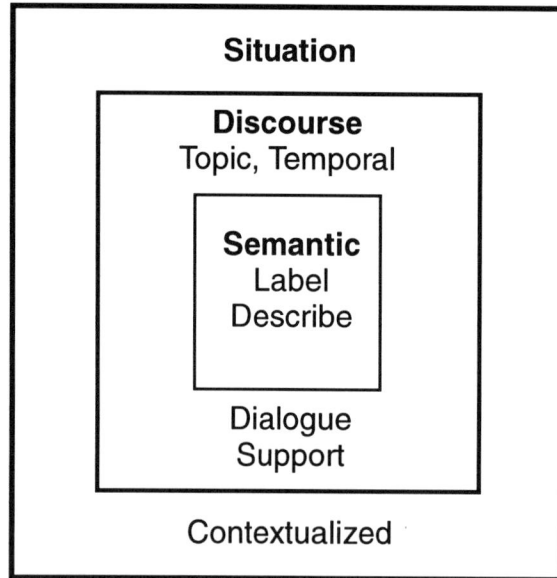

```
┌─────────────────────────────────────────┐
│              Situation                   │
│   ┌───────────────────────────────┐     │
│   │           Discourse            │     │
│   │         Topic, Temporal        │     │
│   │   ┌───────────────────────┐   │     │
│   │   │       Semantic        │   │     │
│   │   │        Label          │   │     │
│   │   │       Describe        │   │     │
│   │   └───────────────────────┘   │     │
│   │          Dialogue              │     │
│   │          Support               │     │
│   └───────────────────────────────┘     │
│             Contextualized               │
└─────────────────────────────────────────┘
```

ADVANCED ORAL LANGUAGE LEVEL

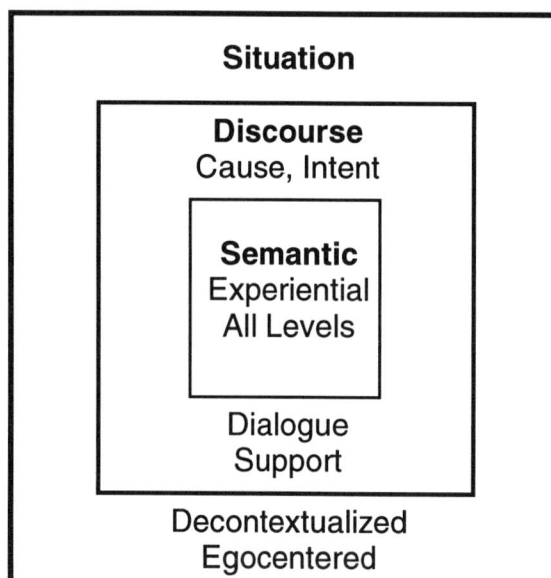

Goal: To use language to label, describe, interpret, infer, and make personal evaluations of experientially acquired information (semantic context); organized in temporally, causally, and intentionally structured discourse that is supported through dialogue with others (discourse context); to refer to meaning at the contextualized symbolic or hypothetical levels (the egocentered decontextualized level of the situational context continuum)

Advanced Oral Language Level

```
┌─────────────────────────────────────────┐
│              Situation                   │
│   ┌───────────────────────────────┐     │
│   │           Discourse            │     │
│   │         Cause, Intent          │     │
│   │   ┌───────────────────────┐   │     │
│   │   │       Semantic        │   │     │
│   │   │      Experiential     │   │     │
│   │   │       All Levels      │   │     │
│   │   └───────────────────────┘   │     │
│   │          Dialogue              │     │
│   │          Support               │     │
│   └───────────────────────────────┘     │
│           Decontextualized               │
│             Egocentered                  │
└─────────────────────────────────────────┘
```

EMERGENT LITERATE LANGUAGE LEVEL

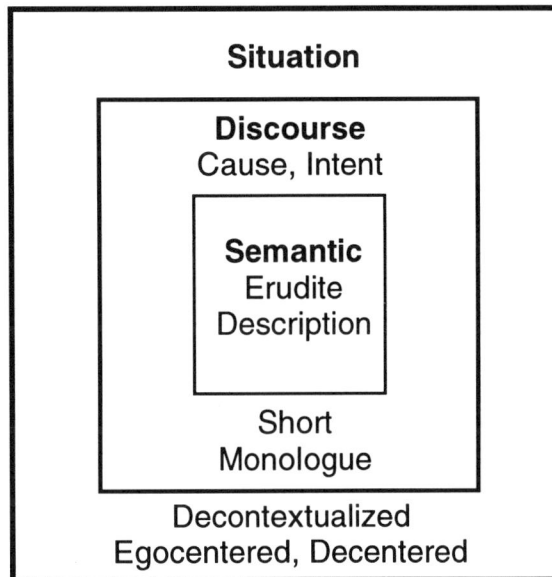

Goal: To use language to refer to experientially acquired knowledge at all levels of the semantic continuum and to label and describe erudite information (semantic context); organized in temporally, causally, and intentionally structured discourse produced in short monologues (discourse context); to refer to meaning at all contextualized levels and the egocentered and decentered levels of decontextualization on the situational context continuum

Emergent Literate Language Level

Situation

Discourse
Cause, Intent

Semantic
Erudite
Description

Short
Monologue

Decontextualized
Egocentered, Decentered

ADVANCED LITERATE LANGUAGE LEVEL

Goal: To use language to refer to experiential and erudite knowledge at all levels of the semantic continuum (semantic context); organized in complex temporally, causally, intentionally, and goal-directed discourse structures produced in monologues (discourse context); to refer to meaning at all contextualized and decontextualized levels of the situational context continuum.

Advanced Literate Language Level

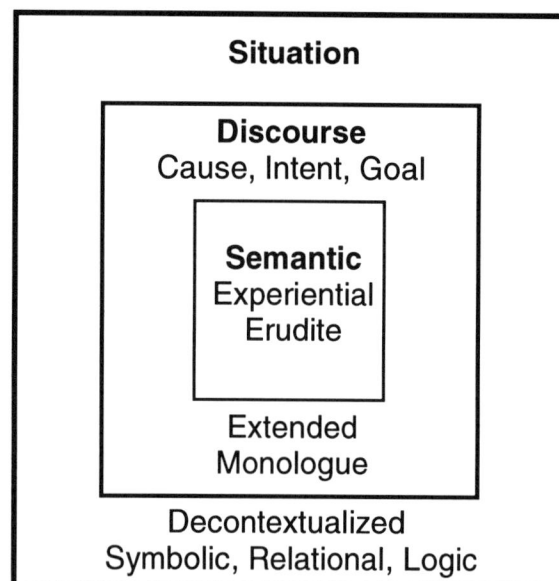

```
┌─────────────────────────────────────────┐
│             Situation                     │
│   ┌───────────────────────────────┐       │
│   │        Discourse              │       │
│   │     Cause, Intent, Goal       │       │
│   │   ┌───────────────────┐       │       │
│   │   │     Semantic      │       │       │
│   │   │    Experiential   │       │       │
│   │   │      Erudite      │       │       │
│   │   └───────────────────┘       │       │
│   │         Extended              │       │
│   │        Monologue              │       │
│   └───────────────────────────────┘       │
│         Decontextualized                  │
│     Symbolic, Relational, Logic           │
└─────────────────────────────────────────┘
```

Objectives

Objectives are behaviors that can be measured or *products* that are representative of the entire complex network of concepts, systems, and skills emerging from the learning *process*. The objectives are arbitrary and merely provide some behaviors that can be sampled to determine whether change is occurring in the child's developmental abilities. The results of such sampling provide feedback to the speech-language pathologist or other special service provider that the intervention is accompanied by developmental changes or that few changes are occurring, in which case the child's program may require reevaluation. Measurement of objectives also serves as a means of accountability to the child and the program.

Objectives are written to *sample* a variety of behaviors across content areas. If the sampled behaviors change, even though they were not discretely targeted and explicitly taught in the Storybook-Centered Curriculum, then it can be assumed that the child has learned and organized a wide range of concepts and systems. It also can be assumed that the child did not learn the concepts in isolation, but rather as part of a complex and integrated network of knowledge. *The objectives should not be used to identify and teach specific skills.* Doing so merely results in teaching a few behaviors without changing the child's underlying system, so that it appears that the child is progressing developmentally when, in fact, the child is only learning a few superficial behaviors. Such changes mask the symptoms of a developmental disorder, but the child's ability to solve problems, organize experience, and independently learn at higher levels of language does not change.

The following objectives provide guidelines for sampling changes in concepts, systems, and behaviors. For convenience, they are organized according to content area. The criteria are open-ended by design, suggesting that, for example, greater syntactic complexity will include some of the structures listed. It is assumed that if some structures are produced in a sample, then others are also within the child's productive competence, since no one structure was taught or emphasized.

CONTENT AREA: READING

Emergent oral language level: Given an episode depicted on a wordless storyboard from the Story Starters Series, the child will be able to:

    a. Dictate a story that specifically labels and describes the characters and the actions

    b. When provided with minimal prompts, dictate a story with a sequence of three actions, including at least one use of a temporal term and the appropriate use of verb tense within sentences

    c. Dictate a story with an MLU of 3 to 5 words

    d. Represent the story using an illustration accompanied by scribbling that the child then "reads"

Advanced oral language level: Given an episode depicted on a wordless storyboard from the Story Starters Series, the child will be able to:

    a. Dictate a story that labels and describes characters and interprets two emotions, causes, states, or attributes

    b. Dictate a story that infers or predicts an outcome or future action

    c. When provided with minimal prompts, dictate a story with a sequence of at least three actions, including at least one use of a causal term and the appropriate use of verb tense coordinated within and across sentences

    d. When provided with minimal prompts, dictate a story with a sequence of at least three actions, including at least one instance of planning

    e. Dictate a story with an MLU of 4 to 7 words

    f. Use developmental writing and spelling strategies to produce approximations of printing that follow a left-to-right, top-to-bottom sequence

Emergent literate language level: Given an episode depicted on a wordless storyboard from the Story Starters Series, the child will be able to:

a. When provided prompts or asked questions, dictate a coherent story that includes the necessary labels, descriptions, interpretations, and inferences

b. When provided minimal prompts, dictate a story with a sequence of at least 4 actions, including causality and at least one instance of planning

c. Dictate a story with an MLU of 4 to 7 words that includes modal verb constructions, infinitive clauses, coordinating conjunctions, and adjective and adverbial phrases

d. Write by creating a text that matches the story shown in the pictures using prephonemic and letter-name spelling in which the first sound and aspects of the syllable structure are represented using approximate letter-sound correspondences

e. Include punctuation marks and capitalization randomly throughout writing

Advanced literate language level: Given an episode depicted on a wordless storyboard from the Story Starters Series, the child will be able to:

a. Dictate as an independently generated monologue a coherent story that includes the necessary labels, descriptions, interpretations, and inferences

b. Dictate a story with a sequence of at least 4 actions, including at least one example of a problem-reaction-plan-attempt-consequence episode

c. Dictate a story with an MLU of 6 to 8 words that includes modal verb constructions, infinitive clauses, coordinating and subordinating conjunctions, and relative clauses

d. Write a text that matches the story shown in the pictures using semiphonetic, letter-name, and phonetic spelling where many sounds and most of the syllable structures are represented using appropriate letter-sound correspondences

e. Inconsistently include punctuation marks and capitalization

CONTENT AREA: MATHEMATICS

Emergent oral language level: Given objects that go together—such as dolls, doll clothes, and dishes—the child will be able to perform a variety of mathematic functions including:

a. Semantically, at the level of indication, match 3 dolls with 3 dishes in one-to-one correspondence

b. Verbally label numbers by counting rotely to 5

c. At the level of description, match articles of clothing by color, size, or shape and find those that are the same

d. Respond to and use mathematical vocabulary referring to global perceptual descriptions along the semantic continuum including size, weight, speed, volume, location, and time. For example: gone, full, more, big, fast, top, up, heavy, or first

Advanced oral language level: Given objects that go together—such as dolls, doll clothes, and dishes—the child will be able to perform a variety of mathematic functions including:

a. Select 3 to 5 dishes from a set of 10 in one-to-one correspondence between numbers and objects

b. Verbally label numbers by counting rotely to 10

c. At the level of description, name clothing or dishes by color, size, or shape and find ones that are the same and different

d. Respond to and use mathematical vocabulary referring contrastively to size, weight, speed, volume, location, and time, including full/empty, more/no more, big/little, fast/slow, top/bottom, up/down, heavy/light, or first/last

e. At the level of interpretation, add or subtract items from one group to create two equivalent groups

Emergent literate language level: Given objects that go together—such as dolls, doll clothes, and dishes—the child will be able to perform a variety of mathematic functions including:

a. Select 5 to 10 dishes from a set of 20 in one-to-one correspondence between numbers and objects

b. Label numbers by counting rotely to 30 and counting backwards from 10

c. Establish groups of clothing or dishes according to two perceptual descriptive dimensions, including color, shape, or size (big red or round blue items), and designate ones that are the same and different

d. Respond to and use mathematical vocabulary referring relatively to size, weight, speed, volume, location, and time, including big-tall-wide-long/little-small-thin-short, fast/slow, top-middle-bottom, up-above-over/down-below-beneath, heavy/light, or first-second-next-last

e. State an interpretation of whether an item needs to be added or subtracted from groups to create two equivalent groups

f. Write numerals from 1 through 5

g. Label pennies, nickels, and dimes and state which is worth more when two coins are compared

Advanced literate language level: Given objects that go together, such as blocks or other manipulatives of different colors, the child will be able to perform a variety of mathematic functions, including:

a. Select up to 50 objects in one-to-one correspondence between numbers and objects

b. At the level of labeling, count by ones and tens to 100 and count by even numbers to 10

c. Record the size of groups using graphs and charts and recognize whether two groups are equivalent

d. Respond to and use mathematical vocabulary describing relative size, weight, speed, volume, location, and time in the context of simple story problems

e. Interpret whether an item needs to be added or subtracted and write a corresponding equation using one-digit numbers

f. Write numerals from 1 through 50

g. Label and then describe the monetary values of coins and count the total value of two coins

CONTENT AREA: ART

Emergent oral language level: Following discussion of a picture from a book in The Story Box® Series the child will be able to:

a. Respond by drawing, painting, or modeling from clay a primitive representation of the pictured character (scribble or clay ball described as the character)

b. Represent at a descriptive level at least one part of the character, such as an eye or leg

c. Use a range of colors, shapes, and sizes of lines or forms to represent the character

d. Use art as an outlet of own creativity rather than to share

Advanced oral language level: Following discussion of a picture from a book in The Story Box® Series, the child will be able to:

a. Respond by drawing, painting, or modeling from clay a representation of the pictured character consisting of eyes, a mouth, arms, legs, or other descriptive features

b. Represent at the descriptive level the spatial relationships between facial features and the orientation of arms and legs relative to the head, although the body may be missing

c. Use colors, shapes, and sizes that approximate the form of the body parts being represented

    d. Use verbal language to label and describe the character, including content (who character is and what character's significance is) and form (color, size, and shapes used to represent it)

    e. Use art functionally to decorate a space or as a gift for another person

Emergent literate language level: Following discussion of a picture from a book in The Story Box® Series, the child will be able to:

    a. Respond by drawing, painting, or modeling from clay a representation of the pictured character containing a distinct head, body, and limbs, with some details added to the eyes, mouth, arms, legs, or other descriptive features

    b. Represent at the descriptive level the spatial relationships between facial features and the orientation of arms and legs relative to the head and the body

    c. Use verbal language to interpret the character's state and to explain character's appearance and actions

    d. Draw or model additional objects or characters that are related to the central character (descriptive list) or are unrelated (collections)

    e. Use the art functionally as a prop for symbolic play or drama

Advanced literate language level: Following discussion of a picture from a book in The Story Box® Series, the child will be able to:

    a. Respond by drawing, painting, or modeling from clay a representation of the character and the event that portrays topically or temporally related information along the discourse continuum, and that includes characters engaged in action or depicted in relationship to objects

    b. Represent at the descriptive level the spatial relationships between and within characters and objects, including correct topological and geometric orientations

    c. Use verbal language to describe the event and to interpret the character's state or actions either sequentially or causally along the discourse continuum

    d. Use shading, texture, or color at the level of interpretation to indicate nuances of meaning

    e. Use the art functionally to symbolize some aspect of a ceremony

CONTENT AREA: SOCIAL STUDIES

Emergent oral language level: Given a book such as *Amazing World Facts* (Ganeri 1991) or other illustrated book covering a broad range of social studies topics, the child will:

    a. Respond by pointing to 10 erudite concepts at the levels of labeling and describing

    b. Verbally label and describe 10 erudite social studies concepts depicted in the pictures

    c. When provided with minimal prompts, state a sequence of 3 erudite facts related to the same topic, including at least one temporal connection between them

    d. Provide labeling or descriptive information about the topic that is decontextualized, representing knowledge learned in a different context at a different time

Advanced oral language level: Given a book such as *Amazing World Facts* (Ganeri 1991) or other illustrated book covering a broad range of topics, the child will:

    a. Verbally label and describe at least 3 erudite social studies concepts depicted in the pictures, organized as a descriptive list

    b. Interpret at least 5 causes, states, or consequences

    c. Infer or predict the activities of individuals in pictured occupations, cultures, geographic areas, and so forth, based on erudite knowledge

    d. Make a personal evaluation of erudite information ("Fire fighters are neat"; "I want to be an astronaut because . . .")

    e. When provided with minimal prompts, state a sequence of three erudite facts related to the same topic, including at least one causal and/or conditional connection between them

    f. Provide labeling or descriptive information about the topic that is decontextualized, representing knowledge learned in a different context at a different time

Emergent literate language level: Given a book such as *Amazing World Facts* (Ganeri 1991) or other illustrated book covering a broad range of topics, the child will:

    a. When provided with prompts or asked questions, give a coherent explanation of a depicted social studies topic that includes the necessary labels, descriptions, interpretations, and inferences

    b. Evaluate the topics ("You should take care of pets"; "You shouldn't eat junk food because . . .")

c. When provided minimal prompts, explain the topic using a sequence of at least 4 facts, including causality and at least one instance of planning

d. Provide a comparison of information from related topics, such as rural versus urban occupations

e. Conduct a 4-step procedure to complete an activity related to a social studies topic

f. Metalinguistically record information discovered using a graph, chart, or drawn symbols, as well as written words

Advanced literate language level: Given a book such as *Amazing World Facts* (Ganeri 1991) or other illustrated book covering a broad range of topics, the child will:

a. Provide as an independently generated monologue a coherent explanation of a social studies topic that includes the necessary labels, descriptions, interpretations, and inferences

b. Evaluate the moral of the topic ("You shouldn't because . . .";
"Don't do because . . .")

c. Explain the topic using a sequence of at least 4 facts, including at least one sequence of a problem-reaction-plan-attempt-consequence episode

d. Provide a critique of information, such as concluding that a city is a better place to live if you like to travel

e. Conduct a 4-step procedure that involves reading and writing to complete a social studies activity

f. Metalinguistically record information discovered and write definitions for new concepts

CONTENT AREA: SCIENCE

Emergent oral language level: Given a book such as *I Wonder How Does the Wind Blow?* (Langley 1991) or other illustrated book covering a broad range of scientific topics, the child will:

a. Respond by pointing to 10 erudite concepts at the levels of labeling and describing

b. Verbally label and describe 10 erudite science concepts from those depicted in the pictures

c. When provided with minimal prompts, tell a sequence of three erudite concepts related to the same topic, including at least one temporal connection between them

d. Provide decontextualized labeling or descriptive information about the topic, representing knowledge learned in a different context at a different time

Advanced oral language level: Given a book such as *I Wonder How Does the Wind Blow?* (Langley 1991) or other illustrated book covering a broad range of scientific topics, the child will:

a. Verbally label and describe a descriptive list of at least 3 erudite concepts from the sciences depicted in the pictures

b. Interpret at least 5 causes, states, or consequences

c. Infer or predict the actions associated with pictured animals, plants, the earth, physics, or health based on erudite knowledge

d. Make a personal evaluation of erudite information ("I like storms"; "I know how to go faster because . . .")

e. When provided minimal prompts, tell a sequence of 3 erudite facts related to the same topic, including at least one causal and/or conditional connection between them

f. Provide decontextualized labeling or descriptive information about the topic, representing scientific knowledge learned in a different context at a different time

Emergent literate language level: Given a book such as *I Wonder How Does the Wind Blow?* (Langley 1991) or other illustrated book covering a broad range of scientific topics, the child will:

a. When provided with prompts or asked questions, give a coherent explanation of a depicted science topic that includes the necessary labels, descriptions, interpretations, and inferences

b. Evaluate the information ("You should take care of the environment"; "You shouldn't waste energy because . . .")

c. When provided minimal prompts, explain the topic using a sequence of at least 4 facts, including causality and at least one instance of planning

d. Provide a comparison of information from related topics, such as summer versus winter weather

e. Conduct a 4-step procedure to complete a scientific experiment

f. Metalinguistically record information discovered using a graph, chart, or drawn symbols, as well as written words

Advanced literate language level: Given a book such as *I Wonder How Does the Wind Blow?* (Langley 1991) or other illustrated book covering a broad range of scientific topics, the child will:

a. Provide as an independently generated monologue a coherent explanation of a science topic that includes the necessary labels, descriptions, interpretations, and inferences

b. Evaluate the moral of the topic ("You shouldn't because . . .";
"Don't do because . . .")

c. Explain the topic using a sequence of at least 4 facts, including at least one sequence of a problem-reaction-plan-attempt-consequence episode

d. Provide a critique of information ("Plants shouldn't be over-watered because . . .")

e. Conduct a 4-step procedure that involves reading and writing to complete a science experiment

f. Metalinguistically record information discovered and write definitions for new concepts

CONTENT AREA: ARTICULATION

Emergent oral language level: Given pictures and text representing an episode of a story from the emergent reading level of The Story Box® Series, the child will be able to:

a. Discriminate among different sounds and sound sequences, as measured by differentially pointing to vocabulary words at the levels of labeling and describing

b. Acquire a large enough vocabulary to begin forming the phonological system of sounds, sound patterns, sound sequences, and syllable shapes characteristic of the language

c. Acquire sufficient syntactic structures for sound sequences and coarticulation patterns across word boundaries to begin to develop

d. Acquire sufficient experience negotiating meaning with a listener and making adjustments, based on both feedback and the need for clarification, to begin to conventionally organize the phonological system

e. Increase awareness of how sounds are conventionally produced by directing attention to the motor productions and phonemic properties of words modeled by others

f. Demonstrate a reduction in the percentage of phonological process errors that result in syllable reduction or phonemic differences of more than one feature from the target sound, even though productions are not yet conventional

Advanced oral language level: Given pictures and text representing an episode of a story from the emergent reading level of The Story Box® Series, the child will be able to:

a. Discriminate among and produce words with more complex sound patterns and syllabic structures, including a vocabulary of words that interpret and infer

b. Acquire morphological forms, including plurals, past tense inflections, possessives, modal verbs, present progressive inflections, comparative morphemes, and other forms that change the phonological structure of words and that must be discriminated on the basis of subtle phonological differences in sound and production

c. Understand how to semantically and syntactically coordinate aspects of time, number, and state within sentences, creating the need to produce a variety of morphemes to mark these meanings

d. Acquire decontextualized uses of language, creating an increased social need to produce words conventionally and to make modifications in pronunciation based on feedback

e. Increase awareness of how sound sequences and multisyllabic words are conventionally produced by directing attention to the motor productions and phonemic properties of words modeled by others

f. Demonstrate an increase in the percentage of words conventionally produced in both syllabic structure and phonemic representation, and a reduction in the percentage of phonological process errors that result in syllable reduction or phonemic simplifications

Emergent literate language level: Given pictures and text representing an episode of a story from the emergent reading level of The Story Box® Series, the child will be able to:

a. Produce words with more complex sound patterns and syllabic structures in the context of telling a story that has at least 4 actions organized by temporal sequence and causality

b. Acquire derivational morphological forms, including prefixes and suffixes that change the phonological structure of words (medic—medicine; medical—medically) and that must be discriminated on the basis of subtle phonological differences in sound and production

c. Evaluate the production of words produced by self and others to judge whether the production is correct or incorrect in syllabic and phonemic structure

d. Demonstrate metalinguistic awareness of letter-sound correspondences and the position of sounds in words when provided support from the visual information present in the print

e. Associate the conventional production of phonemes and sound sequences in words with the print, matching articulation to the cues provided in the print when reading familiar text

f. Modify the production of words when the adult writes the child's production phonetically and engages the child in active problem solving directed at changing the production to be more conventional

g. Demonstrate an increase in the percentage of words conventionally produced in both syllabic structure and phonemic representation, and a reduction in the percentage of phonological process errors that result in syllable reduction or phonemic simplifications

Advanced literate language level: Given pictures and text representing an episode of a story from the emergent reading level of The Story Box® Series, the child will be able to:

a. Maintain correct articulation of all phonemes contextualized to reading the written text

b. Maintain correct articulation of all phonemes contextualized to talking about the pictures

c. Maintain correct articulation of all phonemes decontextualized by talking about topically related events that are not pictured but that share similar vocabulary

■ Specific Intervention Strategies for Facilitating Language Learning

The goal of the speech-language pathologist or other special service provider is to enable children to understand and produce oral and written language at higher levels of discourse structure and semantic complexity with less support from the situational context. This goal is accomplished by engaging children in active language explorations of topics. During these explorations, the interventionist maintains a discourse structure that is more organized than the children can independently maintain by prompting or supplying parts of language that the children do not produce on their own. Within the framework of the discourse structure, the adult also prompts and supports the children's use of language to express higher levels of semantic complexity.

The interventionist maintains an overall discourse structure so that the concepts and language structures the children develop are part of well-organized mental structures (Norris and Hoffman 1990, 1993). As the children become more accomplished at talking about a topic, the discussion is guided to higher levels of discourse organization. Repeated discussions of a topic provide the children with multiple opportunities to discuss the conceptual relationships within the topic at increasingly complex semantic levels. Raising the semantic level of the discussion also increases the children's use of language structures that code the higher levels of semantic displacement. Through these guided discussions, the children internalize topic-related knowledge, discourse structure, semantic complexity, and language forms.

Scaffolding Strategies Used to Facilitate Language Learning

Supplying this discourse support is referred to as scaffolding (Bruner 1983; Cazden 1983). Like the scaffolds that support portions of a building under construction, the interventionist's scaffolding is temporary, supplied long enough to allow the children to develop the language ability necessary to communicate successfully at a particular level of discourse structure and semantic complexity without assistance. The process of scaffolding can be viewed as a three-step cycle, as shown across the top of Figure 4-2.

The first step is called *assessing a whole*. It involves giving the child a relatively unsupported opportunity to talk about a whole topic. Questions such as, "Can you tell this story?" or demands such as, "Explain the experiment to the class" provide opportunities for children to demonstrate their organization of a relatively large text structure. The adult uses the child's response to this challenge to judge the levels of discourse structure and semantic complexity the child is capable of using in discussing the topic. This assessment is essentially a test item. The child's response provides the interventionist with information regarding what scaffolding is needed in the second step. All too often, interventionists appear to administer a sequence of such challenges without taking the second step of scaffolding the answers to the questions.

The second step is a sequence of communicative turns between the interventionist and the child. If semantic complexity is the primary target, the interventionist prompts the child to express information about the topic at higher levels of semantic organization than are typical of the child's language. Or, if discourse complexity is the primary target, the adult prompts the sequential telling of the important components of a narrative or expository text. Following each turn the child takes, the adult provides feedback regarding the semantic appropriateness of the child's language as detailed in the following section.

Within a sequence of turns, the adult's utterances form the scaffold that holds the child's utterances together in a discourse macrostructure. Each set of adult-child turns can be viewed as a means to increase the organization of the child's language system. This scaffolding step will take a relatively large number of turns, as the adult provides the child with many opportunities to organize the conceptual relationships that are important to the discourse structure. It is during this phase that the child learns discourse structure, conceptual relationships, and language structures.

FIGURE 4-2
The Scaffolding Cycle

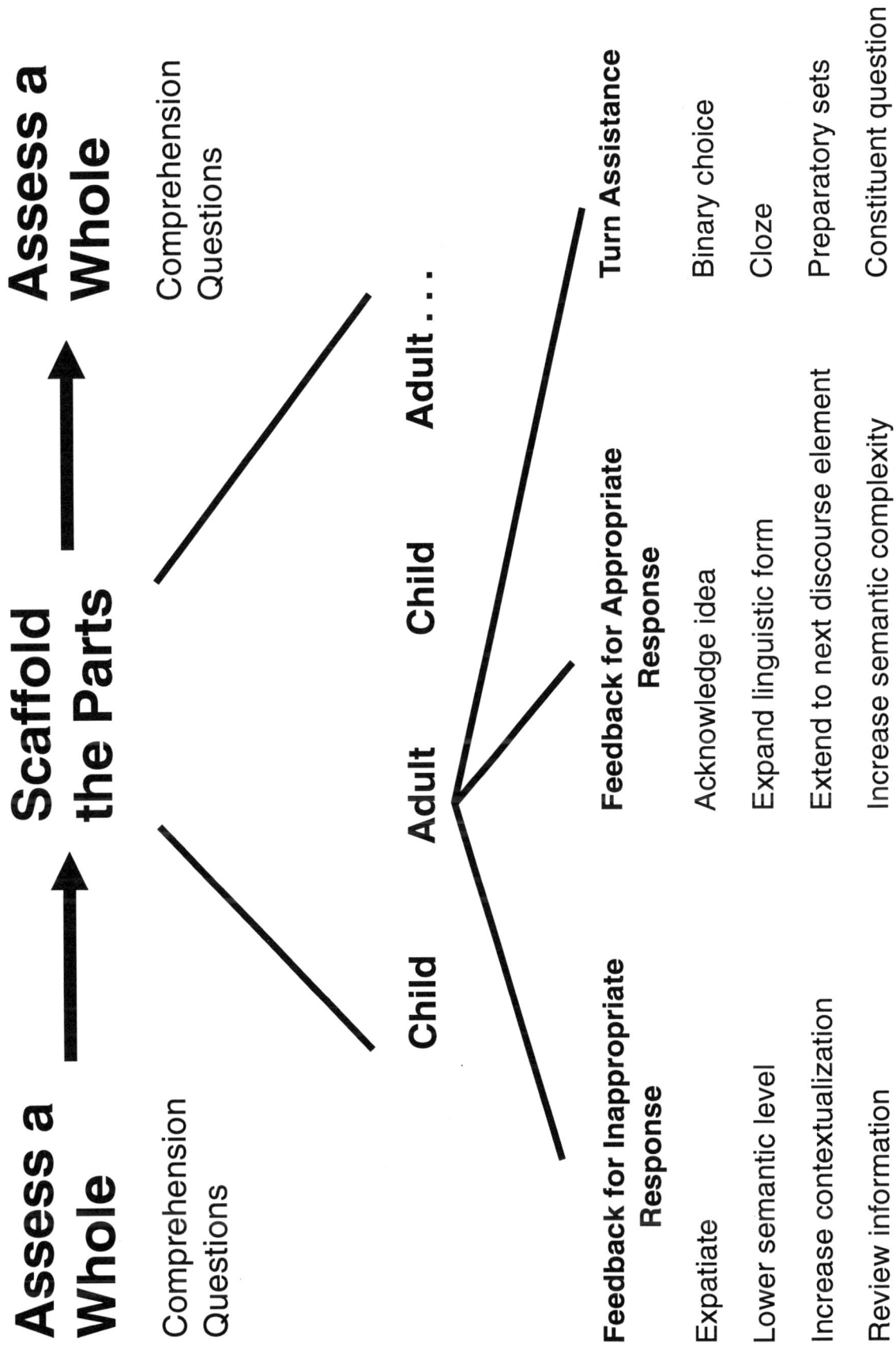

Assess a Whole

Comprehension Questions

Scaffold the Parts

Child   Adult   Child   Adult . . .

Assess a Whole

Comprehension Questions

Feedback for Inappropriate Response

Expatiate

Lower semantic level

Increase contextualization

Review information

Feedback for Appropriate Response

Acknowledge idea

Expand linguistic form

Extend to next discourse element

Increase semantic complexity

Turn Assistance

Binary choice

Cloze

Preparatory sets

Constituent question

The third step is to provide another opportunity for the child to organize the information. This is a test of what the child has learned through the scaffolded interaction. If the scaffolding provided in the second step has been successful, the child's discourse structure, semantic complexity, or both will be better developed than in the first attempt. The facilitator then moves the discussion on to another element of discourse structure or to a higher level of semantic complexity, and the cycle is repeated. If the child's language is not more complex, then the adult will want to discuss the topic again using either more situational context support or lower levels of discourse and semantic complexity.

The two goals, to increase discourse structure and semantic complexity, are interactive. Discourse structure is the macrostructure that organizes the language of stories and expository texts. Semantic relationships form the microstructure of texts, including semantic-syntactic relationships, morphology, and even phonology. The use of these two levels of language organization is discussed in the following section.

INCREASING DISCOURSE STRUCTURE COMPLEXITY

The interventionist must first maintain the discourse organization of the topic being discussed. To maintain the discourse structure of a text, the adult must understand the topic as a sequence of events, as well as understanding the psychological and physical relationships among these events (Labov 1972; Stein and Glenn 1979). While helping the children construct or interpret a text, the adult uses this information as a guide for supplying information that will facilitate the children's communication turns. During poetic discussions, the narrative structure is used as a guide for the sequence of concepts and language to be facilitated. Thus, the discussion develops around the setting, the characters, the event that initiates the story, the characters' plans and attempts, the resolution of the story or episode, and the moral. During transactional discussions, the adult must again understand the sequence of events and essential cause-effect relationships in order to act as the children's guide to understanding the topic. Such transactional discussions will eventually include an overall purpose for the actions, a sequential plan for the actions, the interrelated cause-effect relationships among the actions, and an evaluation of the effectiveness of the plan.

Children with language learning disabilities typically demonstrate poor abilities to organize oral and written discussions of a topic (Merritt and Liles 1987; Miller 1991; Ripich and Griffith 1988). When given an opportunity to talk about a topic, they are likely to shift topics rapidly, constructing only one or two relationships about a topic before moving on to the next. With respect to the discourse dimension of the S-D-S model, these children are producing collections, discourse that does not remain sufficiently on topic. The interventionist helps such children organize information into more coherent discourse by focusing their attention on the important aspects of a single topic.

For example, during a discussion of a storybook, one child may say something about what another child in the group is doing. Knowing that the particular portion of the book is establishing the setting of the narrative, the adult might redirect this child's attention by pointing to the picture (to provide contextual support) and saying, "Tell us what this is." Having elicited an object label, such as "a streetlight," the instructor helps the child add more information to the establishment of a setting by extending that response, "And streetlights are found in the. . . ." When the child responds that streetlights are found in cities, the adult might encourage further elaboration of the setting by saying, "Streetlights are in towns, next to the road so that people can . . . ," attempting to prompt information about the purpose of streetlights. The adult then guides the child in exploring other aspects of the setting that are depicted in the picture or text to aid the child's development of language that is better organized than it was at the start of the session.

As indicated in the lesson plans, once children have organized some information about a topic into a descriptive list, the interventionist leads them toward organizing their observations about the topic into an ordered sequence. This second exploration of the concepts provides some of the redundancy that children with language learning disabilities need in order to internalize conceptual relationships. Ordered sequences related to the setting of a narrative are constructed in accordance with the typical actions of a character. For example, the first character introduced in the book *Stop!* is a milkman. During the discussion of the setting, the adult may lead the children to construct his typical sequence of actions. He or she might provide information by pointing out the relationships between the empty bottles the milkman is picking up and the full bottles he is carrying away from the truck:

> Does the milkman bring empty or full bottles from his truck? . . . First, he brings full bottles. Then, he leaves the . . . bottles and takes the . . . bottles back to the truck.

Further redundancy can be built into the discussion by asking different children in the group to retell the whole sequence that has just been developed to one of the children "to make sure that child heard it all."

The adult uses similar tactics in scaffolding transactional discussions of activities such as cooking. Completing a recipe involves carrying out a sequence of actions in a particular order. Children who have organized this activity only at the level of a descriptive list may be able to assemble appropriate materials such as bowls, spoons, and food items, but will not understand when to add eggs or milk and so forth. Guided by knowledge of the plan of the activity—the recipe—the facilitator can foster the children's development of an ordered sequence. At the same time, the children can be exposed to the use of written language in the form of a recipe. The language used in creating an ordered sequence will be rich in the temporal markers that are problematic for many children with language impairment:

First we need to crack the egg into the bowl. *After* we *have cracked* the egg, we beat it with the fork *until* it is all yellow. . . . (French and Nelson 1985)

When the children in the group are successfully constructing ordered sequences, the facilitator prompts discussion of information about the underlying physical cause-effect relationships in the event to start building a reactive sequence. One can prompt the children to consider the "whys" underlying the sequence of events. In the story about the milkman, the group can discuss the reactions of the milkman and the people who live in the house to seeing empty and full milk bottles:

> The bottles on the curb are empty because the people in the house used the milk. . . . So now, the people have empty . . . and they need more. . . .

Once the facilitator and children have constructed the idea that the people who live in the house have used up the milk and need more milk, they can go on to discuss how the milkman takes care of that need and accomplishes his underlying goal of selling milk to people by bringing full bottles and taking away empty bottles. The sequence of actions in the cooking event would also be discussed with respect to their cause-effect relationships:

> When we hit the egg on the side of the bowi it . . . , and when we beat the egg with a fork it turned. . . .

The interventionist then introduces discussion of problems and the plans that are used to solve them to build an abbreviated structure. Abbreviated structures include statements about the human needs and goals that underlie the actions that appear in stories:

> The people need milk, and it is the milkman's job to bring full milk bottles to the people who have used up their milk, and to take away the empty milk bottles that they have left over.

The interventionist also draws attention to the problems and goals involved in transactional discussions. For example:

> We can't just put the egg into the bowl because we will get pieces of eggshell into our food, so first we need to . . . the egg on the. . . .

The same principles of redundant exposure to higher levels of discourse organization hold for helping children understand and communicate in routine events, including classroom routines. The facilitator may have to help scaffold children's understanding of classroom rules through a process of:

- Recognizing those actions that are appropriate versus inappropriate (a descriptive list)

- Establishing the usual sequence of actions (an ordered sequence)

- Scaffolding the cause-effect relationships that are implied by the rules (a reactive sequence)

- Understanding the teacher's and students' underlying goals (an abbreviated structure)

For example, learning to "raise your hand" to be recognized in a classroom discussion might be facilitated through contrasting this act with inappropriate acts such as walking to the board or yelling out. Then the sequence of actions can be discussed:

> You decide to ask a question, then you raise your hand and wait for the teacher to call on you.

Then the cause-effect relationships can be discussed:

> The teacher needs to be able to see the hands of children who want to ask questions.

Then the underlying reasons can be explained:

> The teacher can't understand more than one child talking at a time, so we can't all talk at once. When you raise your hand, your teacher can pick one child at a time without everyone talking at the same time.

Notice that the semantic relationships entailed in these explanations are sometimes rather complex. It will often be necessary to contextualize such discussions by helping the children actually follow these procedures during a class period.

In summary, the levels of discourse structure are used to guide the development of topic discussions. The interventionist judges the children's independent abilities to structure discourse, and then uses the strategies discussed in the next section to help the children take part in a higher-level organization of the topic. Table 4-4 (page 146) contains examples of children's independently generated stories at different levels of structure and the discussions that might be targeted at that level. As shown in this table, the adult is seeking to guide the children to construct stories that are two stages above their independent level of functioning. For example, if a child is capable of independently producing a collection, the table shows how the facilitator would provide practice in constructing an ordered sequence. Note that, because each discourse structure adds to the levels below it, it contains aspects of the lower levels. While constructing a reactive sequence, children are exposed to the temporal ordering of an ordered sequence and the topic relatedness of a descriptive list.

TABLE 4-4
Examples of Child Independent Levels of Discourse Structure and Facilitator Targeted Levels of Discourse Structure

Child: Collection	Facilitator: Ordered Sequence
There's a milkman and a truck and bottles of milk.	The milkman is carrying milk bottles. First, he brought full milk bottles from his truck. Then he picked up the empty bottles at the curb. Now, he is leaving one full bottle for each empty bottle. Later, he will take the empty bottles back to his truck.

Child: Ordered Sequence	Facilitator: Abbreviated Structure
The milkman brings bottles from his truck. He puts the bottles on the curb. Then he takes the empty bottles away.	The milkman is doing his usual job. First, he stopped his truck and brought two carriers of full milk bottles to the curb. Then, he leaves one full bottle for each empty bottle. After he has replaced the empty bottles, he puts the empty bottles in his carrier and takes them back to the truck. He likes his job.

Child: Abbreviated Structure	Facilitator: Interactive Structure
The milkman is doing his job by bringing full bottles of milk and taking away empty bottles. He likes his job.	The milkman is doing his job of bringing full bottles of milk to people and taking away their empty bottles. Then he meets a cat who spends her day looking for things to eat. The milkman likes cats, so he stops to pour the milk out of a bottle that wasn't quite empty for her to drink.

PROVIDING COMMUNICATIVE OPPORTUNITIES AND MEANING-BASED FEEDBACK

As depicted in the lower portion of Figure 4-2, the facilitator provides scaffolding in the form of oral communication turns that occur between the child's turns. After each child turn, the adult supplies (1) feedback based on the meaning of the child's utterance and (2) a structured opportunity for the child to take the next turn.

Feedback for inappropriate response: A *semantically inappropriate* utterance is an indication that the child has not adequately organized the information available. The adult uses these opportunities to provide information that the child needs through *expatiations*. An expatiation builds on the child's idea semantically (Muma 1978). In normal discourse, participants in a conversation typically add new information from their own perspectives to the other person's comments through expatiations. In scaffolding, expatiations are used to provide information the child needs to understand a topic from the adult perspective. The expatiation is used to provide clarification of semantic relationships that the child has misinterpreted. For example, if a child says, "Milkman sad," the adult might respond, "He looks happy to me. See his mouth, it is bent up at the corners. He is smiling. So, I think he is happy."

In general, these expatiations involve the adult talking about the topic at a *lower semantic level* than the child's utterance (Bloom 1970). In this example, the child interpreted the character's emotional state inappropriately. The adult responded with language at the descriptive semantic level. We recommend beginning discussion of a topic at lower levels of semantic displacement and then moving on to higher levels as the topic is developed. Thus, prior to the child's "Milkman sad" utterance, the discussion should have established which picture the word "milkman" refers to (semantic label) and that the pictured milkman is smiling (semantic description). When the child fails to move on to the interpretation that the milkman is happy, the adult *reviews information* previously established in the conversation to reinforce who the milkman is, that he is smiling and, therefore, that he must be happy (Roser and Martinez 1985).

The adult may also choose to *increase situational contextualization* by referring back to the picture. The language about the milkman and his smile thus will have a stable visual representation that the child can use to help support the development of the more abstract idea that the milkman is happy (Blank, Rose, and Berlin 1978; Westby 1985). Or the children in the group can all take turns smiling and describing their own emotional states as "happy."

While focusing on the semantic aspects of the conversation, the clinician will be providing the child with numerous models of the language structures that are used to code those relationships. Repeated statements about a person's internal emotional states are coded in English using pronouns and copula verbs, as seen in the facilitator's utterances in Table 4-4. It is expected that the child will internalize some of these aspects of English while listening to the clinician and trying to use the clinician's language as a model for later productions (Snow and Goldfield 1983).

When the child's language is semantically appropriate, the adult acknowledges the appropriateness of the child's contribution (Roser and Martinez 1985). For example, if the child says, "Milkman is smiling," the adult may agree by replying, "You're right" or "Uh huh." Or, the adult may tacitly acknowledge the child's turn by giving him or her the time to take another turn. In the case of semantically appropriate utterances that are syntactically incomplete, the adult will also want to provide an *expansion of the linguistic form,* such as, "You're right, the milkman is smiling" (Muma 1978). Again, it is expected that the child will internalize some of the characteristics of the adult language forms as a result of listening to these expansions within the conversation.

Feedback for appropriate utterances: A semantically appropriate child utterance is an indication that the child has organized that portion of the discourse structure at a particular level of semantic complexity. The facilitator will use such opportunities to build more complex language. The conversation can be moved in one of two directions: to increase the discourse structure or to increase the semantic complexity. Discourse structure can be increased by prompting the child to add the *next discourse element.* For example, saying something like "and then . . . ?" will elicit the next event in a sequence. The clinician can attempt to move the child's discussion to a higher level of semantic complexity through an utterance such as, "He is smiling because he is . . ." (French and Nelson 1985; Snow, Nathan, and Perlman 1985).

Turn assistance: On completing a turn, the interventionist supplies the *turn assistance* necessary for the child to take the next turn. A variety of turn assistance strategies are exemplified in Table 4-5, listed in order from most to least supportive. In a *binary choice* utterance, the adult models two utterances, either of which the child could choose to use in entirety to take a turn. Each utterance models language that is above the child's independent capability. For example, the speech-language pathologist could say, "You could say, 'The milkman is smiling,' or 'He is smiling.'" This strategy provides a contextually appropriate use of modeling in which the adult models syntactic, morphological, and phonological forms in the hope that the child's repetition will be more appropriate than a spontaneous production would be. Within the conversation, these modeled utterances are sources of information that the child could use, not merely a task in which the child must repeat these utterances for the sake of repetition. This strategy is often used in efforts to improve a child's speech-sound production. Typically, we will supply a choice such as, "Is this the man's fum? Or his thumb?" which contrasts the child's articulatory form of a word with the adult form. The adult form is provided last so it will serve as a model for the child's production of the word within this communicative exchange (Hoffman, Schuckers, and Daniloff 1989).

Cloze procedure: A *cloze utterance* is similar to a "fill-in-the-blank sentence," in that the adult constructs part of an utterance and pauses to indicate that the child should finish the utterance (Snow, Nathan, and Perlman 1985). A cloze strategy can be used to prompt a label ("He is a . . ."), a description ("The ball is . . ."), or an interpretation ("He is smiling, so he must be . . ."). Table 4-5 shows that by adding pointing, gestures, and phonemic cues, the clinician can help the child attend to the information that should be supplied in the response. By using relational terms, the adult can cue the production of a complete sentence; for example, "The milkman is smiling, so we know that . . ."

To Parse — to portion out
(simplify)   to make smaller

Explanation — adding new information

TABLE 4-5
Strategies for Prompting Children to Use Different Levels of Semantic Displacement

Facilitator Prompt	Child Targeted Response
Binary Choice	
The milkman picks up the empty bottles or full bottles?	Empty bottles. (Description)
The milkman is smiling. Is he happy or sad?	Happy. (Interpretation)
Cloze Procedure	
The milkman picks up the empty . . .	Bottles. (Label)
The milkman is . . .	Picking up the bottles. (Description)
The milkman is smiling. He must be . . .	Happy. (Interpretation)
Every day, the milkman . . .	Picks up bottles. (Inference)
Milkman begins with the sound . . .	Mmm (Metalanguage)
Cloze Procedure with Pointing and Gestures	
The milkman is carrying the . . . [pointing to bottles in picture]	Bottles. (Label)
The milkman is . . . [gesturing action of carrying]	Carrying the bottles. (Description)
Cloze Procedure with Phonemic Cues	
The milkman sees the /k/ . . .	Cat. (Label)
The milkman is /s/ . . .	Smiling. (Description)
He must be /æ/ . . .	Happy. (Interpretation)
Cloze Procedure with Relational Terms	
The milkman is smiling so . . .	He is happy. (Description)
The milkman likes cats so . . .	He gave the cat some milk. (Description)
The milkman picks up the empty bottles and then . . .	He takes them to his truck. (Description)
The milkman pours out the rest of the bottle so . . .	The cat can drink the milk. (Description)
If the milkman gives the cat milk, then . . .	The cat will be happy. (Interpretation)
Preparatory Sets	
Tell us who is bringing the milk.	The milkman. (Label)
Tell us what the milkman is doing.	Carrying the milk. (Description)
Tell us how the milkman feels.	He is happy. (Interpretation)
Constituent Questions	
What did the milkman carry?	The bottles. (Label)
What will the milkman do?	Pick up the bottles. (Description)

Preparatory sets: Rather than supplying the child with part of an utterance, *preparatory sets* focus the child's attention on the concepts that should be included in the next turn in the conversation (Snow and Goldfield 1983). Preparatory sets typically take the form of suggestions such as, "You should tell us how the milkman feels." Preparatory sets can be used to focus on:

- Labels ("Tell us who is bringing the milk.")

- Actions ("Tell us what the milkman is doing.")

- Interpretations ("Tell us how the milkman feels.")

- Inferences ("Tell us what the milkman does every day.")

- Evaluations ("Tell us whether the milkman is a nice person.")

- Metalanguage ("Tell us the sound that begins the word 'milkman.'")

Constituent questions: Like preparatory sets, *constituent questions* focus on the information that is needed, but they require that the child reverse interrogative syntactic forms such as, "What will the milkman do?" as opposed to responding to the more direct form of a preparatory set: "Tell us what the milkman will do . . ." (Ninio 1983).

SUMMARY

The process of scaffolding oral discussions is one that demands that the adult formulate and maintain an overall discourse structure for the conversation. The adult periodically provides the child with opportunities to demonstrate his or her independent organizational abilities through comprehension questions. But most of the adult's efforts are devoted to engaging the child in a scaffolded discussion in which the child is provided many opportunities to interpret and reply to oral language that is integrated into the discourse structure of the topic. The adult's conversational turns are used to increase the semantic abstraction and discourse complexity of appropriate child utterances. The adult responds to semantically inappropriate utterances by providing information necessary to improve the child's understanding of the topic. This assistance is expected to improve the child's semantic understanding of a topic, discourse structure relative to that topic, and language forms utilized in discussing the topic.

Scaffolding at the Advanced Literate Language Level

Scaffolding for older children who are poor readers and writers is modified to focus on increasing the rate and fluency of word recognition and the levels of comprehension along the discourse and semantic continua. A procedure termed *communicative reading strategies* (CRS) is used for this purpose. (See Norris and Hoffman 1993 for an in-depth discussion of intervention for older children.)

A three-step process of interaction takes place in communicative reading strategies.

1. The interventionist establishes the content and intent of the author's message prior to reading the text by using a *preparatory set.* A preparatory set can be provided for any unit of language, such as a sentence, a phrase within a sentence, a difficult word, or a paragraph, depending on the needs of the reader. The preparatory set serves a variety of functions, including activating relevant concepts or background knowledge, simplifying large or abstract units of meaning, or parsing complex grammatical and discourse structures to demonstrate how the form of the language functions to establish relationships of meaning among ideas.

2. One or more readers interpret the author's message by orally reading the text alone or in unison. During this reading, the interventionist monitors the reading for indications that the information either is or is not being meaningfully processed by the learner. Indicators such as word miscues, slow rate of word recognition, frequent decoding errors, poor phrasing, word-by-word reading, intonation that is inappropriate to the meaning of the message, or poor response to comprehension checks suggest that something about the message is unknown or difficult to process.

3. The interventionist provides differential feedback to the reader based on whether the learner's reading suggested that the text was or was not adequately processed for meaning and intent. If the text is read fluently and meaningfully, the interventionist provides feedback using a scaffolding strategy that expands on the idea or models inferences or predictions. This feedback teaches reading comprehension by modeling how the reader must make interpretations that go beyond literal meanings and how the reader uses background knowledge to make sense of text. If the text is not read fluently or meaningfully, the interventionist may choose to teach the unknown language, to activate the reader's background knowledge, to clarify or challenge a misinterpretation, or to model a response to the intended message. The scaffolding strategies are as follows:

Preparatory sets: Preparatory sets are used to assist the child in activating appropriate background knowledge. Skilled readers activate their own background knowledge for a topic before they encounter actual text information (Afflerbach 1987). They form tentative hypotheses about what is going on (interpretations) and what is probably going to happen next (predictions), based on the activation of schemata, or networks of associated information they already possess. For example, given the following text from the theme book *The Grumpy Elephant:*

> "I feel grumpy," said Elephant.

The interventionist might use preparatory sets such as these: "Find out what kind of animal is talking" [pointing to "said Elephant"], and "He's telling you what kind of mood he's in" [pointing to "I feel grumpy"].

Acknowledgment: Acknowledgment provides feedback by confirming what the reader has read and understood. It treats reading as natural communication, in which speakers and listeners take turns and acknowledge that they heard and comprehended what the speaker said (Fitzgerald 1990). Acknowledgment, often consisting of a simple phrase such as "I see" or "OK," encourages the reluctant child to continue reading by confirming the message. For example, an acknowledgment of a text that reads, "I feel grumpy" might be "Oh, he's in a bad mood."

Expansion: Expansion refers to rewording the text information into grammatically more complete sentences (Froese and Kurushima 1979). These more complete sentences generally include relational terms, such as conjunctions (because, so, when), verb tense markers (will, did, should), or adjectives and adverbs. These aspects of language help to explicitly establish connections between ideas, especially for children who have difficulty with implicit meanings. For example, if the text says, "Along came Monkey," an expansion might be, "Along came Monkey into the jungle."

Extension: Extension refers to linking one idea to a second, related idea. It extends the topic to include the next action in a sequence, the consequence of an action or state, or a reaction to a situation. Extensions establish predictions about new information, as well as linking new ideas to previous text. Predictive questions in particular lead to better inferential comprehension (Memory 1983). For example, if the text reads "Along came Monkey. Poor old Elephant," an extension interjected between the reading of the two sentences might be, "Now that Monkey came along, I wonder how he will react to Elephant's bad mood."

Expatiation: Expatiations consist of elaborations on an idea or concept to establish greater meaning, to clarify unfamiliar vocabulary, to explain a metaphor or other figurative language, or to model inferences and interpretations (Readance, Baldwin, and Head 1987; Roser and Juel 1982). For example, if the text reads, "'I feel grumpy,' said Elephant," an expatiation might be, "He does look grumpy. His eyes are narrow and his mouth is frowning. Something bad must have happened."

Association: Associations occur when links are established between information just read and ideas that have been given in previous pages, paragraphs, or episodes (McCormick and Hill 1984). Associations help readers understand that meaning crosses the boundaries of sentences, paragraphs, and pages, and that all known information is integrated in interpreting current actions or states. For example, if the text reads, "Parrot jumped and fell over Giraffe," the interventionist might review the previous page, and make an association such as, "Elephant bellowed, or yelled so loudly, that it scared Parrot. Parrot got so scared that he . . ." [pointing to new text].

Generalization: Generalization links events, morals, or states in the story to similar situations that occur in other contexts, such as the child's own experiences or community, national, or world events. Generalizations help the reader to see how stories impose meaning on experience and teach something about the world and our response to it (Hayes and Tierney 1982). Similarly, reference to familiar experiences can help readers interpret unknown events presented in a text. For example, if the text reads, "Parrot jumped and fell over Giraffe," a statement of generalization might be, "He was startled, just like we were when the fire alarm went off."

Semantic cue: Semantic cues are used to assist the reader to retrieve or recognize a word that is misread or difficult to decode. Synonyms, definitions, or related words are given to help establish the correct network of information and maximize the probability that the correct word will be recognized and retrieved (Risko and Alvarez 1986). If the word is not in the child's lexicon, it can be modeled in a context where synonyms and definitions have already been used in order to build a meaningful network. Semantic cues that might be given when a child miscues on the word "grumpy" are, "This word tells you he's in a bad mood; he's grouchy, unhappy, grumbling at everybody."

Fluent reading: Fluent reading of a sentence or phrase is used to model how the elements of the sentence work together to communicate meaning (Abelson and Petersen 1983). It is used when a child struggles with the text and other scaffolding strategies alone are not successful in helping the child to construct meaning. The child is directed to look at the written words while the interventionist reads, so that the child simultaneously sees and hears how the sentence functions. For example, if the child reads, "I fell gr-, grume, groupy," a fluent reading might be modeled, followed by expatiation or other scaffolding strategy, to help the child associate the words and the meaning.

Parsing: Parsing refers to chunking complex sentences into smaller idea units and processing the ideational relationships within the sentence (Colwell 1982). Its purpose is to help the reader see how the sentence is made up of smaller semantic units and to use the visual input from the text to discover how the complex language works. For example, the sentence, "'Poor old Elephant, I'll dance for you,' Giraffe said" might be parsed, "This is who Elephant was talking to. This is what the long-legged Giraffe was doing. This tells you Giraffe dances because he feels sorry for Elephant."

Paraphrase: Paraphrasing refers to rewording the text after it is read. In the paraphrase, the difficulty of the vocabulary may be reduced, an unfamiliar word can be defined through descriptions or use of synonyms, complex sentences can be reworded in shorter, simpler sentences, and interpretations or other cues to meaning can be given. Paraphrasing enables readers to interpret the passage using language that expresses the meaning at a level more consistent with their language (Palinscar and Brown 1984). For example, the sentence, "'Stop that noise!' bellowed Elephant," might be paraphrased, "Elephant was so upset by all the noise, he yelled, 'Stop that noise!' He yelled it in an angry cry, a loud and mad bellow." While stating the paraphrase, the interventionist points to the parts of the written sentence that correspond to those ideas.

In CRS instruction, the same story is interactively read across several days as outlined in the Storybook-Centered Lesson Plans. Each day, one element of the story is read—for example, only the setting or only the initiating event, or one episode or chapter. During each session, the previously read pages are reviewed and a new part of the story is interactively read. This process allows for repeated readings of difficult text, enabling the children to more independently derive meaning and experience fluency with less scaffolding across readings. As the language and meaning of the text become more familiar, the readers are helped to summarize previously read information rather than reading the pages verbatim and to metacognitively analyze the structure or form that writers use to structure text. The structure of difficult words or words read with miscues are metalinguistically analyzed, using procedures described under Teaching Spelling in chapter 3 (see page 92). The book reading is followed by a Topic Explorations or Thematic Studies activity to establish background knowledge and provide experiences with expository text and the transactional function of language. Writing is incorporated to provide experiences with the expressive mode of written language.

■ Case Example of Language and Reading Assessment

A case example can help to illustrate the use of the SDS model for assessment and intervention planning. In this case example, the child's oral language was examined under conditions of storytelling in response to a picture, before and after scaffolding was used to help the child interpret and organize the pictured information. In addition, a decontextualized but familiar experience was compared to the storytelling. A similar comparison of oral reading before and after scaffolding was conducted, as well as reading under contextualized and decontextualized conditions.

Analysis of Oral Language Samples

The child's oral language was examined by eliciting language samples under three conditions and describing the results using the Situational-Discourse-Semantic (SDS) Model. First, an oral story was elicited using a picture from the Apricot I picture set (Arwood 1985), representing a task in which the language was situationally contextualized to the picture (Level S:IV). The picture depicted two boys fighting and another watching as an adult is attempting to break up the fight. The second sample was elicited in response to the same picture, but under conditions of scaffolding where the examiner assisted the child to organize and talk about pictured events. The third sample represented a change in the task to a decontextualized situational context where the child was asked to recount a personal experience (Level S:VI). Characteristics of the language produced across these three situational contexts were compared.

CONTEXTUALIZED NARRATIVE

The oral narrative was elicited under conditions where the examiner used one picture to model telling a story and a second picture to elicit the child's story. The resulting sample revealed a primitive story consisting of four ideas expressed in sequence using the grammatical conjunction "and."

Adult: I want you to tell me a story about this picture.

Child: 1. And these two people were fighting

2. and this boy is this sitting this feet in there.

3. And this man is coming to . . . is wanting them to stop

4. and he's carrying a first-aid box with him.

One idea (3) represented a character's reaction to the fight, but most of the story consisted of describing scenes from the picture without assigning any significance or purpose to them (2, 4). The child had difficulty linguistically coordinating the man's actions with his purpose, resulting in a false start (3). Within the short story, a topic was maintained but it did not focus on a problem or event. The action sequence was temporally ordered, and one reaction is stated, but it does not unify the story, resulting in a discourse level assignment of D:III (ordered sequence). This level corresponds to the narrative development expected between 2 and 4 years of age according to Applebee's (1978) norms. Semantically, three of the ideas in the story (1, 2, 4) merely described actions depicted, and one (3) provided an interpretation of the motives of the character. No inferences or interpretations that added information to the story were included. The child exhibited difficulty in semantically coding information, as exemplified in idea (2). This story suggests that the child views symbolic information that is presented in pictures statically, bringing little personal experience or background knowledge to the event.

NARRATIVE WITH SCAFFOLDING

To determine the child's potential level of oral narrative production, the examiner provided scaffolding to assist the child in including more ideas and greater complexity and organization. Initially, a more complete story was modeled, and the child was asked to retell it. This retelling included some of the information modeled, but the attempt resulted in severe linguistic difficulty in expressing the more complex ideas. This difficulty was reflected in a high number of false starts, fillers, repetitions, pauses, and ideas tagged to the end of other utterances. The child attempted greater grammatical complexity in order to coordinate multiple ideas but without success.

Adult: [following modeled story] So can you tell me about it?

Child: Um, this went . . . um . . . I mean . . . This one didn't like . . . um . . . these two boys and . . . and this one didn't want any . . . didn't want to . . . to . . . to take their lun . . . lunch and . . . and to take and throw their stuff off their desks so they . . . And this one got . . . and this one got real mad, started to fight. And this one got punched in the . . . stomach. And the . . . and the . . . principal was running over to him . . . to stop the fight and put first aid on their wound spots.

Following the initial retelling, scaffolding was used to talk about individual ideas. The responsibility for linguistically coding the ideas was shared between the examiner and the child. The examiner controlled the order of talking about the events. The child was given a third opportunity to tell the story. This retelling reflected a significant change in the amount of information included, the complexity of the grammar used to organize the ideas, and the semantic specificity of the words used.

Child: 1. The bully went . . . wanted their . . . the boys' lunch money

2. and the boys said, "no."

3. And the bully got mad and started . . . him . . . and he started to fight.

4. And this one got punched in the face

5. and this one got punched in the stomach.

6. And the teacher saw what was hap . . . happening

7. and ran over with a first-aid box

8. so they would stop fighting

9. and heal their wounds with first aid.

This narrative consisted of nine ideas, all of them topic related and focusing on the problem stated in the initiating event (1, 2, 3). The temporal sequences were frequently also causally determined and explicitly stated (2, 3, 6, 7, 8, 9), resulting in a discourse level characterized as a reactive sequence (D:IV). Semantically, only three of the ideas (5, 6, 7) represented descriptions of pictured events. The others required interpretations of internal states (1, 3) or actions preceding or following the depicted state (2, 6, 8, 9). Semantically, each of the ideas was stated specifically and accurately. The child's story retelling following scaffolding reflects a significant change compared to the first story, and indicates that the child requires considerable input to organize with complexity and specificity ideas depicted symbolically in pictures.

DECONTEXTUALIZED EXPERIENCE

The child was asked to talk about a personal experience, which is a decontextualized situational context. Three related topics were present in the recounting: falling off a bike, riding faster than a friend, and changing bikes. The first topic contained five ideas, followed by nine more ideas when asked for additional information.

Child: 1. Um . . . Well, I get to pick out my own 10-speed bike.

2. But I might fall off of it.

3. 'Cause I fell off of my first . . . fell off of my bike yesterday

4. and I fell off of my friend's bike

5. and I hit my chin, my knee, and my elbow.

Adult: Ooh. Did it hurt?

Child: 6. Not when I fell off my friend's bike.

7. But when I fell off of my . . . of my bike

8. cause my seat . . . it's up and I was . . .

9. there's speed bumps . . . um . . . on one of my . . . on one of the streets in my neighborhood.

10. And I was back there with my friend

11. and we were going over them.

12. And when I came back over the high one, I was turning

13. and my bike . . . the tires slid

14. and I fell off

15. and I scraped my knee.

The ideas were told as a reactive sequence with frequent cause-effect relationships between ideas that served to unify the passage to explain how the accident occurred, which corresponds to discourse level D:IV. Few complex sentences were used to coordinate related ideas, however. For example, the child abandoned his attempt (3) to recount that he had already fallen off of bikes twice and instead just listed the two events (3, 4). When he tried to elaborate how the accident happened, he could not integrate the information about the speed bumps with the raised seat, resulting in short bits of information being juxtaposed (7, 8, 9) and expressed with a high rate of linguistic nonfluencies. Almost all of the ideas were comprised semantically of descriptive statements expressed in NP + VP + NP sentence constructions. One idea (2) reflected a possible future event, or a semantic inference, and one (13) interpreted an action. Thus, the child provided more information organized at a higher discourse level for the personal event than for the initial fight story, but both stories were at similar semantic levels.

Analysis of Oral Reading Samples

The child's reading ability was examined by eliciting reading samples under three conditions and describing the results using the Situational-Discourse-Semantic Model. First, an oral reading sample was elicited using text at a first-grade reading level unaccompanied by pictures. The examiner provided the name of the character prior to reading. ("This story is about Red. Read the story to find out who Red is.") This task represents a situationally decontextualized linguistic situation in which all of the context had to be created from the words alone (Level S:VIII). The second sample was elicited using a first-grade level text accompanied by a picture, where the words and illustration provided parallel information (a situational context of Level S:IV). The third sample was elicited using the initial text, but under conditions of scaffolding where the examiner assisted the child to attend to relevant cues of meaning, function, and form while reading. Characteristics of the reading produced across these three situational contexts were compared.

DECONTEXTUALIZED READING

The first reading sample was elicited by presenting the text and asking the child to read the words orally. The text was factual or transactional discourse, organized as a descriptive list (Level TD:II). The sentences ranged from five to nine words in length, many with dependent clauses such as infinitives, indirect objects, and conjoined phrases. The resulting sample revealed reading characterized by miscues (in bold type) on 28% of the words, slow rate (1 min. 40 sec.), and monotone pitch. Most of the ideas (1, 3, 5, 6) semantically required interpretations of feelings, attitudes, or beliefs, while the remaining ideas described actions.

1. It is fun to have a **big** (dog) like Red.
2. He can **help** (play) **thel** (ball) with me.
3. He **like** (likes) to **red up** (ride in) the car with us.
4. I **cale** (call) and he comes.
5. Red **he** (inserted) is a good **big** (dog),
6. and we **tern** (are) good to **heem** (him).

Analysis of the child's miscues reveals that he has a small vocabulary of high frequency words that he accurately recognizes, although with effort as reflected by the slow rate and poor intonation. The child's difficulty processing written information at this level was further demonstrated by the inability to coordinate multiple cues to decipher unknown words. The child frequently attended to grapho-phonemic cues presented by the word or predicted a word based on grammar (1, 2, 3, 5), resulting in the choice of an adjective where a noun phrase occurred and the insertion of a subjective pronoun (5). However, when the resulting word choice did not maintain syntactic or semantic sense within the total context of the sentence (1, 2, 3, 5) or resulted in a nonsense word (2, 4, 6), he did not revise his prediction. These unmonitored miscues resulted in grapho-phonemic miscues such as the confusion of b/d ("big" for "dog")—a discrimination error common in emergent readers—and assimilations of words encountered earlier based on phonemic cues ("red" for ride, assimilated from [1]).

The miscue produced in the first sentence resulted in failure to establish the topic of the passage, and thus limited the background knowledge the child could activate to assist word recognition and comprehension. This limited the ability to coordinate multiple cues and to interpret the passage, so that when asked questions about what he had read, the child inappropriately identified that Red is big and helps.

CONTEXTUALIZED READING

The second reading sample was elicited in response to an illustrated text that was fictional (the poetic discourse function). The text was written as an ordered sequence of events (Level PD:III), where each monster in the story in turn demonstrates a special talent at a party. The text is repetitive across episodes, with a descriptive question asked and answered. The syntax of the sentences is fairly complex because of the question and relative clause transformations, and the nonspecific referents including "that," "it," "do," "what," and "this" that compose most of the content words. In this context, the child was able to accurately read and comprehend the text.

1. What can this little monster do?

2. It can sing.

3. That's **wet it can** . . . what it can do.

The reading rate and intonation produced in this sample reflected fluent reading, even for words that had been read word by word in the decontextualized passage. The child was able to coordinate cues from multiple sources, reading difficult words such as "monster" and "sing" using grammatical, semantic, grapho-phonemic, and pictured information to formulate predictions. When a miscue occurred (3), the child was able to use the total context of the sentence to evaluate and revise his prediction.

DECONTEXTUALIZED READING WITH SCAFFOLDING

To determine the child's potential level of oral reading for decontextualized information, the examiner provided scaffolding to assist the child to activate appropriate background knowledge, parse complex sentences into constituent ideas, and produce relevant interpretations and inferences. Each of the six sentences was interactively read using communicative reading strategies (Norris 1991). When the child was asked to reread the passage, accuracy of word recognition (1 miscue), reading rate (25 seconds), and intonation all improved, reflecting independent reading of this passage.

The child was asked to metalinguistically analyze the structure of difficult words by generating a spelling. These attempts were phonetic, characterized by the presence of phonetically correct initial and final sounds, but use of vowels and consonants that were not conventional for the actual spelling. His attempts included:

- **halp** for help
- **liek** for like
- **bol** for ball

While the child was able to implicitly analyze the structure of words and differentiated between questions and statements when reading, his explicit metalinguistic knowledge was limited. In addition to limited knowledge of word structure, the child was unable to respond to questions such as, "What is a word?" or "Which sentence asks a question?" This indicates that the child does not have sufficient competence with reading to be explicitly aware of component elements, and in turn cannot efficiently use this metaknowledge to parse sentences, evaluate miscues, and coordinate multiple reading cues. A whole language approach, in which all levels of language are addressed in an integrated manner, should be used both to build on existing abilities and to facilitate the emergence of higher levels of language.

■ Summary

The Storybook-Centered Curriculum is designed to be used flexibly to meet the needs of kindergarten or early childhood teachers who choose to implement whole language, of programs that are seeking to include children with special needs in the regular classroom, and of speech-language pathologists and other special service providers working on teaching language and facilitating learning that peers acquire naturally during the preschool years. Methods for adapting the curriculum to meet the needs of children across a wide range of abilities are described in this manual, supported by specific suggestions for talking about information at different levels of difficulty along the semantic, discourse, and situational continua provided on each daily Storybook-Centered Lesson Plan. The Storybook-Centered Curriculum is designed to be adapted, modified, and revised to meet the needs and interests of individual teachers or special service providers and their students. Favorite activities, special events, personal interests, and current topics all can and should be incorporated into the curriculum to reflect the teacher's own Tender Loving Care.

Scaffold Strategies to Mediate

Direct attention to imp elements
Provide feedback to questions & comments
Assist child to talk
Provide related remarks

Provide timely prompts

Encourage cooperative learning

Assist child to formulate question

Engage child in problem solving

Provide elaboration & expression

Model both implicit & explicit meaning

Provide progressively less assistance

Techniques for Supporting
- Modelling
- Instructions in small steps
- Sensori-Motor experiences
- Decrease language input
- Prompts
- Decrease in complexity

Storybook: when 1st start out discuss & talk about;
" what would you put on your picture?"
" what words would you write to go with your pics"

References

Abelson, A. G., and M. Petersen. 1983. Efficacy of "talking books" for a group of reading disabled boys. *Perceptual and Motor Skills* 57:567-70.

Adams, M. J. 1990. *Beginning to read: Thinking and learning about print.* Cambridge, MA: The MIT Press.

Afflerbach, P. 1987. How are main idea statements constructed? Watch the experts. *Journal of Reading* 30(6):512-18.

Allen, J., E. McNeill, and V. Schmidt. 1992. *Cultural awareness for children.* New York: Addison-Wesley.

Applebee, A. N. 1978. *A child's concept of story: Ages 2-17.* Chicago: University of Chicago Press.

————. 1991. Environments for language teaching and learning: Contemporary issues and future directions. In *Handbook of research on teaching the English language arts,* edited by J. Flood, J. M. Jensen, D. Lapp, and J. R. Squire, 549-58. New York: Macmillan.

Aram, D. M., B. L. Ekelman, and J. E. Nation. 1984. Preschoolers with language disorders: Ten years later. *Journal of Speech and Hearing Disorders* 27:232-44.

Arwood, E. L. 1985. *Apricot I language kit.* Portland, OR: Apricot.

ASHA Committee on Language Learning Disabilities. 1989. Issues in determining eligibility for language intervention. *Asha* 31(3):113-18.

Baumann, J. F., and E. J. Kameenui. 1991. Research on vocabulary instruction: Ode to Voltaire. In *Handbook of research on teaching the English language arts,* edited by J. Flood, J. M. Jensen, D. Lapp, and J. R. Squire, 604-32. New York: Macmillan.

Bickmore-Brand, J. 1990. *Language in mathematics.* Portsmouth, NH: Heinemann.

Blank, M., S. Rose, and L. Berlin. 1978. *The language of learning: The preschool years.* New York: Grune and Stratton.

Bloom, L. 1970. *Language development: Form and function of emerging grammars.* Cambridge, MA: The MIT Press.

Britton, J. 1982. Writing to learn and learning to write. In *Prospect and retrospect: Selected essays of James Britton,* edited by G. M. Pradl, 94-111. Montclair, NJ: Boynton/Cook.

Brown, R. 1973. *A first language: The early stages.* Cambridge, MA: Harvard University Press.

Bruce, B. 1981. A social interaction model of reading. *Discourse Processes* 4:273-309.

Bruner, J. 1983. *Child's talk.* New York: Norton.

Bryan, T. 1986. A review of studies on learning disabled children's communicative competence. In *Language competence: Assessment and intervention,* edited by R. L. Schiefelbusch, 227-60. San Diego, CA: College-Hill Press.

Calkins, L. M. 1986. *The art of teaching writing.* Portsmouth, NH: Heinemann.

_____. 1991. *Living between the lines.* Portsmouth, NH: Heinemann.

Cazden, C. 1983. Adult assistance to language development: Scaffolds, models, and direct instruction. In *Developing literacy: Young children's use of language,* edited by C. Cazden, 3-18. Newark, DE: International Reading Association.

_____. 1988. *Classroom discourse.* Portsmouth, NH: Heinemann.

Charlesworth, R., and K. K. Lind. 1990. *Math and science for young children.* Albany, NY: Delmar Publishers.

Chomsky, C. 1980. Reading, writing, and phonology. In *Thought and language/ Language and reading,* edited by M. Wolf, M. McQuillan, and E. Radwin, 51-71. Cambridge, MA: Harvard Educational Review.

Clay, M. M. 1991. *Becoming literate: The construction of inner control.* Portsmouth, NH: Heinemann.

Colwell, C. G. 1982. Paragraph processing: A direct-functional-interactive model. *Reading Improvement* 19:13-24.

Creaghead, N. A. 1992. Classroom interactional analysis/script analysis. In *Best practices in school speech-language pathology,* edited by W. A. Secord and J. S. Damico, 65-72. San Antonio, TX: The Psychological Corp.

Davidson, A. 1983. *Maths and me: Helping your child with mathematics.* Auckland, New Zealand: Shortland Publications.

Ferreiro, E. 1986. The interplay between information and assimilation in beginning literacy. In *Emergent literacy: Writing and reading,* edited by W. H. Teale and E. Sulzby, 15-49. Norwood, NJ: Ablex.

Ferreiro, E., and A. Teberosky. 1982. *Literacy before schooling.* Portsmouth, NH: Heinemann.

Fisher, B. 1991. *Joyful learning: A whole language curriculum.* Portsmouth, NH: Heinemann.

Fitzgerald, J. 1990. *Reading comprehension instruction 1783-1987: A review of trends and research.* Newark, DE: International Reading Association.

French, L., and K. Nelson. 1985. *Young children's knowledge of relational terms: Some ifs, ors, and buts.* New York: Springer-Verlag.

Froese, V., and S. Kurushima. 1979. The effects of sentence expansion practice on the reading comprehension and writing ability of third graders. In *Reading research: Studies and applications,* edited by M. L. Kamil, 95-99. Clemson, SC: National Reading Conference.

Ganeri, A. 1991. *Amazing world facts.* New York: Mallard Press.

Gentry, J. R. 1982. An analysis of developmental spelling in GYNS AT WRK. *The Reading Teacher* 36:192-200.

_____. 1989. *SPEL . . . is a four letter word.* Portsmouth, NH: Heinemann.

Gibbs, D. B., and E. B. Cooper. 1989. Prevalence of communication disorders in students with learning disabilities. *Journal of Learning Disabilities* 22:60-63.

Golden, J. M. 1990. *The narrative symbol in childhood literature: Explorations in the construction of text.* New York: Mouton de Gruyter.

Goodman, K. S. 1982. *Language and literacy: The selected writings of Kenneth S. Goodman,* vol. 2: *Reading, language, and the classroom teacher,* edited by F. V. Gollasch. Boston: Routledge and Kegan.

_____. 1986. *What's whole in whole language?* Portsmouth, NH: Heinemann.

_____. 1993. *Phonics phacts.* Portsmouth, NH: Heinemann.

Hayes, D. A., and R. J. Tierney. 1982. Developing readers' knowledge through analogy. *Reading Research Quarterly* 17:256-80.

Hill, S., and T. Hill. 1990. *The collaborative classroom: A guide to co-operative learning.* Portsmouth, NH: Heinemann.

Hoffman, P. R. 1990. Spelling, phonology, and the speech-language pathologist: A whole language perspective. *Language, Speech, and Hearing Services in Schools* 21:238-43.

Hoffman, P. R., and J. A. Norris. 1989. On the nature of phonological processes: Evidence from normal children's spelling errors. *Journal of Speech and Hearing Research* 32:787-94.

_____. 1994. Whole language and collaboration work: Evidence from at-risk kindergartners. *Journal of Childhood Communication Disorders* 16(1):41-48.

Hoffman, P. R., G. Schuckers, and R. G. Daniloff. 1989. *Children's phonetic disorders: Theory and practice.* Austin, TX: PRO-ED.

Holt, B. G. 1991. *Science with young children.* Washington, DC: National Association for the Education of Young Children.

Hudson, J. A., and L. R. Shapiro. 1991. From knowing to telling: The development of children's scripts, stories, and personal narratives. In *Developing narrative structure,* edited by A. McCabe and C. Peterson, 89-136. Hillsdale, NJ: Lawrence Erlbaum.

Kamii, C. 1988. *Number in preschool and kindergarten: Educational implications of Piaget's theory.* Washington, DC: National Association for the Education of Young Children.

Labov, W. 1972. *Language in the inner city.* Philadelphia: University of Pennsylvania Press.

Langley, A. 1991. *I wonder how does the wind blow?* New York: Derrydale Books.

Lasky, L., and R. Mukerji. 1990. *Art: Basic for young children.* Washington, DC: National Association for the Education of Young Children.

Lehr, F., and J. Osborn. 1994. *Reading, language and literacy: Instruction for the twenty-first century.* Hillsdale, NJ: Lawrence Erlbaum Associates.

Lehr, S. S. 1991. *The child's developing sense of theme: Responses to literature.* New York: Teachers College Press.

Loban, W. 1976. *Language development: Kindergarten through grade twelve.* Urbana, IL: National Council of Teachers of English.

Martinez, M., and N. Rozer. 1985. Read it again: The value of repeated readings during storytime. *The Reading Teacher* 38:782-86.

Maxwell, S. E., and G. P. Wallach. 1984. The language-learning disabilities connection: Symptoms of early language disability change over time. In *Language learning disabilities in school-age children,* edited by G. Wallach and K. Butler, 15-34. Baltimore: Williams and Wilkins.

Mayesky, M. 1990. *Creative activities for young children.* Albany, NY: Delmar Publishers, Inc.

McCabe, A., and C. Peterson. 1991. *Developing narrative structure.* Hillsdale, NJ: Lawrence Erlbaum Associates.

McCormick, S., and D. S. Hill. 1984. An analysis of the effects of two procedures for increasing disabled readers' inferencing skills. *Journal of Educational Research* 77:219-26.

McGee, L. M., and D. J. Richgels. 1990. *Literacy's beginnings: Supporting young readers and writers.* Boston: Allyn and Bacon.

Memory, D. M. 1983. Main idea prequestions as adjunct aids with good and low-average middle grade readers. *Journal of Reading Behavior* 12:37-48.

Merritt, D., and B. Liles. 1987. Story grammar ability in children with and without language disorder: Story generation, story retelling, and story comprehension. *Journal of Speech and Hearing Research* 30:539-52.

Miller, J. 1991. *Research on child language disorders: A decade of progress.* Austin, TX: PRO-ED.

Monroe, M. 1951. *Growing into reading: How readiness for reading develops at home and at school.* New York: Scott, Foresman and Co.

Morrow, L. M. 1988. Young children's responses to one-to-one story readings in school settings. *Reading Research Quarterly* 23:89-107.

Morrow, L. M., and J. K. Smith. 1990. The effects of group setting on interactive storybook reading. *Reading Research Quarterly* 25:213-31.

Muma, J. R. 1978. *Language handbook: Concepts, assessment, and intervention.* Englewood Cliffs, NJ: Prentice-Hall.

Neidecker, E. A. 1980. *School programs in speech-language: Organization and management.* Englewood Cliffs, NJ: Prentice-Hall.

Nelson, K. 1985. *Making sense: The acquisition of shared meaning.* New York: Academic Press.

_____. 1991. Event knowledge and the development of language functions. In *Research on child language disorders: A decade of progress,* edited by J. Miller, 125-42. Austin, TX: PRO-ED.

Nelson, N. W. 1992. Targets of curriculum-based language assessment. In *Best practices in school speech-language pathology: Descriptive/nonstandardized language assessment,* edited by W. A. Secord and J. S. Damico, 73-86. San Antonio, TX: The Psychological Corporation.

Ninio, A. 1983. Joint book reading as a multiple vocabulary acquisition device. *Developmental Psychology* 19:445-51.

Norris, J. A. 1988. Using communication strategies to enhance reading acquisition. *The Reading Teacher* 41:368-73.

_____. 1989a. Facilitating developmental changes in spelling. *Academic Therapy* 25:97-108.

_____. 1989b. Providing language remediation in the classroom: An integrated language-to-reading intervention method. *Language, Speech and Hearing Services in Schools* 20:205-19.

_____. 1991. From frog to prince: Using written language as a context for language learning. *Topics in Language Disorders* 12:66-81.

_____. 1992. Learning to talk through literacy: Whole language for handicapped preschoolers. In *Perspectives on whole language: Past, present, potential,* 148-56. Columbia, MO: Instructional Materials Laboratory, University of Missouri.

_____. 1993. Early sentence transformations and the development of complex syntactic structures. In *Communication development: Foundations, processes and clinical applications,* edited by B. Shulman and W. Haynes, 293-340. New York: Prentice Hall.

Norris, J. A., and J. S. Damico. 1990. Whole language in theory and practice: Implications for language intervention. *Language, Speech, and Hearing Services in Schools* 21:212-20.

Norris, J. A., and P. R. Hoffman. 1990. Language intervention within naturalistic environments. *Language, Speech and Hearing Services in Schools* 21:102-9.

_____. 1993. *Whole language intervention for school-age children.* San Diego, CA: Singular Publishing Group.

_____. 1994. Whole language and representational theories: Helping children to build a network of associations. *Journal of Childhood Communication Disorders* 16:5-12.

Palinscar, A. S., and A. L. Brown. 1984. Reciprocal teaching of comprehension fostering and comprehension activities. *Cognition and Instruction* 1:117-75.

Pappas, C. C., B. Z. Kiefer, and L. S. Levstik. 1990. *An integrated language perspective in the elementary school: Theory into action.* White Plains, NY: Longman.

Phillips, V., and L. McCullough. 1990. Consultation-based programming: Instituting the collaborative ethic in schools. *Exceptional Children* 56(4):291-304.

Piaget, J. 1952. *The language and thought of the child.* London: Routledge and Kegan Paul.

_____. 1954. *The construction of reality in the child.* New York: Basic Books.

Read, C. 1986. *Children's creative spelling.* Boston: Routledge and Kegan Paul.

Readance, J. E., R. S. Baldwin, and M. H. Head. 1987. Teaching young readers to interpret metaphors. *The Reading Teacher* 40:439-43.

Reid, J., P. Forrestal, and J. Cook. 1990. *Small group learning in the classroom.* Portsmouth, NH: Heinemann.

Ripich, D. N., and P. L. Griffith. 1988. Narrative abilities of children with learning disabilities and nondisabled children: Story structure, cohesion, and propositions. *Journal of Learning Disabilities* 21:165-73.

Risko, V. J., and M. C. Alvarez. 1986. An investigation of poor readers' use of a thematic strategy to comprehend text. *Reading Research Quarterly* 21:298-316.

Roser, N., and C. Juel. 1982. Effect of vocabulary instruction on reading comprehension. In *New inquiries in reading: Research and instruction.* Thirty-first yearbook of the National Reading Conference, edited by J. A. Niles and L. A. Harris, 110-18. Rochester, NY: National Reading Conference.

Roser, N., and M. Martinez. 1985. Roles adults play in preschoolers' response to literature. *Language Arts* 62:485-90.

Schirrmacher, R. 1988. *Art and creative development for young children.* Albany, NY: Delmar Publishers.

Scott, C. M., and D. L. Erwin. 1992. Descriptive assessment of writing: Process and products. In *Best practices in school speech-language pathology: Descriptive/ nonstandardized language assessment,* edited by W. A. Secord and J. S. Damico, 87-98. San Antonio, TX: The Psychological Corporation.

Scott, J. 1992. *Science and language links: Classroom implications.* Portsmouth, NH: Heinemann.

Secord, W. A., and E. H. Wiig. 1991. *Developing a collaborative language intervention program.* Lockport, NY: Educom Associates.

Short, K. G., C. Burke, and J. Harste. 1991. *Creating curriculum: Teachers and students as a community of learners.* Portsmouth, NH: Heinemann.

Simon, C. S. 1985. The language-learning disabled student: Description and therapy implications. In *Communication skills and classroom success: Therapy methodologies for language-learning disabled students,* edited by C. S. Simon, 1-56. San Diego: College Hill.

Sinatra, G. M. 1990. Convergence of listening and reading processing. *Reading Research Quarterly* 15:115-30.

Smith, F. 1985. *Reading without nonsense.* New York: Teachers College Press.

_____. 1990. *To think.* New York: Teachers College Press.

Snow, C. E., and B. A. Goldfield. 1983. Turn the page, please: Situation-specific language acquisition. *Journal of Child Language* 10:535-49.

Snow, C. E., D. Nathan, and R. Perlman. 1985. Assessing children's knowledge about book reading. In *Play, language and stories,* edited by L. Galda and A. Pellegrini, 167-81. Norwood, NJ: Ablex.

Staton, J., R. Shuy, J. Peyton, and L. Reed. 1988. *Dialogue journal communication.* Norwood, NJ: Ablex.

Stein, N. L., and C. G. Glenn. 1979. An analysis of story comprehension in elementary school children. In *Advances in discourse processing.* vol. 2: *New directions,* edited by R. O. Freedle, 53-120. Norwood, NJ: Ablex.

Straw, S. B. 1990. Reading and response to literature: Transactionalizing instruction. In *Perspectives on talk and learning,* edited by S. Hynds and D. L. Rubin, 129-48. Urbana, IL: National Council of Teachers of English.

Sulzby, E. 1985. Children's emergent reading of favorite storybooks: A developmental study. *Reading Research Quarterly* 20:458-81.

Sulzby, E., and L. B. Zecker. 1991. The oral monologue as a form of emergent reading. In *Developing narrative structure,* edited by A. McCabe and C. Peterson, 175-214. Hillsdale, NJ: Lawrence Erlbaum.

Sunal, C. S. 1990. *Early childhood social studies.* Columbus, OH: Merrill.

Tannen, D. 1982. The oral/literate continuum in discourse. In *Spoken and written language: Exploring orality and literacy,* edited by D. Tannen, 1-16. Norwood, NJ: Ablex.

Taylor, H. 1993. The whole language classroom: Factors contributing to effective storybook reading. Master's thesis. Louisiana State University.

Teale, W. H., and E. Sulzby. 1986. *Emergent literacy: Writing and reading.* Norwood, NJ: Ablex.

Temple, C., R. Nathan, N. Burris, and F. Temple. 1988. *The beginnings of writing* (2d ed.). Boston: Allyn and Bacon.

Vygotsky, L. S. 1962. *Thought and language.* Edited and translated by Hanfmann and Vakar. Cambridge, MA: The MIT Press.

Waters, S. 1993. Discourse structure in a kindergarten classroom: An examination of whole language interactions. Master's thesis, Louisiana State University.

Wells, G. 1985. *Language, learning and education.* England: NFER-NELSON.

_____. 1986. *The meaning makers: Children learning language and using language to learn.* Portsmouth, NH: Heinemann.

Westby, C. E. 1985. Learning to talk—talking to learn: Oral-literate language differences. In *Communication skills for classroom success: Therapy methodologies,* edited by C. Simon, 183-213. San Diego: College-Hill Press.

_____. 1994. The vision of full inclusion: Don't exclude kids by including them. *Journal of Childhood Communication Disorders* 16(1): 13-23.

White, T. G., M. F. Graves, and W. H. Slater. 1990. Growth of reading vocabulary in diverse elementary schools. *Journal of Educational Psychology* 82:281-90.

Whitin, D. J., H. Mills, and T. O'Keefe. 1990. *Living and learning mathematics: Stories and strategies for supporting mathematical literacy.* Portsmouth, NH: Heinemann.

Yaden, D. B. 1988. Understanding stories through repeated read-abouts: How many does it take? *Reading Teacher* 41:556-60.

Yaden, D. B., L. B. Smoklin, and A. Conlon. 1989. Preschoolers' questions about pictures, print convention, and story text during reading aloud at home. *Reading Research Quarterly* 24:188-214.

Appendix:
Reproducible Class Profiles

Social Studies Checklist
Science Checklist
Mathematics Checklist
Art Checklist
Reading Checklist
Language Arts Checklist

Social Studies Checklist

Date:

Rating Scale

0 = Not at all
1 = Given objects
2 = Given pictures
3 = Given prompts
4 = Spontaneously

STUDENTS' NAMES

History (tells about)

Holidays
Traditions
Personal history
Seasons

Political Science (demonstrates)

Friendships
Sharing
Cooperation

Geography (tells about and/or shows)

Farm/city
Clothing
Regions/boundaries
Maps
Direction/space
Globe

Psychology (tells about, controls)

Moods
Self-image
Fears
Aging/development

Sociology (tells about)

Family
Neighborhood
Community
Responsibilities
Environment

Economics (tells about)

Buying/selling
Classroom needs
Personal needs
Community needs
Resources
Occupations

Anthropology (tells about and participates in)

Culture
Foods
Music
Games

Science Checklist

Date:

STUDENTS' NAMES

Life Science (tells about)

Plants		
Animals		
Development		
Ecology		

Physical Science (manipulates materials to show understanding of)

Mass		
Force		
Motion		
Energy		
Machines		

Health Science (tells about, makes healthy choices)

Body parts		
Body systems		
Foods		
Nutrition		
Growth		

Earth Science (tells about)

Minerals		
Weather		
Solar system		

Observation Skills (tells about, demonstrates)

Collection		
Comparison		
Classification		

Measurement (tells about, demonstrates)

Length		
Weight		
Volume		
Temperature		

Recording Findings (tells about, demonstrates)

Pictures		
Graphs		
Maps		
Oral language		
Written language		

Mathematics Checklist

Date:

STUDENTS' NAMES

Numbers (demonstrates, tells about)

Matching sets					
One-to-one correspondence					
Counting to 30					
Number recognition to 30					
Writing numerals to 10					

Operations (demonstrates, tells about)

Conservation					
Ordering					
Patterning					
Comparing					
Adding					
Subtracting					
Equivalence					

Measurement (demonstrates, tells about)

Volume					
Weight					
Distance					
Time					

Sets and Classification (demonstrates, tells about)

Shape					
Size					
Space					
Color					
Same					
Different					

Recording (demonstrates, tells about)

Graphs					
Charts					
Calendar					

Money (demonstrates, tells about)

Naming coins					
Coin values					
Counting pennies					
Recognizing $ and ¢					

Art Checklist

Date:

Rating Scale	STUDENTS' NAMES						
0 = Not at all 1 = Given objects 2 = Given pictures 3 = Given prompts 4 = Spontaneously							

Representation (demonstrates, tells about)

Body image							
Objects							
States							
Symbolic representations							
Abstract expressions							

Media (demonstrates, tells about)

Clay							
Cloth							
Paper							
Art materials							

Topological Form (demonstrates, tells about)

Spatial orientation							
Spatial relations							
Whole-to-part							

Geometric (demonstrates, tells about)

Shape							
Size							
Line							
Color							
Texture							
Space							

Format (demonstrates, tells about)

Sculpture							
Drawing							
Painting							

Function (demonstrates, tells about)

Create							
Express							
Decorate							
Ceremony							
Symbols							
Props							

Reading Checklist

Date:

Rating Scale	STUDENTS' NAMES					
0 = Not at all						
1 = Given objects						
2 = Given pictures						
3 = Given prompts						
4 = Spontaneously						

Oral Language (demonstrates)

Label objects, characters						
Describe actions, states						
Describe by characteristic						
Interpret meaning from cues						
Infer/predict from cues						
Evaluate, justify, explain						
Tell story with temporal, causal, intentional links						

Print Knowledge (demonstrates)

Left-to-right concept						
Top-to-bottom concept						
Whole-word concepts						
Oral-written word correspondence						
Recite familiar story verbatim						
Use reading intonation						
Use formal grammar						
Know function of punctuation						
Know function of capitals						
Know title page, author						

Metalanguage (demonstrates)

Concept of wordness						
Identify, produce rhymes						
Sound-letter correspondence						
Sound-letter-word matching						
Phonemic segmentation						
Phoneme substitution						
Syllabic structure						
Sounds in syllables						
Associate words with initial consonant						
Recognize small written vocabulary						

Emergent Reading (demonstrates)

Read story verbatim						
Read verbatim, some words						
Attempt word recognition						
Reading strategies imbalanced						
Read at preprimer level						
Read at primer level						

Language Arts Checklist

Date:

Rating Scale	STUDENTS' NAMES						
0 = Not at all							
1 = Given objects							
2 = Given pictures							
3 = Given prompts							
4 = Spontaneously							

Dictation (demonstrates)

Represent ideas in writing							
Dictate complete ideas							
Written language style							
Elements of story grammar							
Maintain topic							
Purpose for writing							
Aware of conventions							
Participate in spelling							

Writing (demonstrates)

Left-to-right concept							
Top-to-bottom concept							
Whole-word concepts							
Rapidly shifting topic							
No sentence patterns							
No planning, spontaneous							
No permanence of ideas							

Spelling (demonstrates)

Use drawing, writing							
Use scribbles, lines, shapes							
Attempt to copy letters							
Initial consonants for whole word							
Letter names and sounds							
Random letters for syll. structure							
Vowels spelled perceptually							
Testing and experimentation							
Small vocabulary of words							

Punctuation (demonstrates)

Use punctuation randomly							
Emphasize word with punctuation							
Use punctuation at end of sentence							

Handwriting (demonstrates)

Letter forms approximated							
Random white spaces							
Develop pencil grasp							
Print many letters							
Attempt letter orientation							
Attempt uniform size							

Develop your students' language, social, and storytelling skills with these other effective products . . .

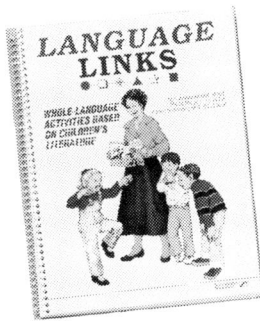

LANGUAGE LINKS
Whole-Language Activities Based on Children's Literature
by Karalee Ameel, M.Ed., Paula Paganucci, M.Ed., and Karen Rohovsky, M.A., CCC-SLP

Promote literacy with these activities based on the content of 20 vocabulary-rich stories. Strengthen the listening, language, and thinking skills that improve your students' performance in the classroom. Thirty-six activities for each of the 20 books listed cover Vocabulary, Predicting, Questions for Critical Thinking, Social Skills, Math, and Extended Activities. Plus, work on short-term memory, story comprehension and analysis, evaluation, classification, and sequencing skills.   **Catalog No. 7782-YCS $39**

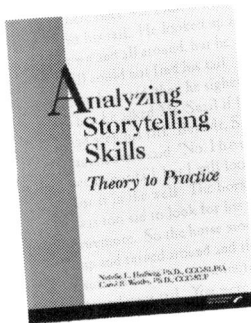

ANALYZING STORYTELLING SKILLS
Theory to Practice
by Natalie L. Hedberg, Ph.D., CCC-SLP/A, and Carol E. Westby, Ph.D., CCC-SLP

Look to these well-known authors for storytelling analysis based on leading research. You'll understand the relationship between narratives and language development and eight different ways to analyze stories. Find out how to collect stories, prepare stories for analysis, interpret language data, and analyze stories.   **Catalog No. 7495-YCS $45**

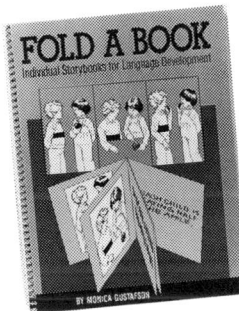

FOLD A BOOK
Individualized Storybooks for Language Development
by Monica Gustafson

Integrate whole language into the classroom! It's easy with this new twist to sequencing stories. Develop oral language and literacy in the classroom collaborative environment. Students fold a book from a standard-size sheet of paper, place illustrated panels in order, and the story-writing process begins!   **Catalog No. 7755-YCS $29.95**

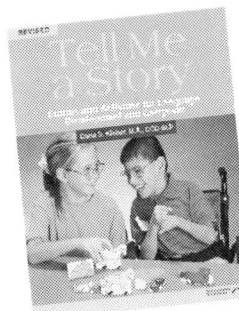

TELL ME A STORY (Revised)
Stories and Activities for Language Development and Carryover
by Carla S. Kleber, M.A., CCC-SLP

Your favorite interactive speech and language therapy tool has just gotten better! Help your students meet individual goals with 26 *new* stories. Get them talking with thematic stories students will identify with. Plus, you'll have manipulatives that are clearly organized—making them easier to use!   **Catalog No. 7178-YCS $49**

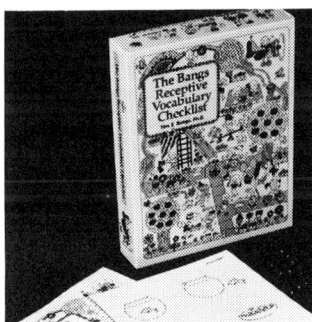

THE BANGS RECEPTIVE VOCABULARY CHECKLIST
For Preschool and Kindergarten Children
by Tina E. Bangs, Ph.D., CCC-SP/A

This vocabulary checklist helps identify language deficits in preschool and kindergarten children. You'll have 95 vocabulary words and phrases children normally acquire in a developmentally sequenced order between the third birthday and entry into first grade. Use the child's performance results to select and write receptive vocabulary goals and objectives for IEPs.   **Catalog No. 7597-YCS $49**

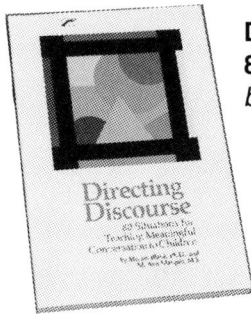

DIRECTING DISCOURSE
80 Situations for Teaching Meaningful Conversation to Children
by Marion Blank, Ph.D., and M. Ann Marquis, M.S., CCC-SLP

These context-appropriate activities provide topics and sequences for guiding children to higher levels of language functioning. The lessons are presented in pairs—a simple version for children 3 to 4 years old and a more complex version for children 5 to 8 years old. Lessons are further organized into five activity areas—Organization of Objects and Materials, Transformation of Materials, Perceptual Analysis of Material, Games and Motor Activities, and Dramatic and Written Representation. Suggestions for other lessons that follow the same format are included.

Catalog No. 7403-YCS   **$29**

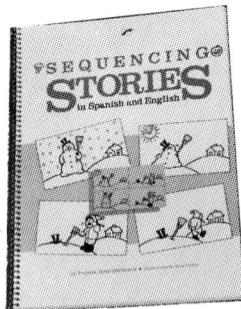

SEQUENCING STORIES
In Spanish and English
by Pamela Meza Steckbeck, M.A.

Here are 20 sequencing stories and activities in English and Spanish that will help teach important skills to your Spanish-speaking, ESL, bilingual, or children who have language disorders. You read each four-part story aloud. Children then recall and retell stories in the correct sequence, ordering corresponding pictures as they go. Use them with confidence even with limited Spanish proficiency.   **Catalog No. 7462-YCS**   **$22**

READ TO ME, TALK WITH ME (Revised)
Language Activities Based on Children's Favorite Literature
by Barbara M. Lockhart

Get an up-to-date list of 225 popular titles in children's literature. New books and stories help you create a partnership with parents to reinforce language skills taught in school. Send home these open-ended, fun activities to involve parents in their child's language and reading development. Plus, add a special dimension to your home carryover program with new books and activities focusing on cultural diversity.

Catalog No. 7165-YCS   **$39.95**

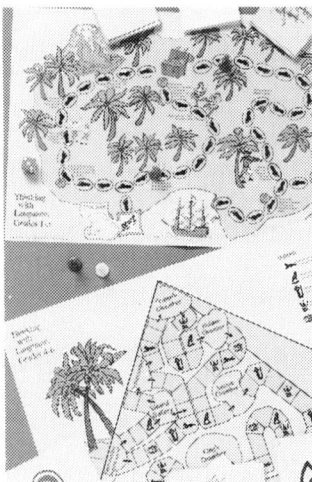

THINKING WITH LANGUAGE, GRADES 1-3
The Pirate Treasure Game for Building Language Skills
THINKING WITH LANGUAGE, GRADES 4-6
The Pyramid Treasure Game for Building Language Skills
by Elaine Burke Krassowski, M.S., CCC-SLP

Help children improve their reasoning skills by playing these fun card-and-board games! These thematic games use semantic, pragmatic, and metalinguistic approaches to encourage thinking skills in your clients with language disorders. Achieve primary goals, including word retrieval, organization, word association/reasoning, clustering, and problem solving.

Thinking with Language, Grades 1-3, Catalog No. 7804-YCS   **$44**
Thinking with Language, Grades 4-6, Catalog No. 7805-YCS   **$44**

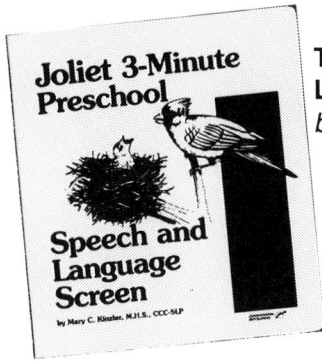

THE JOLIET 3-MINUTE PRESCHOOL SPEECH AND LANGUAGE SCREEN
by Mary C. Kinzler, M.H.S., CCC-SLP

In just 3 minutes you can identify your students who may need special services before kindergarten. This easy-to-use, quick-to-administer screen differentiates individuals with intact skills from those with suspected problems in phonology, grammar, and semantics. You'll have two versions of an Individual Screen Form—one for testing children 2½ to 3 years old and another for testing children 3 to 4½ years old. Record responses directly onto the appropriate form. Transfer that record to either the Class Record Form or the new space-saving computerized recordkeeping program.

Catalog No. 7800-YCS $55

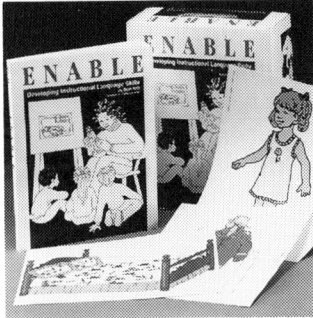

ENABLE
Developing Instructional Language Skills
by Beth Witt, M.A.

Help your preschool children develop the effective listening skills they need for future academic success with this complete question-answer competence kit. You'll receive an extensive manual containing stories, reproducible checklists, and assessment materials. You'll also get full-color manipulatives, including 41 puppet cutouts!

Catalog No. 7476-YCS $129

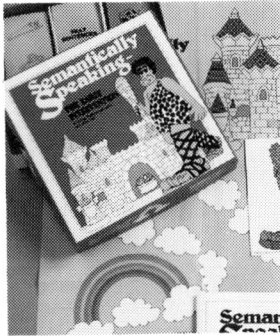

SEMANTICALLY SPEAKING™—FOR EARLY INTERVENTION
by Elaine Burke Krassowski, M.S., CCC-SLP

This board game is similar in format to the others in the *Semantically Speaking*™ series—but for your PK, kindergarten, and first-grade children. Students will improve their abilities to receive, organize, and convey information in five word categories: food, clothing, animals, tools, and household items. You'll also be able to teach a basic vocabulary students need for successful daily communication, and expressive and receptive language skills as well.

Catalog No. 7675-YCS $45

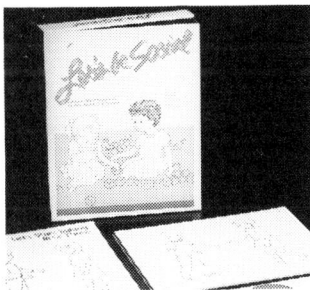

LET'S BE SOCIAL
Language-Based Social Skills for Preschool At-Risk Children
by The Social Integration Project, adapted by Linda Levine, Ed.D.

Here's a 10-week fieldtested curriculum to use in your preschool classroom. Initiate social interaction skills through teacher-led direct practice, skill discrimination exercises, modeling, and instructional activities. Follow the easy-to-use lesson plans to focus on a new skill each week.

Catalog No. 7571-YCS $39

LANGUAGE STORIES
Teaching Language to Developmentally Disabled Children (Revised)
by Anne Byrne McGivern, M.A., Margery Lewy Rieff, Ph.D., and Barbara Floyd Vender, M.S.

Here are carefully written stories for your developmentally delayed students who currently may use two- to three-word sentences. The 60 stories combine low-level vocabulary and controlled syntax with high-interest topics. The text comes with 350 illustrated cards to reinforce the narratives.

Catalog No. 7402-YCS $75

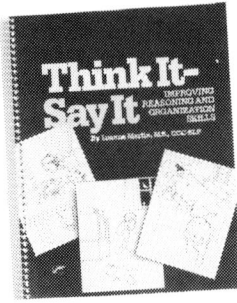

THINK IT—SAY IT
Improving Reasoning and Organization Skills
by Luanne Martin, M.S., CCC-SLP

No preparation is needed with these visual, flexible materials! Reproducible pictures and questions help you teach verbal reasoning and language organization skills to your clients with cognitive or language impairments.

Catalog No. 7648-YCS   **$29**

CARRYOVER FOR KIDS
Parents as Partners
by Linda Serway, M.S., CCC-SLP

Encourage carryover at home with 114 creative activities for learning language. These reproducible letters give you portable and practical suggestions to send home. Each sheet offers a half-page overview of the skill presented, and a half-page Home Activity Plan for implementing each skill. Individualize activities as needed for maximum parent involvement.

Catalog No. 7756-YCS   **$29.95**

ORDER FORM

Ship to:

INSTITUTION: _____

NAME: _____

OCCUPATION/DEPT: _____

ADDRESS: _____

CITY:_____ STATE:_____ ZIP: _____

☐ Please check here if this is a permanent address change.

Telephone No._____ ☐ work ☐ home

Payment Options:

☐ My check is enclosed.

☐ My purchase order is enclosed. P.O.# _____
                                (Net 30 days)

☐ Charge to my credit card. ☐ VISA ☐ MasterCard ☐ Discover

Card No. ☐☐☐☐☐☐☐☐☐☐☐☐☐☐☐☐

Expiration Date: Month_____ Year _____

Signature_____

QTY.	CAT. #	TITLE	AMOUNT

Please add 10% for postage and assured delivery. 8% for orders over $500.
Arizona residents add sales tax.
Canada: Add 22% to subtotal for shipping, handling, and G.S.T.

Payment in U.S. funds only.	**TOTAL**	

MONEY-BACK GUARANTEE

You'll have up to 90 days of risk-free evaluation of the products you ordered. If you're not completely satisfied with any product, we'll pick it up within the 90 days and refund the full purchase price! *No questions asked!*

We occasionally backorder items temporarily out of stock. If you do not accept backorders, please tell us on your purchase order or on this form.

FOR PHONE ORDERS

Call 1-800-866-4446. Please have your credit card and/or institutional purchase order information ready. 9 AM–6 PM Central Time
Voice or TDD / FAX (602) 325-0306

Send your order to:

Communication Skill Builders
a division of The Psychological Corporation
3830 E. Bellevue / P.O. Box 42050-YTS / Tucson, AZ 85733